Perilous Journey

Perilous Journey

A Mother's International Quest to Rescue Her Children – A True Story

Patricia Sutherland

New Horizon Press
Far Hills, New Jersey

Patricia Sutherland
        Perilous Journey: A Mother's International Quest to Rescue Her
        Children – A True Story

Cover Design: Robert Aulicino
Interior Design: Susan M. Sanderson

Library of Congress Control Number: 2002101395

ISBN: 0-88282-226-8
New Horizon Press

Manufactured in the U.S.A.

2007   2006   2005   2004   2003 / 5   4   3   2   1

Dedicated to
my mother

Author's Note

This book is inspired by and based on the actual experiences of Patricia Sutherland. The personalities, events, actions and conversations portrayed within the story have been reconstructed from extensive interviews and research, utilizing court documents, letters, personal papers, press accounts and the memories of participants. In an effort to safeguard the privacy of certain individuals, their names have been changed and, in some cases, otherwise identifying characteristics have been altered. Events involving the characters happened as described; only minor details have been altered.

Table of Contents

Introduction. ix

Prologue. xv

Chapter 1   New Year's Resolutions. 1

Chapter 2   Of Myths and Fairy Tales. 15

Chapter 3   Building Sand Castles 33

Chapter 4   Lullaby and Good Nights 47

Chapter 5   Birth of a Prince 73

Chapter 6   True Confessions. 83

Chapter 7   Good Fortune and Bad 95

Chapter 8   The Same Differences. 105

Chapter 9   Lost Dreams and Foolhardy Plans. 123

Chapter 10   Futile Wishes, Dire Realities 135

Chapter 11   Yin and Yang 145

Chapter 12   Fleeting Reunion 155

Chapter 13   Vigils of Hope, Vigils of Despair. 163

Chapter 14   Concrete Pipe Dreams 183

Chapter 15   Deportation and Other Threats 197

Chapter 16   Toward Decision Day 211

Chapter 17   Mission Impossible. 221

Chapter 18   Crushing Blows 233

Chapter 19   One Step Forward, Two Steps Back 253

Chapter 20   Countdown. 263

Chapter 21   The Perilous Journey 277

Chapter 22   Destination: Freedom. 295

              Epilogue 313

Introduction

Between 2500 and 3000 B.C., settlers migrated to the Malay peninsula in southeast Asia, becoming the forebearers of today's Malaysian population. Many lived in the coastal regions and traded with Chinese, Indian and other seafarers. Some of these traders espoused the religion of Hinduism. This faith blended over time with the local animist beliefs. After the Muslims conquered India, they spread the religion of Islam to the land that is now Malaysia. There, in the fifteenth century, Islam acquired a firm hold on the region when the Muslim Mudzaffar Shah overthrew his Hindu half brother and became the ruler of the powerful city-state of Melacca. The tenets of Islam have become a grip that has tightened in recent years.

Thereafter, Melacca, which had become a valuable meeting point where Chinese, Arabs, Malays and Indians traded, was periodically conquered by the Portuguese, the Dutch and then the British, whose rule was interrupted by the Japanese invasion and occupation from 1942-1945 during World War II. Throughout and after the war, the people of Malaysia made it known that they no longer wanted to be a British colony.

In 1957 the country won its independence from Britain and became the Federation of Malaysia (its official title) that same year. At first, Malaysia consisted only of the territory located on the Malay peninsula, but it was soon joined by the former colonies of Sarawak and Sabah located on the island of Borneo in 1963. The island of Singapore also joined the Federation in 1963, but left two years later. The tiny principality of Brunei, entirely surrounded by Sarawak, declined to join the Federation and to this day remains an independent state.

Today, Malaysia's population is predominately Malay with Chinese and Indian minorities. Muslims hold most senior government positions and run the bureaucracy. By constitutional definition, all ethnic Malays are considered to be Muslim and Islam is the official state religion.

Malaysia's government is a constitutional monarchy. The nominal head of state is the *Yang di-Pertuan Agong* ("the paramount ruler"), customarily referred to as the king. Surprisingly, the king does not serve for life—a new king is elected every five years from among the nine sultans of the peninsular Malaysian states. All real power in the country lies in the cabinet led by the prime minister. This minister must be a member of the lower house of parliament whose party commands a majority in that body.

Malaysia's premier political party, the United Malays National Organization (UMNO), has held power in coalition with other parties ever since the country achieved independence from British rule. The country's current Prime Minister is Dr. Mohamed Mahathir, a UMNO stalwart who assumed office in 1981. In September of 1998, the Prime Minister fired his heir apparent, Deputy Prime Minister Anwar Ibrahim, because of a dispute over Ibrahim's proposed economic reforms. When Ibrahim countered by publicly attacking Mahathir's administration, he was jailed on trumped-up allegations of corruption and sex crimes.

Mahathir suffered for this rash action in the country's elections in 1999. Four opposition parties formed a coalition to counter him and, although it could not topple the UMNO's majority in parliament, the coalition did make significant electoral gains. One of the parties in that coalition was the National Justice Party (Keadilan) led by Wan Azizah Ismail, the wife of the deposed and imprisoned Anwar Ibrahim. A second was the Islamic Party of Malaysia (PAS), a fundamentalist group that called for the founding of an Islamic state.

Malaysia and Women's Rights

Although Islam preaches that men and women are equal in the eyes of Allah, many Islamic societies grant men a privileged position over women. Malaysia is no exception to this. The inequality between the sexes in Malaysian society perhaps is best seen in the workings of its judicial system.

When Malaysia first won its independence from Britain, it retained from its colonial past a legal system based on English common law. However, it supplemented this system with a body of Islamic law that is administered by the Syariah Court, which is composed of Muslim clerics.

This islamic court applies only to Muslims and considers matters of personal status, such as marriage, divorce, religious orthodoxy and so on. Zairah Anwar, a Malaysian and the Executive Director of Sisters in Islam, wrote in the September 1997 issue of *AsiaWeek*, "Intolerant and repressive teachings are slowly creeping into Malaysian society. Nowhere is this more true than in matters relating to women's rights and fundamental liberties."

Sometimes the Syariah Court must settle an issue where the established law is unclear or undecided. In these cases, the Court refers the matter to a *mufti* (religious leader) who will pronounce a *fatwa* (ruling) based on precedent and a strict reading of the Quran. In Malaysia's Syariah Court, these *fatwas* have the binding force of law. At a meeting in Washington, D.C. in October of 2000, Ms. Anwar noted that her country's government had become increasingly religious. "In the 1990s there was far more religion (in the state) than ever before," she said. "There are more Islamic schools and Islamic institutions and existing laws have been amended."

One striking example of the increased stridency came in 1991, when three Muslim girls were arrested for participating in the Miss Malaysian Petite Contest. One of the little known *fatwas*, it turned out, banned women from participating in beauty pageants.

Since Islamic law ultimately derives from the teachings of the *Quran*, most Muslims are loath to criticize it. However, many Muslim women feel they are discriminated against and treated unfairly. Among their criticisms:

A man may unilaterally divorce his wife outside of court simply by stating his intention to divorce three times. However, a woman may not divorce her husband without applying to the law. Women who initiate divorce must navigate an extremely complex legal process that often is beset by bureaucratic difficulties and delays.

The all-male Muslim clerics are reluctant to grant a divorce to a woman without the agreement of her husband. The court will often insist on mediation and will postpone proceedings should the husband be absent. Furthermore, many of the court's judgments will ignore precedence in order to favor male plaintiffs or defendants.

The court will often insist that women be represented by lawyers, even though this is not required by law. Women who do seek lawyers often find that they cannot afford competent representation. In addition, many male lawyers advise their female clients that they should drop their cases and simply go back to their husbands.

Malaysia allows each of its states independence in deciding how it will adjudicate Islamic law. This has led to a great many differences in interpretation from state to state. For example, a man must fulfill four conditions to practice polygamy in Selangor, but need not do so in Tregganu. To make matters worse, a decree given by the Syariah Court in one state is unenforceable in another. Thus, a man ordered to pay child support in Kuala Lumpur may avoid doing so by moving a few miles across the border to Petaling Jaya. Many men have taken advantage of this to circumvent the law altogether.

Although women's groups have raised grave concerns and proposed remedies, change has yet to come to Malaysia's powerful Syariah Court which invariably favors Muslim men over women.

Malaysia and Anti-Western Sentiment

Malaysia's attitude toward Western influence is highly ambivalent. On one hand, Malaysia is one of the "Asian Tigers" which has embraced Western-style capitalism and, as a result, seen its economy boom. On the other hand, Malaysia has also seen a corresponding rise in Islamic militancy and anti-Western fervor. The fundamentalist party PAS has slowly increased its political power by calling for an Islamic state and denouncing the West. Yet Malaysia's most virulent expression of anti-Western sentiment can be found not in its politics but in its underground terrorist organizations.

The pervasive terrorist group Al-Qaeda gives enormous sums of money to fund Islamic militant groups throughout Southeast Asia, including Malaysia's own Kumpulan Mujahideen Malaysia (KMM). This extremist organization was founded in the 1980s by the son of PAS leader Nik Aziz. Young Malaysians who joined the group were given paramilitary training and told that they would be used to protect PAS leaders in the event of a government crackdown. In truth, KMM was raising an army to overthrow the government and establish an Islamic regime. It should be noted that, although KMM leaders have publicly supported PAS and its ambitions, PAS has officially denounced KMM.

Through the 1980s and early 1990s, KMM's political concerns were primarily domestic. However, things changed radically in the mid-90's when two Indonesian *ulema* (teachers) joined the group. These two men, Abubakar Ba'asyir and Riduan Isamuddin (more commonly known as Hambali), articulated a vision of Islamic militancy that was heavily influenced by the teachings of Osama bin Laden. Malaysian authorities have positively identified Abubakar Ba'asyir as one of the leaders of the Malaysian Mujahidin Council, a militant religious group linked to Al Queda. The two men urged the KMM to devote itself toward the founding of a pan-Asian Islamic state that would encompass Malaysia, Indonesia, the Philippines, Singapore and Brunei. These clerics influenced the KMM members into believing that jihad is everything in Islam and that the practice of Islam is not compatible with the concept of democracy.

Toward this end, Hambali waged a campaign of terror throughout Southeast Asia. Police in Singapore uncovered a KMM plan to bomb American targets in their city, as well as their intention to order nine tons of a chemical explosive. Indonesian police arrested a Malaysian named Taufik Abdul Halim in a Jakarta shopping mall shortly after the bomb he was carrying exploded and blew off one of his legs. Inside Malaysia itself, the KMM robbed mini-marts, attacked a police station and exploded a bomb inside a Hindu temple.

KMM's methodology is to attack non-Muslim targets and any Muslims they deem to have deviated from their own narrow interpretation of Islam. They do so in order to polarize public opinion and depict Western influence as antithetical to Muslim belief. This was most strikingly borne out in their assassination of Joe Fernandez, a Malaysian office-holder from the state of Kedah. Fernandez was a Catholic rumored to have attempted to convert Muslims to his Christian faith—the merest suspicion of this was enough pretext for KMM to have him killed. KMM views the Western ideals of democracy, pluralism and religious tolerance to be dangerously heretical.

In May 2000 an attempted bank robbery by members of KMM went awry. Two KMM men were captured during the hold-up and eventually gave information that led to a massive police crackdown of the group. Over the next few months, the Malaysian government arrested thirty-eight members of the KMM and reportedly is still on the lookout for two hundred more.

Malaysia's links to world terrorist organizations were exposed after September 11, 2001. Shortly after Osama bin Laden's terrorist attacks on the United States, the world learned that Al-Qaeda members had frequently met in Malaysia to discuss their plans. The most notorious of these meetings occurred in January 2000 in Kuala Lumpur. In attendance were Nawaf Alhazmi and Khalid Almihdhar, two of the terrorists on board the plane that crashed into the Pentagon. The roommate of a third hijacker also attended, along with Zacarias Moussaoui, the so-called "twentieth hijacker" prosecuted in Virginia. Moussaoui is known to have taken several trips to Malaysia over the past ten years. *Time* reported that, while there, Moussaoui was provided with a letter supporting his covert identity as a marketing consultant for a Malaysian company. The cover was provided by Yazid Sufaat, a former Malaysian army captain and trusted lieutenant of a militant Islamic cleric in neighboring Indonesia long associated with the jihad in Afghanistan. Yazid currently is being detained by Malaysian authorities for ordering four tons of ammonium nitrate, the same explosive used by Timothy McVeigh in the Oklahoma City bombing.

Although Al-Qaeda has never used Malaysia as a launching pad for terrorist attacks, it considers the country a convenient place in which to meet and plan. Perhaps just as importantly, the group also chooses Malaysia when it wants to meet with radical Islamic organizations from Southeast Asia. No doubt this is because Malaysia permits visa-free entry to citizens of most Islamic nations. One U.S. official has gone so far as to call the country "a perfect place for terrorist R and R."

But only a little of Malaysia's convoluted political history and none of its underlying links to terrorism were known by Patty Sutherland as she first daydreamed, then embarked upon the exotic journey on which she hoped to finally meet her Prince Charming...

Prologue

Following is a portion of a marital summary written in January, 1995 for Tuan (Sir) Haji Sulaiman, Malaysia's top Syariah Court lawyer, in the hope that he would agree to represent me in my fight to obtain custody of or visitation rights with my children.

My name is Noor Faridah Sutherland Binte Abdullah. I converted to Islam on 27 February, 1990 and married Prince Mahmood Shah Bin Prince Mohammed Archibald of the Johor royal family the next day, in Melacca, Malaysia. To circumvent the Melaccan residency requirement, Mahmood used the address of a friend in Melacca. He alleged this was necessary because his cousin, the Sultan of Johor, might have interfered if we had married in Johor. A valid concern, as Mahmood had forged a letter from his first wife, Aziza, who lived in Brunei, about their divorce.

Our first child, Princess Mariam Nabila, was born in Johor Bahru on 28 September, 1990 and on 15 February, 1992, I bore a son, Prince Iskandar Shah (seventh in line to the Sultanate). We made our home on Mahmood's family's small resort island, Rawa, nine miles off the coast of the village of Mersing, in the State of Johor. We also maintained a house in Johor Bahru.

I have endeavored to be a good Muslim wife, though my husband never gave me guidance in Islam. Although he professed a great and enduring belief, he rarely prayed, fasted during Ramadhan, read the Koran or went to the Mosque. To his credit, though, we did not eat pork and he did tithe every year as prescribed. Solely through my own initiative, I read books to better my understanding of the religion.

I was raised in a small village in the United States. My parents, both educators and practicing Christians, raised me to believe in one God, whom I now call Allah. It was effortless for me to embrace Mohammed as the final, true Prophet foretold in the Old Testament. Recently, I have begun to pray and read the Koran daily.

I first learned my husband was unfaithful when Iskandar was a baby. Mahmood did not know I knew for a long time, because I was afraid to confront him. Recently, I was told that my husband had bedded dozens of women during our marriage. I was also told Mahmood regularly seduced women tourists on the island while I was sleeping with the children. Further, he had a reputation for picking up bar girls whenever he was in the city on business. To maintain his facade and my ignorance, he must have told me hundreds of blatant lies. I am thankful I did not contract a heinous disease from my husband, who was supposedly my protector. I no longer trust Mahmood and have been repulsed by his touch; however, I have maintained a pleasant façade and steeled myself against despair for the sake of the children.

Furthermore, I have come to realize my husband is an alcoholic. He drank beer or whiskey to excess every night throughout our marriage. He boasted that before he met me he drank a fifth of Black Label Scotch every day and did not have a problem with alcohol since he now drank less than that. He often became verbally abusive when drunk and I grew to fear him and his handgun, which he compulsively wore beneath his shirt during the day and kept under his pillow at night.

I would like to stress here that Mahmood did try to be a good parent to our children. Unfortunately, because of his dysfunctional childhood, he had no aptitude for the task. He insisted upon strict, inappropriate discipline and would harangue the children over the smallest infraction. He had no patience for tears, made promises he had no intention of keeping and teased the children mercilessly, thinking such cruelties were good for them. When I tried to reason with him, he humiliated me in front of the children, furious that I dared to challenge him. Yet, he was very generous with toys and treats, often too generous. He spoiled the children. Sadly, Mariam and Iskandar were tense and reserved in his presence. Further, it was uncharacteristic of him to show any concern over their daily needs, yet he harangued and blamed me if anything went wrong with them.

I attempted to communicate my increasing unhappiness to my husband in the hope that our marriage could be salvaged. All things considered, I still loved him. However, he mocked my feelings, threatened me and began spending longer and longer periods of time away. Still, when we were together, I endeavored to maintain family harmony.

In the spring of 1994, Mariam, Iskandar and I went to Michigan to visit my family. Mahmood encouraged us to go and refused to consider coming with us. I discussed my despair over the marriage with my family. I believed Mahmood no longer cared for me and I had to admit I was afraid to return to Malaysia with the children. I suspected that, if the marriage ended, he would send me away and keep the children from me.

When Mahmood and his brother, Prince Ibrahim Alang, were three years old and eighteen months respectively, their mother, Faridah Margaret, the progeny of a Thai servant and Scottish planter, had been compelled to leave them and Malaysia. The boys' father, Prince Mohammed Archibald, was an irresponsible, womanizing, alcoholic who had made her life unbearable. He would sooner have shot her than share his sons or his property with her. Instead, once she was gone, he gave Mahmood and his elder half sister, Princess Maria, who also had been separated from her Malay mother, to their grandparents in Australia. Ibrahim Alang, because he was too young for the ship passage, was sent to the Sultan's palace to be raised with the Crown Prince. He and Mahmood were told that their mother was dead. The two of them did not see or have any factual information about their mother until they were grown. Further, the Sultan himself had sent his first wife, an Englishwoman, away and forbidden any contact between her and her two children, one of whom was the Crown Prince.

This callous disregard within Mahmood's family for a mother's rights filled me with great trepidation. Now my worst fears have come true and I am separated from the two people I love the most, my two small children. Please help me...

chapter one

New Year's Resolutions

January 1, 1989

My New Year's resolution is certain this year: Find a life. But how? Fill out the graduate school application that has been yellowing on my desk these many weeks? Seek fulfillment in good works? Run an ad in the personals? *Bright, attractive, angst-ridden, irreverently neurotic, divorced, childless twenty-eight-year-old blonde BA with an '85 Toyota and $2,000 in the bank seeks Mr. Right and/or fulfilling occupation. All fascinating responses will be pondered.*

January 5

I went to dinner in Leland this evening with Janice Mullen, fellow ennui sufferer. She has invited me to come aboard to go abroad. I bit my tongue hard as I sputtered out a resounding "YES, tell me how? Tell me what, when? WHERE?"

"Our destination is uncharted," she says, "our option's the world."

"I can do this," I bubbled, babbled, burst with relief.

Tentative date of departure: March 1; Return: maybe never; Itinerary: whim-driven.

I need a passport, shots, backpack, sleeping bag, hostel card, money belt and plane ticket. I can sell my car, Fiestaware, vintage compact collection and complete set of *Mother Earth News* back issues.

January 20

I am a woman obsessed, perpetually, ecstatically, intentionally obsessed. I have a stack of books from four different libraries on everything from cheap travel to elephant safaris. It seems I have been preparing for a long time, at least mentally. We had our first shots: typhoid and yellow fever. They were wonderfully painful. The doctor ordered anti-malarial pills and the vaccination for an ugly strain of meningitis sweeping through Nepal. Next week is cholera and the second typhoid. My passport application is in the mail and the Chicago Immigration Office where I mailed it promises materialization of said passport in two or three weeks.

January 22

I suffered a long, excruciating anxiety attack last night that unnerved me. I was restless and troubled, unable to shake its grip until 4:00 A.M. As I struggled to pinpoint the source of my worries, I realized the reality of this trip was finally hitting me. A little fear and a few misgivings are normal and healthy, I told myself, though a lingering and wretched panic attack is surely cause for concern. Am I doing the right thing? What if I fail? How do I fathom the unfathomable? Thinking and writing about the tangibles of this trip are effortless, but I am unable to get my mind around the intangibles. I do know that, when taking a leap into the unknown, some anxiety is a perfectly ordinary reaction to a perfectly extraordinary action.

I crave the profound change of habit/culture/people/values this trip will provide. I have been in such a rut lately, doing what is safe, easy and conventional. I am bored with conventional food, conventional travel and conventional men.

I want this adventure to spawn the passionate, soul-blowing, hyper-intense love of my life. I want a husband with brilliance, wealth and easy laughter. I want servants, laughing children, a big beautiful house amid tropical breezes, great fun and a great love. For this, I will give up all that I have been saving deep within me and in return I want to be happy and fulfilled. Ah, dreams...

January 24

Today I bartered my eighty-three back issues of the *Mother Earth News* for a sleeping bag, which last had been used at the summit of Mt. McKinley (or so I was told) I found a cool twenty-five dollar backpack at a thrift shop and I intend to fill it with funky, functional clothes for all climates and cultures.

I have phoned every 1-800 bucket shop from New York to Los Angeles and I'm a tad overwhelmed by the options. Janice left the flight plan up to me and has been no help. She says yes to everything. An eighteen-hour bus trip to NYC and a one-way flight to London for ninety-nine dollars? "Sounds great," she says. Hitchhiking to the West Coast and charming our way onto a cargo ship to Shanghai? "Splendid." Filling a suitcase with Levi's and Twinkies and flying to Moscow for a one thousand dollar profit on our first-class airfare? "Sure, whatever." Smuggling AK47's into Beirut? "Let me think about that one." She is extraordinarily blasé—a side effect, I suspect, of having four thousand dollars in cash to my two.

My mantra has become, "I will not stress about money." The backpackers' travel guides know their stuff and confidently declare that one can live comfortably throughout most of the Third World for about five dollars a day. Between youth hostels, eating local food and traveling by bus or train, I can go exactly four hundred days with my two grand. And when it is dwindling down to pocket change, I will find one of the ubiquitous jobs available to young, strong Americans, like teaching English or harvesting grapes.

My passport arrived yesterday and I've been thinking it would make a great earring. With my youth hostel card dangling from the other ear, I might start a trend.

January 28

We got our second typhoid and cholera shots today. I just called Janice and she's flat on her back moaning. I have my numb, swollen right arm resting on a notebook and am writing with Herculean effort. I cannot lift my arm and any movement makes me gasp. I have no intention of changing my clothes until the pain decreases. As unpleasant as this is, I don't mind it a bit! In this pain is the ever-present realization of its function: *Travel without Typhoid*, a jolly good thing.

February 1

Janice and I are buying around-the-world tickets for $1,899. After four thousand phone-calls, four hundred bizarre to banal options discarded, forty anxiety attacks and four nightmares about being caught in a Bangladeshi tidal wave, running for cover during a coup, rotting in a Chinese prison and getting lost in Katmandu, I finally struck a deal with a sweet Turkish guy in a Los Angeles bucket shop. My affluent and ever generous elder brother will pay for my ticket, bless his businessman's soul. The tickets are good for 365 days with up to twenty different stops and a slew of workable restrictions I must hammer out on my own with the airline. Not today, though, as I am exhausted by the two and a half hour telephone call to finalize the purchase and in shock by the implications of the term, "non-refundable." Actually, there are waves of excitement intermingled with the waves of trepidation. WE ARE GOING!

February 6

There are two people coming to look at my car today. It is time to say goodbye to it. When I got the car, new and shiny and ready to roll, it was the fulfillment of my youthful dreams. My stand-up-comedian boyfriend and I spent many, many traveling miles between comedy clubs in it when I should have been in graduate school classes. It sat in Mother's yard when I moved to the Caribbean and met a Navy SEAL who became my husband. We sold the car to my brother Matt over the phone from our home in Norfolk, Virginia, and he sold it back to me when that marriage self-destructed after fourteen tumultuous months. Then, it served as my taxi when a friend drove me down to Ann Arbor, where I checked myself into treatment at University of Michigan for anorexia. After I finished the pro-scribed therapy and hopefully was on my way to handling my problem, it fetched me. Now I was selling my darling Toyota to further me along on the road to my geographic dream cure. Farewell, old friend.

February 7

I got the price I wanted for the car. The buyer comes this afternoon to take away my earthbound wheels. I converted my final alimony check into traveler's checks.

My menstrual blood flowed today for the first time in eight months. I have been worrying about it more than I'll admit. It stopped before I went into treatment and the doctors assured me that it was a consequence of the anorexia and would return as I gained some weight and my health improved. Well, bummer, because now I must shop for tampons, an expensive rarity in most countries. Hey, there is a bonus: I may also get my sex drive back. Yikes!

I've been working on our itinerary with the airline. We had our choice of hemispheres and the northern seemed most logical. The first five tentative legs of our odyssey are Detroit to Los Angeles (Janice will go to San Francisco) to Honolulu to Hong Kong to Singapore to Bangkok. When we want to go below the equator, we'll buy the tickets locally or hop on a boat.

February 28

In thirty hours we drive to Detroit to catch our flights to the West Coast where Janice and I will spend five days with relatives and friends respectively and then meet up at LAX for our flight to Hawaii.

I got my final shot yesterday, gamma globulin for hepatitis. I have two thousand dollars in American Express travelers checks and $283 in cash, giving me, I figure, an additional fifty six and two-thirds days of travel, on top of my initial estimate of four hundred days. I have filled the backpack with exactly the prescribed stuff and lashed the sleeping bag bungee cords to the outside. I am ready to go right this very minute but, alas, our bon voyage party is tonight and I have another box to fill and put into storage and all day tomorrow to live through.

March 1

I am in California staying with Aunt Emily and Uncle Bob and eating lemons and grapefruit off the trees in their backyard. My aunt and uncle insisted I see Crystal Cathedral and Disneyland, a tad too contrived for my style, though people watching at both places was priceless.

Last night I slept fitfully, plagued by distressing thoughts: What if I lose my money, my backpack and my nerve? What if Janice loses her money, her backpack and her nerve? I tell myself to submerge these doubts right now, take a long walk in the sun and hum a few bars of "Leaving on a Jet Plane." Excellent idea.

March 6

My aunt and uncle drove me to the Los Angeles airport and Janice and I met at the ticket counter as planned. In my seat, with seat belt fastened, I intend to recline a bit and devour a few magazines or flirt further with the cute guy across the aisle. My adventure of a lifetime has begun!

March 7

We arrived in Honolulu at 2:00 A.M. and walked to a nearby park where we spread out our sleeping bags on the grass. There was no one around and we slept like lava rocks for three hours, got up with the sun and stumbled back to the airport. There we stashed our backpacks in lockers, cleaned up for a half-awake tour of Honolulu and caught the free airport shuttle into town.

The fifteen-dollar-a-night youth hostel has a two-week waiting list and the free campground is closed until Friday. There is nothing else remotely near our budget so we've set ourselves up in an empty gate at the airport. The backpacker's "bible" recommends this as a pleasant, carpeted, hassle free domicile and we vehemently concur. The workers are friendly and the lavatories ideal for a paper towel bath and hair wash in the sink. The lights are pleasantly dimmed here at our chosen suite and the posted flight schedules list gates so we know we have this gate for at least twelve uninterrupted hours.

We're spread out, enjoying the food we bought earlier in town, while we organize our stuff and search for deals in the tourist guidebook. During the day tomorrow, our belongings will again get stashed in lockers while we return to town for people watching, groceries and a camping permit. Then, after another marvelous night here, we can head for the North Shore to camp.

March 12

Dear Mother,

Aloha from the Kaiaka State Recreation Area and Campground on the North Shore of the big island. We arrived here two days ago after checking out of gate 15 at the airport. After a long and scenic bus ride across the island, we hitchhiked with a surfer dude who brought us to the campground. We found the perfect waterfront site and pitched our tent. As the only campers here, we were a tad nervous until the maintenance couple came by and assured us the area is safe. A mongoose also came by and we spent a half-hour watching him nose around.

There is a small town about a mile down the road with great, cheap restaurants and a plethora of hippie surfer dudes and chicks drawn to the best waves in the world at Sunset Beach. We spent yesterday there with our mouths hanging open in awe at the expert surfing and humpback whales breaching. We were joined by a South African and Dutch couple who have been everywhere and had endlessly inspiring stories to tell.

Today we leave because the glamour of camping has worn off, due to its bugs, dampness, cramped, uncomfortable sleeping and early darkness (6:45 sunsets). We are returning to the airport and the tourist throngs of Waikiki Beach for our last two nights in Hawaii.

Love and Kisses, Patty

March 18

Dear Mother,

I am eating a breakfast of yogurt, chopped apples, raisins and granola in a building on top of a grass-carpeted hill overlooking the spectacular Hong Kong Harbor, which some call Hong Kong's soul. Looking down on them, the sea blue waters become bullet gray in the distance. We are in a small cafeteria full of young people from around the world. We are the only Americans, though almost everyone speaks English. Janice and I are planning a day of touring and seeing museums in Kowloon with Carl, a German guy to whom we've been talking as we drink our coffee.

We arrived here Thursday morning after a delightful eleven-and-a-half-hour flight. We flew Singapore Airlines for the first time and the flight was unparalleled luxury. Upon takeoff from Honolulu, sarong-bedecked attendants bedazzled us with steaming towels and engraved menus, portending a gourmet feast, which did not disappoint. The toilets were stocked with toothbrushes, toothpaste, combs, razors, perfumes, lotions and mouthwash. They handed out playing cards and had postcards and aerogrammes that they graciously offered to mail anywhere. We felt like we were living in the bounty of luxury.

When we first arrived, we walked around in a daze for a couple hours. The streets are packed with shops and kiosks and hawkers and peddlers and buskers and beggars and tourists. The noise is deafening, but the sights exciting. Fortuitously, finding the right bus was a cinch, because the guidebook warned that there would be a grueling forty-minute uphill walk to the hostel once it dropped us off. Well, for fifty-five minutes we trudged up steep, ancient steps wobbling from fatigue and the weight of our packs. When we saw the amazing view of this history-packed city from the hilltop, all was forgiven, though we found out later that we could have come by taxi for less than a dollar!

Later, we took our first hot showers in over a week and settled into our $2.50 dormitory bunks. After a twelve-hour sleep we woke up manic to see more of the city and, with Janice counting, we flew down the 1208 steps and spent most of yesterday absorbing on Hong Kong's culture. We saw Sung Dynasty Village, giving us a glimpse of ancient China, and visited the jewel-colored tableaux of legends and mythology at the Tiger Balm Gardens. When you juxtapose the history and majestic modern skyscrapers with dog and cat carcasses hanging in the butcher shops, fruits and vegetable we couldn't name, Chinese medicine shops with $10,000 Ginseng roots on display and tiger penises behind the counter, you become aware of the eclectic mix of old and new which is today's Hong Kong. The saddest and strangest sight was the hundreds of old men and women permanently stooped over, carrying huge loads and looking as though they had just walked out of a seventeenth-century village.

A man approached Janice and me in a coffee shop where we had stopped for a bite. His name was Tan and he was a marriage broker. He works for a bunch of wealthy local men looking for American women willing to take a couple years out of their lives to go through the elaborate theatre of a serious, flawless, airtight courtship and matrimony—love and sex optional. The reward for these men is United States citizenship: a priceless commodity with the Chinese scheduled to take over in a few years. I'm sure you can guess what our rewards would be. Yes, lots and lots of money and a priceless education. These men, he assured us, are urbane, speak impeccable English and we can go out with as many as we need until we find one we like enough for the 'Show.' What a strange world this is.

While out today, we will apply for Chinese visas. The People's Republic of China is so close and cheap that everyone here has gone or is going and we have decided to join a couple leaving tomorrow for a few days in Gangzhou. I'll keep you posted.

Love, Patty

March 23

My Darling Zoe,

Happy Birthday from China, best buddy, and read on for a vicarious odyssey. I am sitting in the common room of our youth hostel with Andrew (a cute Irishman), Mark (a cuter Australian) and Janice. We arrived an hour ago.

Our Chinese adventure began at the border after an hour's train ride from Hong Kong. Customs required a half-dozen different, silly forms and constant passport flashing. Once cleared, we searched for the train to Gangzhou. We had been told the trains ran until 10:00 P.M. and it was only 9:30, but the last train had pulled out ten minutes prior to our arrival.

Hordes of people surrounded us, staring and/or pushing local currency in our faces, hoping we would sell them Hong Kong dollars or F.E.C.'s. That acronym, my dear, is for the Foreign Exchange Currency the official-looking government workers made us buy at the border to spend in special tourist shops. Ah, but we knew from our guidebook that they are much more fun to trade, at great profit, for local yuan in the streets.

Rather than take a taxi to Gangzhou we decided to improvise and find a room in Shenzen, a border town we knew nothing about. So, laughing all the way, we set off walking through the streets. Finally, after pricing a few places and finding them all outrageously expensive, we settled on one, although the only room available was a double. We have two large twin beds, a television, a private bath with hot water, a thermos full of strong tea and a friendly porter. Yes, we got all this, plus clean sheets and towels, for less than eight U.S. dollars each, still too much.

We went out for a delicious but hilarious meal, which entailed lots of pointing, nodding, strange flavors, textures, chopstick gyrations and an audience of local people. We were so entertaining to them, we could have charged admission. Afterwards we slept, girls in one bed and boys in the other. We woke up at eight, caught the noon train and traveled third class, stuffed into an unpadded, vintage WWII car for two hours with pungent, pleasant, petite people. We were the only Westerners on the train and everyone wanted to practice saying "hello, Coca-Cola, Michael Jackson," the extent of their English! The scenery was spectacular: a watercolor of rice paddies on terraced hillsides tended by farmers in big, flat hats leading their water buffaloes.

When we arrived, we pushed through the crowds, made our way into the city, found the neat guesthouse recommended by our backpacker's guide, checked in and went off to see the sights.

Later, we walked along a putrid river, breathing air dense with pollution, eating delicious pastries and smoking awful, fifteen cents a pack, filterless cigarettes. We rented bikes and rode in a mass of gawking people to a park on the river. There we hired a boat and were followed and harassed by unpleasant young men saying, "hello, USA, bye-bye," without smiling. It was eerie. On the way back to our guesthouse at rush hour, we got caught in the midst of a fast moving sea of bicycles with no room to maneuver and no way to escape. It was both terrifying and exhilarating.

March 26

I'm back in Hong Kong now. Mark had to leave for Sydney today so we caught the night ferry back and Mark and I enjoyed a rousing game of backgammon surrounded by snoring Chinese.

As I write this, Mark is on his way home to his prison guard job in Australia while Janice and I are back at the hostel on the hill, packing up. We're going to hang out at the airport and hope to catch a standby flight to Singapore without too much hassle or too many hours or days of waiting.

Love, Patty

Postscript bulletin: We slept in a quiet corner of this cacophonous airport and now, sixteen hours after arriving, it is 10:00 A.M., March 27th, and we are booked on a flight leaving for Singapore in one hour.

March 31

We spent two days in Singapore. It was clean, safe and determinedly dull. We were more than ready to move on and, after a little research, we hopped on a bus to Malaysia. After we were dropped off at the Malaysian border, the spit-shined driver of the spit-shined Mercedes bus politely pointed us towards visa and customs. Without looking back, we plunged into the crowd.

Instantaneously, we were accosted from every direction by leering men, saying, "Hello, what your name? Where you come from? You want change money? Where you go? You like me?"

Holding our passports tightly, we maneuvered our way through this chaotic mass of people, cars and booths marked with strange words and exotic script. Finally, after wondering if we'd taken a wrong turn and were caught in an airlift or political rally, a Good Samaritan spoke to us in English and got us to the right booth.

The stamping of our passports took a few seconds and then we found ourselves in front of Abdul, the Customs Lothario. He wanted to know all about us, but most importantly, whether we would go out with him when we returned to Singapore. To appease this man who could rip our bags apart, dissect each item and probably strip-search us as well, we played along. We told him the name of our guesthouse, took his phone number and got out of there in a hurry. When we looked back, he was surrounded by men laughing and slapping him on the back.

This is a Muslim country and had we been thinking or paying attention to the guidebooks' warnings, we would have dressed differently. My sleeveless dress showed some cleavage and Janice was wearing a miniskirt. We set ourselves up for harassment and that is what we got. The stereotype of the wild and easy Western woman preceded us and I do hate to perpetuate a stereotype. From here on out we will dress modestly, except on the beaches, of course!

Onwards. We found the bus to the main station in Johor Bahru, only to learn the nonstop buses to Mersing, a coastal village, were not running. We were referred to an ominous and ancient-looking vehicle, without a door or glass in the windows, that would give us a transfer halfway through the trip. Throwing caution to the wind, we climbed aboard.

The roads are narrow; the drivers are maniacs. The noise and vibration of the vehicle made thinking blessedly impossible. The driver repeatedly slammed on his brakes and swerved off the road to pick up new passengers. When we thought the bus surely could not hold another person, it stopped and picked up a family of seven! I loved every death-defying minute and saw my first pixie-like monkey just hanging out by the side of the road. The countryside was filled with a combination of rubber and palm oil plantations interspersed with burned-out land, cleared and waiting to be turned into more rubber or palm oil plantations.

We arrived in Mersing unscathed. As we disembarked from the bus, we were met by a ferry boat captain looking for passengers. We said we would be happy to take his boat to Tioman Island in the morning if he would steer us to a nice place to spend the night. Well, our nice place was on the main street of this noisy town with dogs that never shut up and roosters who start crowing hours before dawn. The nice part was the room was only $1.75, I experienced my first squat toilet and it's only a short walk to catch our boat so I am vociferously not complaining!

Janice, sporting bloodshot eyes like mine, was smiling ruefully as we waited at the dock. Our 9:00 A.M. ferry did not leave until 10:30 and I promptly fell asleep for four of the five-hour, twenty-six-mile trip to Tioman. I lay on my back on the deck under a cloudless, equatorial sky, sans sunblock.

Here I sit, in the three-tabled restaurant a few feet from our primitive room where Janice slumbers. I am on the Malaysian island of Tioman, surrounded by locals, curious to see if the hot coffee with cream I just ordered with great fanfare and confusion will accurately materialize. Aaah, my coffee has arrived and it appears, as usual, I'll be drinking strong instant coffee sweetened and whitened with copious amounts of condensed milk. I'm eating a strange little packet of milk biscuits, a cookie-like confection I bought for ten cents. They're quite good dipped in the coffee.

2 April

Dear Mother,

Notice that I switched the day and month around above? That is the way most of the world does it and I make the same damn mistake every time I fill out a form here, which is often. So, from this day forward I am going to put the day first on everything. Now allow me to bitch about the metric system. I feel like a moron not understanding meters and kilograms and so on. Why America continues to use an archaic, illogical system is beyond my understanding.

Enough about that, as I am in a state of tranquility and can't be bothered with petty things. Tioman is reputedly one of the ten most beautiful islands in the world and I blissfully nod in agreement. The pristine beach stretches on forever and is dotted with small resorts consisting of a few bungalows, open-air cafes and mellow, happy Malays. According to brochures, the island itself is thirteen kilometers long and nine kilometers wide with a beautiful dense rainforest in the interior, populated by trees and flora of every shade of green imaginable. Portions of the movie *South Pacific* were filmed here because of its charm and beauty.

Janice and I are sitting in the South Pacific Café, a short walk from our bungalow. I'm drinking local (palm oil and salt enhanced) brewed coffee with condensed milk and listening to Malaysian music on the radio. I am nursing a severe sunburn I picked up on the ferry ride over. The swelling and blisters will soon pass and fail to dampen my blissful demeanor. However, a certain little species of fauna is causing me a speck of trouble. A spider monkey is gleaning my scalp while I write. His name is Bloody Monkey and he is an incorrigible pain in the ass. I have been alternately cleaning up after him or yelling at him for his havoc-causing habits of pee-ing on, stealing, breaking, tipping over or eating my stuff all morning. Nevertheless, he is adorable and I expect to never tire of watching him whilst I loll away the weeks at Mango Grove, Batik and Bungalows, our new home. I am learning how to make batik fabrics and will surprise you with one of my creations soon.

Love, Patty

chapter two

Of Myths and Fairy Tales

17 September 1989

Tonight we attended the wedding reception of a local man and a British woman. The two hundred or so Malays were dressed in their finest sarongs and silky pajama-like outfits and the hundred-plus tourists wore their best T-shirts. A band of drums and guitars was playing traditional and Western music and the beach was packed with dancers. There was sweet black tea to drink, little pastries to eat and eligible bachelors to meet. The young, attractive bride and groom wandered around smiling and chatting. The man's family owns the festive resort where the wedding and reception were held and the newlyweds will live there. Sounds enchanting and I fantasize that soon I too will meet the man of my dreams.

18 September

The Fates assured that we'd be up in time for our 9:00 A.M. departure on the slow boat back to Mersing. I went inside, lay down on the boatman's stinky foam mattress and fell asleep. I was awakened by a mysterious lack of ferryboat engine vibrations and its put-put-put.

Janice poked her head in the door to say Alang, one of the guys we met at the wedding, was outside with his Hydrofoil requesting permission to kidnap and take us to the island of Rawa. I nodded sleepily, grabbed my backpack and we jumped across to a gleaming white behemoth of a boat that dwarfed the ferry and left it rocking pitifully in its wake. I went down into the cabin and continued my nap.

Ten minutes later, Janice woke me bubbling with enthusiasm about Alang, Rawa and the other merits of our detour. "Look out the window. Have you ever seen anything so beautiful? He is having a chalet prepared for us, they are serving breakfast right now in the restaurant, the beach is world class and we are his guests and should forget about paying for anything," she gushed.

Feeling magically refreshed, I jumped up excitedly and we disembarked onto a long wooden jetty. I noticed my backpack, about fifty yards ahead, being carried toward a group of enchanting chalets by a servant who seemed to have materialized out of thin air.

Before I could say, "Destiny is afoot a few feet from here," we were in the restaurant and I was shaking hands with Alang's brother, Mahmood. I stared as he held my hand a second too long and gazed into my eyes. What was it about his five-foot-nine-inch, slightly overweight though gorgeous frame, beautiful dark hair and chic mustache, sensual brown eyes, sexy accent and seductive smile that immediately attracted me? I wasn't sure but something strange and magical had me noticing, in the restaurant's bamboo framed mirror, how badly I needed a haircut, eyebrow pluck, skin exfoliation, makeup application and contact lens insertion. Then the four of us sat down and coffee, tea, juice, eggs, toast, pancakes and a huge plate of fruit were placed in front of us. At one point, the two brothers excused themselves and chatted privately by the bar. Another servant was summoned and the small duffel bag that had been sitting by Mahmood's chair quickly disappeared, to my odd relief. I found out later he had intended to leave that morning and changed his plans when Alang asked him to stay and entertain Janice's friend.

When they returned to the table, plans were made for a foray to the private chalets at the end of the island. Janice and I were escorted to our chalet where we showered, changed into beachwear and giggled like schoolgirls. I already knew I was positively smitten with Mahmood and Janice was definitely not smitten with Alang, though she was enjoying his company.

Before you could say, "Love is in the air, the surf, the sand and coral," we were admiring the shoreline as a speedboat raced us toward our appointment with destiny—no, lunch—at Omar's Place. Omar is their younger half brother who owns the two chalets and awesome kitchen/den/deck/beach bungalow, into which we soon found ourselves settling.

A supply boat had been following ours and, as we opened wine bottles, two workers scurried about, preparing a barbecue feast.

As we ate, Alang and Mahmood began quietly discussing what sounded like a family problem. As they talked among themselves for a few minutes, I distinctly heard the words "prince" and "princess." When I put my hand on Mahmood's arm and looked questioningly at him, he laughed and then Alang joined in. The brothers almost sheepishly admitted they were princes of the royal family of Malaysia, but then said no more. Imagine that! I was beginning to feel like Cinderella...

I found both backgammon and Scrabble boards and challenged my handsome prince to three out of five for the former and a hundred point head start on the latter. After many hours of stiff competition, scintillating conversation, romantic sighing and divine eating we looked up and noticed the sun was setting. Janice and Alang were deeply engrossed in what sounded like a discussion about agriculture.

Mahmood took my hand. We walked down to the tiny beach and, while the sun was in its apex of decline, he kissed me. I quivered, I quavered, I quaked and in my thoughts I said, *I am really quite taken by you, Mahmood, and am most willing to let you have your way with me tonight, if you would be so kind.*

22 September

We floated through the next few days, separating only to use the toilet. Fortunately, we were able to spend long stretches of time in his room, admiring his shell collection. We swam, snorkeled and fished off the end of the jetty. We played hours of backgammon, where he had the upper hand, and Scrabble, where I had to increase his head start to two hundred points. We ate fabulous meals, often the only time we saw Janice and Alang, who were off in a romantic haze of their own.

This morning, while playfully wrestling with me in the surf, Mahmood stepped on a sea urchin. He stumbled out of the water, dizzy with pain.

I counted forty-five black spikes imbedded on the sole of his foot while three workers took turns beating them vigorously with a wooden paddle. This had to be done to dissolve the barbed, bacteria laden spikes and dissipate the poison. I squeezed lime wedges over the bleeding, swelling foot to disinfect the wound. More than two hours were spent on this torturous remedy while Mahmood carried on, unperturbed by the pain, entertaining me with tales of far worse. Finally, he told the workers to take the rest of the day off and called for a Johnny Walker Black on the rocks for himself and a Stoli martini for me. His foot had ballooned to twice its normal size and I was in awe, as he didn't miss a beat in continuing the royal treatment of an infatuated guest.

24 September

At breakfast, the four of us decided to head over to the mainland and down to Johor Bahru, as we all had business to attend to. Within the hour we were on the Hydrofoil, gliding over the South China Sea, speeding toward Mersing, nine miles away.

Mahmood took me to meet his friend Dr. Linus, who gave me a B-12 shot and loaded me up with antibiotics and other useful drugs for a worsening sore throat and fever. I noticed that, right before we left, he gave Mahmood a handful of sleeping pills, but I said nothing. Then we found Janice and Alang and we were soon off by plush Mercedes taxi to Johor Bahru.

I have learned a little more about the man of my dreams. He is forty-four years old, has a nineteen-year-old daughter and a forty-two-year-old wife in Brunei from whom he is long separated. He has lived in Brunei for twenty years and has two very successful businesses, selling fire and safety equipment to the Brunei government and Shell Oil, which has the monopoly on Brunei oil.

Mahmood told me he has been spending more and more time on Rawa lately, as he and Alang are determined to wrest total control of the island from their six younger half brothers and sisters, since only Mahmood and Alang are legitimate heirs; the others really had no right to inherit their father's estate. Their father, Prince Mohamed Archibald, married a British waitress he met in London. Because they never got around to converting her to Islam or having a proper Muslim marriage ceremony until it was much too late, there now is a lengthy legal battle over who are the legitimate heirs to the father's fortune and much ugliness has emerged.

In Johor Bahru, we checked into the Tropical Inn, went across town to the Holiday Inn and had an incredibly savory Chinese dinner of garlic eel, scallops in oyster sauce, sea cucumbers and red bean pancakes for dessert. Afterwards, we hung out in their lounge and met up with Yem, the Crown Prince. 'Yem' is actually an acronym; his real name is exceedingly long. He was there with a cousin, Shah, Mahmood's youngest half brother, Samad, as well as a few henchman/bodyguards and a gorgeous model who is a former Miss Philippines. The next in line to be Sultan of Johor was a pleasant, personable, august prince. We chatted, but I didn't dare forget for a moment with whom I was bantering. Had he felt compelled to say, "How dare you speak to me that way, you impertinent commoner! Off with your head!" I'd have understood and gone willingly to my demise.

We didn't stay long because Mahmood and Alang were worried Yem would make demands on them and saying no is not an option. Also, Mahmood and I were anxious to be alone.

26 September

Yesterday, I got my hair cut while the guys and Janice had shampoos. I look ever so much better!

Today, I saw a new side of Mahmood. We were in a restaurant and a group of young men who were very high on something came in and began to aggressively flirt with me. They ignored my, "Go away, please," and one of them grabbed me, which sent Mahmood into pistol-whipping action. I watched in amazement as he pulled out a gun and whacked the guy over the head with it. Luckily, there was no blood, though he did knock the guy out. We left the restaurant in haste. I was pretty shaken up, though I felt like the damsel in distress of an old western novel whose man has stood up for her honor. It made Mahmood seem even more like the prince of my dreams. Afterward, we went back to the hotel for the rest of the day.

Both Mahmood and I knew our feelings for one another were deepening. We held each other and came to the conclusion that we were undoubtedly, indubitably, irrefutably falling in love.

He is, though I try to dissuade him, totally convinced I am the most exquisite woman ever created. He believes everything I say and do is brilliant. I tell him no more than half is, but he is incorrigible. The more I tell him about my eccentricities and my past, the more he appears to care. He dotes on me, waits on me, is tender and caring and he buys me really awesome presents like a huge bottle of Joy perfume, exquisite gold jewelry and clothes. I have no memory of ever being with a man who is so wonderful in so many ways. In every way, actually. Name a wonderful quality and he has it. And he is smart; his vocabulary and his grasp of math and science are superior. He has a marvelously open mind, a witty, irreverent sense of humor and he is a wonderful lover.

27 September

We took Alang to the airport and he flew home to Kuala Lumpur. Janice was not sad for long, though, because we were off to Singapore, under the wing of Mahmood. Janice and Mahmood get along swimmingly and she and I are closer than we've ever been, so all the stars are in alignment.

Our first stop in Singapore was the office of Mahmood's travel agent, Ilene. Janice and I have been thinking about going to Indonesia, but we were a day late for the bimonthly boat. Just as well, because Ilene found us cheap airline tickets from Singapore to Jakarta, leaving October third.

We took Janice to Skyscraper, our favorite guesthouse, then he and I checked into the Equatorial Hotel, an art deco treat. It was there, tentatively, that Mahmood and I began to talk about the future.

In short order, we agreed ours was True Love and we were Soul Mates and we would Get Married, Have Babies and Live Happily Ever After. Mahmood said he would handle all the details; I smiled demurely.

29 September

Today, Mahmood discovered I had only eight hundred dollars left and he went into shock. He could not fathom how I was able to live on so little and he immediately wrote me a check for one thousand dollars to spend in Indonesia. He also asked me very politely to stop traveling after this trip, which brought tears of joy and relief to my eyes. I suspect the cause for my feelings was a combination of backpacker's burnout and true love.

Mahmood must leave for Brunei on Saturday and I will move into the guesthouse with Janice. We will spend the time preparing for Indonesia. A few more days and we fly away!

4 October

Zoe, my most beauteous best friend and confidant, I have only a minute to dash this note off to you. Please accept my deep, deep, deep remorse for postal paralysis, new-news negligence and missive misdemeanors. I have been so busy falling in **"LOVE"** with the **"MAN"** and this is not just any love and he is not just any man. No, no, no, this is a love and he is a man that warrants bold, underlined, quotation-marked, embossed, glow-in-the-dark gold leaf capital letters. And...he's a prince. Yes, a real prince, literally as well as figuratively.

With that tantalizing tidbit, I must leave you for now. More to come.

Love, Patty

7 October

Dear Mother,

Please accept my profound apologies for the letter lapse of these past three weeks and chalk it up to all that has been happening to me. Suffice it to say, I have fallen in love...and with a prince of Malaysia, no less.

I am sitting in an open-air restaurant, drinking sublime Balinese coffee and watching a tissue skinned old woman change the exotic fruit, orchids and incense on a little altar by the door. The wonder of Bali is beyond compare.

Janice and I flew on Wednesday from Singapore to Jakarta, in a plane packed with Indonesian workers returning to their villages. The two-hour flight had the ironic feel of a local bus trip, though there were no chickens on board.

We spent one night in Jakarta, a noisy, exciting city with refreshing character. The next afternoon we climbed onto a train and oh, what a journey we had to Denpasar! Thirty hours passed in a haze of clove cigarette smoke and a sleepless daze of fussing babies and chatty students wanting to practice their English. We perched uncomfortably on narrow, wooden seats staring out our tiny windows at mile after mile of palm oil and rubber plantations interspersed with stretches of untended land, quaint villages and bustling cities.

We arrived in Denpasar, capitol of Bali, thoroughly disoriented, exhausted, sore to the very core of our being. Allah was beneficent, though, because our subsequent two-hour minibus ride out to the beach accompanied by interesting fellow passengers was marvelous fun and we effortlessly found a gem of a guesthouse. We slept for twelve hours and woke up ready to shop!

Mahmood, my new love, wants me to replace my wardrobe with clothes suitable for the Consort of a Prince. Please note that was written tongue-in-cheek. Seriously though, I'm tired of the frayed, stained, funky stuff I've traveled with and lately, my things barely even pass muster for a grungy backpacker. Once I return to his side, I need to have a more conservative, chic wardrobe. He has a tailor friend in Singapore who is going to make me the right stuff when I go back. But for now, the batiks of Bali are calling out to me and I am in love and have money to spend. Ahhh, bliss. I'll write more later…

Janice and I spent eleven hours looking at ten thousand different pieces of rayon or cotton fabric dyed and sewn ten thousand different ways. I bought one dress, two shirts, a belt for the dress and two pairs of earrings. There is twice as much jewelry and half as many leather goods as there are clothes from which to choose. The prices are so low they rival a good thrift shop and remind me sadly that such things are possible only when there are the sweatshops in the neighborhood. Someone is making a fortune here and it sure ain't the village seamstresses.

Most of the tourists are extroverted Australians with a can of beer in one hand and a cigarette in the other. Most of the locals are exploited hawkers, just trying to put rice on the table by selling defective knock off watches, ugly jewelry and stupid toys. There is also an inordinate number of stunning, young, poorly dressed women with sickly babies slung over their backs begging us to buy braided leather bracelets.

The Balinese are mostly Hindus, with some Animists, Muslims, Christians and Buddhists mixed in. There are tiny, elaborately carved temples and offerings are made everywhere to the local gods. In doorways and tree stumps, on counters and sidewalks, one trips over flower garlands and fruit bowls, incense and small statues of Shiva or Ganesh. When I bought the shirts yesterday, the shop owner kissed the money and then touched it to all her racks of clothing, explaining that the gesture was for good luck.

I'm going to end this missive, as it is time now for me to write a love letter to Mahmood. This month apart is excruciating but necessary, as he is in Brunei officially ending his marriage and trying to free up some time by delegating business. Now, please don't harp about rebound relationships. The man with the perfect resume does not exist and Mahmood's marriage has been dead for years. He is a darn near perfect specimen, mark my word.

Love and kisses, Patty

14 October

Zoe darling,

I am a basket case of unhinged anticipation as I count the seven hours until my scheduled telephone conversation with Mahmood, the man I love. We set this up, as going thirty days without his voice seemed inhuman. He has been getting almost daily letters from me, but I have had no way, until today, of hearing, of knowing whether he still worships me! I finally found a place where I can make the call. It's a big, complicated, expensive undertaking and I must succeed or I shall kill myself, clutching a buzzing receiver to my ear, hanged by the neck from the phone cord.

I told Mahmood I am willing to do whatever he asks of me once we are reunited on the 29th and, happily, I have no clue what is to become of me next. I only have conjecture and a multitude of very surreal dreams as my subconscious mind struggles to do what my conscious mind can't. True Love and infatuation are close cousins, differentiated only by the test of time. I want certainty. One definition of anxiety is the inability to predict the future. What if he blows me off on the phone or isn't even there or tells me his wife won't give him a divorce or that she'll ruin him if he sees me again or maybe she's killed him or is screening all his calls?

In my panic, I am sleeping poorly, have chronic diarrhea, no appetite, a perpetually knotted stomach and a mind obsessed. On the other hand, I am excited, optimistic and contented in my love and his worthiness. Here are a few possibilities, some realistic, some ridiculous, of my lovesick circumambulations:

One: He could get amicably divorced.

Two: Rather than divorce the first wife, with the loss of face that entails, she would give him permission to marry again and I would become his second wife. Then he would set her up with a home to live out her life quietly. The question is, could I live with this, even if he would never "be with" Azizah, wife number one?

Three: We could marry and live in Brunei, a tiny country on the island of Borneo, owned by the Sultan of Brunei. He is the wealthiest man in the world until his oil reserves run out in twenty-five years. In his little Sultanate of 200,000 people, there are no taxes, no poverty and medical care is free. The country is almost completely ethnic Malay and Muslim with a few thousand Shell Oil employees, British teachers and palace tutors. The populace is quite conservative except for the upper echelon, which is laid back and progressive. Polo is very popular and Mahmood plays and has horses. He also dives and hunts and used to be a fixture at the palaces, but he's not into that anymore. He wants a quiet life and lots of children, especially sons as he has only a daughter. I may end up in Brunei, playing polo and having babies.

Four: We could marry and settle in Rawa, the island Mahmood partly owns, where we met. He wants to build a home there to live in some, most or all of the year. The island has thirty-five chalets and thirty-five workers on twenty-six acres of coconut trees, an idyllic beach and a pristine coral reef. There are dogs, dozens of cats, a pet goat, monkeys, a baboon, chickens, monitor lizards and snakes. Can you imagine a more wonderful place to raise children? With a few servants, a huge library, the water, fresh air and Mary Poppins, life would be loverly.

These are the top four potentialities and enough for now. Janice has been an invaluable sounding board. She really likes Mahmood and is supportive of our relationship. Though she would rather have me continue the journey with her, she understands and will continue traveling alone. She has no illusions about a future with Alang and when their fun together runs its course, she is heading to Katmandu.

Mahmood wants to see the world and we've talked about traveling together. He has no interest in doing it with a backpack and budget, though, and I can live with that.

I am going to eat mangoes, read *The Prince of Tides*, shop for Christmas presents, sunbathe hedonistically and get a massage now to wile away the six remaining hours until it's time for me to call Mahmood. I'll return to this letter afterwards, so please excuse me.

Post-telephone call platitudes: He loves me absolutely, misses me terribly, pines for me incessantly and is also counting the hours until our reunion. This priceless nine-minute conversation had a twenty dollar price tag and took over an hour of red tape and waiting.

Janice and I leave for Ubud tomorrow, a town north of here known for its handicrafts and ambience.

Love, Patty

16 October

The sun has yet to rise on this Monday morning. We are in Ubud, a small town in the center of Bali. Our two-room guesthouse is threadbare and eerie. A dirt-poor, simple and most peculiar family runs it. One of the seven children is a midget, another a severely retarded deaf-mute, two others seem a tad off and there is an old man who babbles conversationally with great arm movements.

They served me an omelet yesterday that had a strange taste and now I am too sick to leave. I suspect, in my delirious state of dehydration from vomiting and dysentery, that serving rancid food is their strategy for keeping guests longer. I bought the family a can of milk last night when I crawled down the road to buy cigarettes and they shed tears of gratitude, as did I, because black coffee is not my cup of tea.

I just popped three grams of vitamin C, purged my bowels of a watery substance, drank a liter of bottled water, ate two small bananas, took a bucket bath and feel awful. I wish I were recuperating in an air-conditioned, bug-free room on a bed longer than five feet, with a mattress thicker than one quarter inch and unstained sheets that didn't smell. Poor, pitiful me.

19 October

I was sick but a day and we quickly hightailed our way out of Ubud on the nicest bus we could find. The four-hour trip through gorgeous, ear popping highlands to Lovina Beach was a joy and we are safely cloistered in a clean, delightfully normal establishment with fresh smelling eggs. Lovina Beach is a mellow, quiet, untouristed small town and we have decided to stay right here for the next ten days until we return to Jakarta to catch our flight to Singapore. Janice and I are going to read books on the beach while getting two dollar massages and count the ever decreasing hours until we are reunited with our menfolk.

31 October

Janice and I found a plush, three-meals-included bus for the twenty-nine-hour return trip to Jakarta from Bali. Our day in Jakarta was spent inhaling thick pollution, avoiding death on chaotic, lawless streets, jostling our way through shops crowded with aggressive hawkers and having an all-around cultural experience. The two hour flight back to Singapore was uneventful and my airport reunion with Mahmood was divine. I was a quivering bundle of nerves until I looked into his eyes and saw my glorious future in his beatific smile. There is not a shadow of a shadow of a doubt he is my soul mate and we will be happy together, happy forever, happily raising happy children.

Unfortunately, Alang was unable to make it to the airport, but plans are in place for us to fly tomorrow to Kuala Lumpur to meet up with him. We took Janice to the Skyscraper guesthouse and Mahmood and I went to our favorite hotel, The Equatorial, for the night.

We opened a bottle of champagne, Mahmood proposed, I said yes and he gave me a stunning emerald and diamond ring. He shared his thoughts about how to proceed, I sighed in agreement and we went to bed and made glorious love.

3 November

Yesterday, we collected Janice, flew first class to Kuala Lumpur and were met at the airport by Alang. He took us to an opulent downtown hotel, we had dinner and then he left us at a nightclub to run home for a while. The 'while' turned into six hours; Mahmood confessed his brother was notoriously late and unreliable. Finally, the three of us took a taxi back to the hotel.

Alang showed up at noon today and we all flew to Johor Bahru. We will spend one night there, drive up to Mersing in the morning and stay a night at a guest house run by a charming man named Khalid.

6 November

We came across the water on the Hovercraft, a most romantic vehicle, and here I sit on Rawa, eighteen blissful hours later.

Princess Maria, Mahmood and Alang's older half sister, the only offspring of their father's first, short-lived, teenaged marriage, has just joined me with her monkey, Sapphire. Maria prefers to be called Chu and she doesn't like her monkey to be referred to as a monkey, but rather as her child. She is forty-six, has a home in Johor Bahru and has worked as a Club Med "Gracious Host" these past few years. Gracious Host is the best translation from French for the people who mingle with and help the guests at the resort.

Chu has a nonstop, stream of consciousness, do not interrupt, accept hearing the same long anecdote half a dozen times, feel free to write while I'm talking as long as you look up and nod regularly, conversational style, but she also has poignant stories about Mahmood when he was very young and they lived in Australia and England. And she has fantastical tales of the supernatural as well as tedious tales of Sapphire's toilet training. I am able to get a word in edgewise every hour or two and she seems quite taken with me as her brother's love. Mahmood says she will be an invaluable help to me in navigating my way through his culture and family. Furthermore, she can cook the most labor intensive, awe-inspiring, world-class Malaysian dishes. Today, she intends to find a worker to help her collect leaves from a couple dozen different island plants to meticulously wrap around fish fillets for Mahmood's favorite dish. I just offered to help and she's glowing.

The Rawa chalets, restaurant and dive shop are overseen by Prince Hassan, a younger half brother and, according to Chu, evil incarnate. Apparently, his goal in life is to torture and/or kill her Sapphire. Last Chinese New Year, for example, Hassan and Yem, the Crown Prince, tied firecrackers to Sapphire's tail and lit them. Chu says she was so angry she attacked Hassan with her fists and yelled at Yem, a brave act. Sapphire still has nightmares and panic attacks when she hears loud noises, poor furry child.

Hassan is hyperactive, tall and skinny, never smiles, ignores Chu, Mahmood, Janice and me, fawns over Alang and, most interestingly, is thirty-four and unable to read or write! He grew up on the island and he never wanted to go over to the mainland for school, so he never did. He has letters and newspapers read to him surreptitiously, as he tries to maintain a literate façade.

The incredible facts and foibles of the Johor Royal Family are mind boggling and I have no doubt what I've learned is barely a surface skim and the murky pool is bottomless.

There are over forty direct descendants of the first Sultan of Johor, Abu Bakar, who was put on the throne by the British in the mid 1800s. Nearly half of the forty are Mahmood, his brothers, sisters and their progeny. These descendants carry the title Tunku, a gender neutral term meaning Prince or Princess. The Tunku is only passed down through the men, though daughters carry the title. Mahmood is the eldest son of the second eldest

son of the eldest sons on back to the first Sultan. The family members have
not been big breeders over the generations, which probably is a good thing,
because, to keep the bloodline pure, cousins and even brothers and sisters
have married each other. Mahmood is sixth in line to the throne after the
Crown Prince, his two young sons, his brother and first cousin. Because
Mahmood would not marry the Sultan's daughter, his second cousin,
twenty plus years ago, he and the Sultan are estranged. Mahmood tells me
he married Azizah, his first wife, and settled in Brunei to get away from
family problems. This is a sketchy but fairly accurate overview of his family
situation.

Mahmood and I will return to Singapore shortly and he will fly to
Brunei on the fifth. I will go there on the sixth, escorted by his friend
Andre, to stay for ten days in the home of one of Mahmood's employees.
My presence there is to be the height of discretion and no small risk for
Mahmood, since his estranged wife is having a hysterectomy and they are
still settling their divorce agreement which hopefully will be over post
haste. He wants me to see where he has lived for the past twenty years as
Brunei may end up being my home or a place I visit often. We both prefer
the idea of my living in Johor Bahru and Rawa, but anything is possible.

Janice is going to stay on the island while we are gone, being enter-
tained by Chu and hopefully Alang, if he can get away from Kuala Lumpur.
Janice tells me he confessed he is still married. In fact, he introduced her to
his wife, Lorraine, and their four children, at Khalid's guesthouse in
Mersing. The children range in age from two to nine and are very cute and
precocious. Janice and Lorraine spoke only a few words, but Janice thought
she was nice. Janice told Alang she is not interested in breaking up a family
or looking after him. She has found he needs constant attention and super-
vision.

Mahmood assures me that as soon as his first wife is better and the settlement formalized, we'll be announcing our engagement.

10 November
Bandar Seri Begawan, Brunei Darussalam
My most esteemed friend Zoe,
Salutations from yet another new and exciting postmark. Note that
every stamp and piece of currency this country produces has a flattering

likeness of his Royal Highness, Sultan Bolkiah etc., etc., etc. The addenda to his name go on for three pages and the additions to his main palace go on for three miles like the zeros on his bank account and the jewels on his wives.

I am staying in a modest little house as the guest of Boy, his girlfriend Dalia and their baby. Boy is Mahmood's technician and Dalia does some cleaning and secretarial stuff for him. They are both really sweet and I am a happy camper.

My first night in town Mahmood took me to the Yacht Club, introduced me to a bunch of Westerners and we had a few drinks. Alcohol is illegal in Brunei except in designated places for consumption by foreigners only. There was a sign on the wall stating that it is a major offense to serve drinks to Muslims. When I asked about it, Mahmood and his friends laughed, explaining the alcohol ban was really a joke, unenforceable and unenforced.

Azizah's hysterectomy was a success and she returns home tomorrow. Though his first wife's surgery was minor and she and Mahmood have not been together as a couple for several years, we are being discreet for the sake of her family. Hopefully, as Mahmood predicts, it will all be over very soon and he'll be free to marry me. His friends seem happy he's found someone and I do hope you also are convinced this is going to be a good thing for me.

During the days, Mahmood comes by on his lunch hours, tea times and at fivish. One day he sent a woman to take me to the museum and she returned the next day to take me to the one shopping center in town. I had a wallet full of money and did not find a single thing to buy until I went into the grocery store. The prices were exorbitant, but the selection of Western foodstuffs had me salivating greedily. I went on a cart-filling spree, wantonly ignoring pricetags, as I snatched muesli, Triscuits, Edam cheese, strawberries, yogurt, broccoli, Brussels sprouts and a cornucopia of other comestibles. Dalia found me some room in the fridge and Mahmood and I have been breakfasting and lunching in style.

We go out for dinner every evening and, since the first night, I've been to the British Teacher's Club, the British Club and the VIC Club, which means Veterans in Combat, I think.

The teachers were great fun to banter with. They had hilarious stories to tell about the state of education in oil rich Sultanates, where the pay is high and the interest in learning is low. Most of the parents have little education and the kids don't see much value in it. Truancy is rampant, homework is rarely done, school is more social than academic and the kids treat teachers like servants. With Big Daddy Oilbucks taking care of them, they don't really need to work, and if they do, they can get a cushy civil service job, literacy optional. According to the teachers, the average Bruneian prefers to spend his or her day watching illegal satellite television, planning the next shopping trip to Singapore and eating deep-fried shrimp crackers.

Yesterday we were up early and set off for Kota Kinabulu, on the other end of the country, a sixty-seven-mile trek over perfect roads. We saw a variety of lush tropical trees, oil fields, only new-looking cars and vast stables, tracks, buildings and the exceedingly huge palace with sparkling towers and domes and its very own polo field on which His Highness fulfills his passion.

Zoe, I must finish this letter and start preparing for my darling's forty-fourth birthday, today, right here, very soon, so pardon my abrupt departure and know I remain,

Your devoted friend, Patty

14 November

I am leaving Brunei in the morning. Despite some pleasant attributes, Mahmood and I are both convinced we do not want to live in Brunei when we marry. He will need to travel back and forth for at least a year or two, because he has many business interests here, but I can live in Malaysia, which I prefer. We remain more deeply in love with each other than is humanly possible, and life just keeps getting better.

I am going to Michigan for most of December, we have decided. Mahmood was so overwhelmed by the rose and Hallmark card I gave him on his forty-fourth birthday, he told me I should go home for Christmas. He won't come with me. His asthma can't take cold weather and he refuses to consider traveling anywhere that gets colder than seventy degrees Fahrenheit, so even in July, the Michigan climate makes him nervous. We will work out my itinerary when we get to Singapore and odds are I'll be home for Christmas. Mahmood intends to spend the month finding a place for me to live in Johor Bahru and getting year-end stuff done for his businesses in Brunei.

While brainstorming the other night we came up with what will be my Muslim name for conversion and marriage. We have decided on Noor Faridah Sutherland Binte Abdullah. 'Noor' is a family name meaning 'light,' 'Faridah' was his mother's Muslim name, 'Sutherland' is a legal necessity, 'Binte' means 'daughter of' and 'Abdullah' was one of the Prophet's followers who said all converts could use his name. I will still use my Christian name for most stuff; the other is mainly a traditional formality.

Mahmood is here and we are going to cook prime rib, Brussels sprouts and mashed potatoes for our final dinner in Brunei. Dessert will be the last of the huge box of Godiva chocolates he gave me and we have a rollicking evening of Scrabble planned. He gets better every day and he beat me for the first time yesterday, which actually means I beat him by less than 200 points. He feels he has a valid right to a Scrabble handicap, because he does not speak American English or know all the two letter words or have a handle on seven-letter-word strategy.

November 29

Dear Zoe,

I leave for Michigan in two days and I am giddy with anticipation and loaded down with copious quantities of Christmas contraband to convey.

We left Brunei on the 15th and spent four nights in Singapore getting me fitted for new contact lens, new glasses and new clothes. Then we moved across the causeway to Johor Bahru and checked into the Holiday Inn for another four days of avoiding the Crown Prince or getting caught by the Crown Prince and having to drink and/or dine with him and his entourage. We spent one day driving around to see where Mahmood was born and other family landmarks like palaces and mausoleums. Another day was spent meeting friends of his who will help me set up a life here.

The next day we went to Rawa with the complete Thanksgiving dinner we had ordered from the hotel and, for the first time in his life, Mahmood participated in the great American tradition, Thanksgiving. He noted that the gorging part was quite similar to what goes on every evening during Ramadhan, when Muslims break their fast. Janice and Chu, who has experienced Thanksgiving a few times with American friends, joined us.

Janice is ready to move on as she is annoyed with Alang, who did not come to Rawa once while we were in Brunei. She is in Singapore now and

Mahmood and I are going tomorrow to meet with her for a day before we all fly off in different directions on the first of December. Katmandu, Brunei and Michigan respectively.

In Scrabble news, Mahmood's game is improving at a phenomenal rate. He has a razor-sharp memory, an uncanny knack for anagrams and the ability to draw the letters he needs out of the bag. I strongly suspect he is using magic, but I have yet to catch him chanting incantations over the letter bag. We average three games a day and Chu begs to play too, but she is hopelessly awful. We employ different strategies to avoid playing with her. We hide in empty chalets, make lame excuses, complain of headaches or indulge her and attempt aversion therapy through humiliation. She is just too darned good-natured for it to work, though.

Darling Zoe, I eagerly await our reunion and first Scrabble game in nine months. You will lose, of course!

The weather has been marvelous, though the monsoon season officially started last week. The resort is shut down now for two months and I'm the only Western person here. There are a dozen workers hanging around to do maintenance and take care of us.

Words fail to express the flawless perfection of my love for Mahmood, of his love for me, of our mutual compatibility in all ways. I am truly blessed. And True Love, as you well know, can cause excessive platitude usage which spawns goofy prose and annoying justifications for the afore-mentioned, compelling desperate users to employ verbiage filled, run-on sentences, as they attempt graceful exits from finally finished correspondence, culminating in customary closures.

Love and kisses, Patty

chapter three

Building Sand Castles

30 December 1989

My holiday in Michigan has ended and my thirty hours of planes and air-ports has been endured. I got off the plane in Singapore bedraggled and bedazzled by impending visions of Mahmood's embrace. Shooting through Customs and Immigration, I grabbed my baggage and went out to meet my man. Lo and behold, he was nowhere to be seen. I wandered around for a half-hour, growing ever more frantic, and then I phoned Andre's house. Andre answered and told me Mahmood was fast asleep, having confused 1:00 A.M. on the thirtieth for 1:00 A.M. on the thirty-first. I took a taxi to the house and discovered that the love of my life had taken a sleeping pill ear-lier and was just about comatose. I managed to keep him semi-conscious for an hour as I bounced off the walls, but it was such an effort, I relented and let him go back to sleep. For the next three hours, I read every magazine in the house and watched him sleep. At dawn, I woke him again and had to start over, because he'd forgotten everything beyond our hello kiss. But he was duly remorseful and after a proper consummation of our thirty days separa-tion, I forgave him all.

Later, we played seven games of Scrabble on the new deluxe board I brought from Michigan. I dropped my handicap to one hundred points and he still won four of the games. He denies doing any homework or practicing while I was gone, but his improvement is just too profound. I am officially dropping my handicap down to fifty points. He is as passionate about the game as I am, and, as his scores improve, an entirely new Scrabble universe is opening up before us. We intend to buy every book we can find on the game, memorize both the two and three-letter word lists and do anagram puzzles daily. We are genuinely giddy with anticipation. This alone should convince any skeptics we are true soul mates, two peas in a pod, two letter tiles in a bag.

We also found time to unpack my luggage and my gifts for him. He was enamored of everything. We found a one-hour photo shop and had my seven rolls of film from the trip developed. The pictures turned out great. The distribution of the eleven Rolex watches to my family members on Christmas morning made for some priceless photos. More priceless, though, were the shots of people's expressions when I confessed they were knock-offs.

Mahmood is in awe over how supportive and easy-going my family is about him and our relationship. He can't believe no one blinked an eye about him being Muslim, brown-skinned and fifteen years my senior. Truly, we are blessed to be loved by such open-minded and progressive people.

He is finally here and all mine. We are free to begin our life together...

31 December

Mahmood left me at 9:00 this morning to do a million things and returned at 5:00, dead on his feet. I, on the other hand, slept until noon, lolled around happily and drank copious amounts of good room service coffee. What was he doing all day without me? He was organizing, supervising, brainstorming and possibly even indulging in manual labor, as my new and glorious pad takes shape. There is so much to do before I can move in and Mahmood and Foo Chee Kim, a man who works for him, are not allowing me to help. I beg and grovel and show them my muscles but they just shake their heads, wink conspiratorially and chide me to be patient.

On New Year's Eve we stayed in and feasted on pork free pate, cheeses, fruit, Champagne and Scrabble. We were asleep by eleven. New Year's Day was uneventful and my final jet-lagging day of time-zone readjustment. Mahmood and I have been on opposite schedules since I got back and it does get bothersome. We both love watching the other sleep, though, which has compensated.

2 January 1990

We came across the causeway into Johor Bahru midday yesterday and went straightaway to my new pad. Foo Chee Kim took possession of it on the first and the lease will stay in his name to circumvent any 'potential non-sense,' as Mahmood calls it. Foo is going through a rough patch financially and Mahmood is compensating him generously for his valuable assistance. His wife works full-time and they have three school-aged daughters. He is an active Buddhist and looks after famous monks when they come to town.

The house is in a quiet Chinese neighborhood five minutes by taxi from downtown. According to Mahmood and Foo, Chinese neighbors are the best, because they mind their own business, whereas Malays would be peeking in my windows and setting up a round-the-clock gossip vigil.

The house is cement over brick and there is a high brick wall around the property. As one pulls in off the street, there is a padlocked iron gate that opens to a double carport. Another large padlock opens the exterior decorative iron door that matches the gate and there is a deadbolt on the thick, wooden main door. All the windows sport iron grates. I was a bit freaked out by so much security. I explained to Mahmood and Foo that in Northern Michigan we never lock our house or cars or even take the keys out of the ignition. They were truly amazed because, like 99 percent of those here in Malaysia, they assume every place in the United States is over-run with serial killers, drug fiends and rogue cops. Not surprising, because eight out of ten television imports are cop shows and the other two are *Oprah* and *Beverly Hills 90210*. Also, the news here loves to focus—no, obsess—about American crime, racism, Hollywood and political scandals. The misconceptions people have about us are always bemusing and some-times downright frightening.

I walked around the house viewing the three bedrooms and two large bathrooms, the lower level kitchen and the room for another one upstairs, the spacious living/dining rooms on both floors and a tile fishpond under the stairs.

The house has not been lived in for quite some time and it was a dusty, musty, junk-strewn mess. Foo hired five guys to clean and paint and they started this morning,

After the tour of my palace we said goodbye to Foo, checked in to the Holiday Inn and played our first game of Scrabble in my new home country. Then we went out to our favorite restaurant for our favorite entree of garlic eel. We also savored scallops with dried chilies, mixed vegetables with fermented tofu and a cute grouper we pointed to in the huge tank on the wall.

As we were finishing up our red bean pancakes, an acquired taste I've come to enjoy, Foo came by and they whisked me off to a Malaysian nightclub.

We walked into a stadium-sized room with an oversized stage, dance floor and seating for hundreds. The blaring music, a mix of punk, country, rock and Chinese love ballads, was obnoxious. There were oversized disco balls hanging from the rafters and an excess of multi-hued spotlights maniacally roaming over the room.

Young men in black suits and women in short, cleavage-baring dresses and too high heels were so plentiful they kept running into one another. Approximately thirty-seven of them escorted us into one of a couple dozen small glassed in rooms where we were seated on black vinyl loveseats. The glass and chrome coffee table was quickly overflowing with a bottle of Chivas, a siphon, an ice bucket, glassware, stirrers, napkins and bowls of salty snacks. The seventeen people who weren't carrying things into the room were mixing us drinks, asking me stupid questions in terrible English and hitting on Foo and his friend Bernard, who had joined us.

To clarify, the women were prostitutes and the men were keeping an eye on them. These women, some in their teens, were all skinny and hard looking with too much make-up on. Foo told me they were a mix of heroin or pill addicts, students, single mothers, illegals from China and/or the property of the local Mafia. If I'd been able to speak Chinese, I would have attempted some consciousness raising.

Mahmood and I left Foo and Bernard, deep in conversation with four girls, to watch the floor show. There were a dozen dancing singers backing up a well-done striptease, right down to shoes and jewelry. This was followed by a bizarre half-hour of frenzied dancers and at least six costume changes, all of them elaborate and tacky. I felt worn out and a little sickened. Mahmood and I left and were in bed by 2:00 A.M. He woke at 5:30, watched me sleep until 6:30, then he got me up, because he couldn't wait another minute to play Scrabble, make love and eat breakfast, in that order!

12 January

Mommy dear,

I am in love with the finest man on earth. For three-and-a-half days last week I lazed around the hotel room while he was off supposedly agonizing over workmen, water troubles and cracked plaster, to such an extent that things like a bed, a table and a stove could not be dealt with. Or so I was told and believed.

At noon on the fourth day, he told me to put on scruffy clothes and pack up as we were moving in to sleep on the floor and clean my new house. I happily agreed, as I'd been begging to help since the beginning.

We arrived and the front room looked like hell. It was littered with empty paint cans, boxes and tools. But when I walked into the back living area, I was literally floored with shock and dropped to my knees.

My prince had prepared me a palace. Everything was complete. There was a gorgeous white bed already made up with beautiful linens, a matching vanity with chair, a wardrobe and dresser. Around the corner were a kitchen table with place mats and four chairs, shelves full of dishes and glassware and a fully stocked kitchen with rice cooker, stove and refrigerator. I knelt on lovely blue wall-to-wall carpeting and admired white, freshly painted walls.

When I finally stood up and wandered around in a stupor, my eyes welled up with tears. There were vases overflowing with fresh flowers, adorable knick-knacks and romantic gifts he'd hidden in nooks and crannies. Mahmood and Foo watched me, relishing every minute of my surprise and idiotic rapture. I was speechless, overwhelmed with joy and love at my darling's thoughtfulness, great taste, generosity and love for me.

We have been here a week now and it just gets better and better. The workmen, laid-back, cheerful Indonesian illegals, are slowly getting the front room and downstairs livable. We went on a shopping spree and bought a blender, microwave oven, stereo, television and a pantry and bookshelves at an antique store. In the grocery store we filled two shopping carts and at the photo shop we bought ten rolls of film. You can expect visual confirmation of my ecstasy in a couple weeks.

Mahmood is a great cook and has fixed dinner every night since the first, when I made instant oatmeal and fruit salad. I am slowly learning to cook Asian and, as his assistant, I get to chop all the vegetables, crush the spices, ginger and stinky fermented shrimp paste in a stone mortar with a pestle, bone the fish, peel the prawns and wash all the dishes. We always have fresh rice, sliced tiny chilies in soy sauce and we always eat with our hands.

We do most of our shopping with the locals at the night market now. There are a few hundred vendors selling everything from clothes to Chinese medicine to freshly plucked chickens and ducks. The market is out-doors in a huge field a couple miles from our house. I could stay for hours, eating red bean or corn ice cream and watching the guys milk cobras. The venom is a cancer-curing aphrodisiac.

We can't decide whether to get me a roommate until we are married, a servant or Mahmood's sister Chu. Mahmood refuses to allow me to live alone, which is serendipitous as I don't want to. We are leaning toward Chu as there really isn't enough to do to keep a servant busy and roommates can be so awkward. She is on Rawa now and, as Mahmood has some business in Mersing to attend to, we are off in the morning.

Love, Patty

1 February

My favorite mother,

Note the flip side of this postcard is an angle of Rawa you haven't seen yet. The back of the island is a rocky cliff and the drop is about two hun-dred feet at its highest. Tragically, a Canadian tourist accidentally fell to her death there a few years ago. She was a teenager climbing on the rocks with her younger brother, who was so traumatized by watching her fall that he sat paralyzed for hours until they found him. There is a path that runs along the edge and no fence or warning signs. The view of other islands, like Tioman, is excellent from up there and the temptation to get too close to the edge is a strong one. Mahmood and I have taken a picnic lunch and the Scrabble board up there a couple times.

We returned to Johor Bahru last night after an idyllic thirteen days of sylvan pursuits on Rawa. The island doesn't open to tourists for another few days so it was quiet, with just a few staff, Chu, her monkey Sapphire and we two lovebirds. I apologize for not writing while we were there, but my letter would have been a monotony of 'ate, played, swam, kissed, smiled, slept, Scrabble.'

When you write me, please address the letters to P.C.S. An English name attracts attention and the less I get, the better. Technically, we are doing nothing wrong, but Mahmood is concerned that the Sultan, who is notorious for interfering, might find out and try some nonsense. Now that I'm a fixture, we purposely avoid the Holiday Inn and Yem, but odds are high we will be running into Mahmood's family and friends while out. Anyway, don't worry, he's really just trying to avoid gossip and company. Once Mahmood's family realizes he has a house and a wife in Johor Bahru, they will want to visit us and invite us over and Mahmood is determined to avoid that fate as long as possible. I'm too happy to care one way or the other, though I am curious to meet these people he carries on about.

I am thrilled to hear that Bobby will be here in a week. Can't wait to see my brother!

Happy Birthday and I love you, Patty

8 February

Auntie Zoe,

Do you remember, back in 1986, when I was a Navy wife living in Norfolk, Virginia and I had the desire to get pregnant? I couldn't conceive so Uncle Sam paid for my husband and me to undergo a slew of tests culminating in minor exploratory surgery of my reproductive organs. It was determined that there was some scar tissue from a past one week-infection with P.I.D., acquired while engaged and practicing safe sex with an unsafe IUD. It was further determined that the infection probably had nothing to do with my infertility, because my real problem was that I did not ovulate. The stymied experts theorized the only way I could make a baby was by taking fertility drugs. By this time, my marriage was heading downhill fast so I dropped the whole thing and have not bothered to use birth control since.

Do you find this a peculiar way to start a letter? Is it pregnant with possibilities? Is your fertile mind hatching theories? Have you conceived of an embryonic insight? Shall I carry on, planting more seeds?

I quit coffee, cigarettes and alcohol five days ago. I phoned my mother five days ago. I would have phoned or written you earlier, but I am really, really busy as I am converting to Islam and getting married in two and a half weeks.

A week ago I casually mentioned to Mahmood that I was feeling very strange. My period was three weeks late and I'd been writing the symptoms off as premenstrual nuttiness. My breasts were swollen and tender, my sex drive had disappeared and I felt so tired all the time. I jokingly suggested pregnancy and he jumped on it. Before you could say, "Home Pregnancy Test," we had one working on the back of the toilet. It was positive, an obvious dud, I thought, so we went out and bought another one, which was also positive. I was not moved a whit and concluded the results were caused by a premenstrual hormone surge. Mahmood thought otherwise and was acting all crazy excited and carrying on something awful. To satisfy him, I agreed to see our buddy, Dr. Raj, the next day and have another test.

The petri dish offered up what Raj and Mahmood called irrefutable proof, coagulation! I still could not quite grasp it and drilled Raj for half an hour with a multitude of "What about this?" and "What if that?" questions. He and Mahmood found my behavior hilarious until I finally relented and said, "Okay, let's say I really am pregnant. WHAT NOW?"

That afternoon, Mahmood phoned an old ham radio buddy of his who lives in Melacca. He asked him if he could pull some strings with the local Qadi to get me converted and married, there in Melacca, ASAP. Haji Ibrahim Axford, a former Brit, caught the drift immediately and assured Mahmood he'd handle everything. He called the next day to say the Qadi could perform the conversion on 27 February and the wedding the next day. He and his wife, Maimunah, have offered us their house for the ceremony and their names as witnesses on the documents. Haji Ibrahim will act as my Spiritual Father, which means he'll pseudo adopt and then give me to Mahmood at the wedding. Legally, we should be marrying in Johor, but Mahmood doesn't trust the Sultan and doesn't want any family members besides Chu involved. He did give Alang a call whose reaction was "Well, well." I look forward to meeting Lorraine and hope we hit it off. She was a backpacker from England when she met Alang ten years ago and I'd love to hear her story. Apparently, after they'd been living together a few months on an island near Rawa, the Sultan found out and forced them to marry.

Serendipitously, Chu showed up in Johor Bahru the next morning. Mahmood immediately confided in her and she has taken me under her wing. She found the seamstress and helped me pick out fabric for clothing. I was fitted for two traditional, hand-stitched Malay dresses with elastic waists, to wear for conversion and marriage. She took me to a small, dimly-lit shop patronized by village women and I bought an assortment of scarves, blessed oil, henna and some childi en's workbooks on Arabic and Islam. Chu has no experience with pregnancy, but that doesn't stop her from giving me constant advice and comment. I don't mind, since I don't know anything either, and her chatter makes nice background noise.

The day after, I put a scarf over my head and sat down with notebook, pencil and an Islamic teacher to begin memorizing two Arabic prayers, the Tenets and the Pillars of Islam. For my conversion I have to recite at least the most basic prayer in Arabic and answer a bunch of questions. The teacher comes every evening for an hour. He's nice but very serious and if I haven't done my homework, he glares.

Yesterday, I had my first antenatal checkup. Mahmood and I got to see the placenta, a tiny speck on the ultrasound. Dr. Chia Hong Soong advised me to rest a lot, stay away from crowded places and stop taking B vitamins until after the tenth week. I weighed 134 lbs. on the clinic's scales and have another twenty-five or thirty to go. I'm devouring the book *What to Eat When You're Expecting*, which is helping to calm my neurotic fears about food, fetuses and how a former anorexic can possibly enjoy eating for two. The book stresses whole grains, low fat and natural foods and was written by an expert, so it must be good. Actually, it's fantastic and will be my dog-eared tableside bible these next eight months.

Foo and Mahmood went over to Singapore last night to get Bobby and drop Mahmood off at Andre's, because his flight out to Brunei was early this morning. Mahmood got to tell Bobby about my pregnancy and our impending marriage, which I think was unfair, don't you? Well, my brother waltzed in here at 3:00 A.M., wide-awake and manic to talk. Had I not discovered I was pregnant and all, the arrival of a brother would be big, big news. But now it's only really sweet and nice he's here and great I have his company with Mahmood gone.

Well, Mahmood is now in Brunei to try to sort out the most prudent way to dissolve his businesses and avoid his first wife. She and her family could make things very uncomfortable for me and, with a fetus on board, I really need to be married now so that we can say I conceived on the wedding night and the baby was a little early. It's a minor issue that could become major if someone wanted to challenge my baby's legitimacy in court, for an inheritance, say. Otherwise, no one cares, and pregnancy before marriage is common here.

Mahmood is in turmoil, because he wants to bring his daughter, Zahara, to Malaysia to live and he's nervous about how she'll react to me, and, eventually, the baby. And yet, he is also the happiest and most excited expectant husband and father imaginable.

One final and important item before I close this sacred text. The Malay have a tradition Mahmood is determined to follow. **Not one thing is to be bought before the baby arrives.** No clothes, rattles, diapers or even nursery preparation. Nothing! To do so tempts fate and pisses Allah off, with unspeakable repercussions. Mahmood is dead serious and I empathize with where he's coming from. Cards and letters are cool, though, so please write.

Love, Patty and zygote

Postscript: We still do not have a telephone after nearly a month of waiting. Even being a prince who is able to pull strings is useless in this bureaucratic country. Were there heads to bang together, Mahmood would have bonked, but the culprit is Telekom Malaysia, a government-owned entity overstaffed with underpaid and unskilled workers.

13 February

Mother dear,

Have you recovered from the shock of my pregnancy? I haven't either. It's real and wonderful and scary and weird and magical and thrilling and it gets me out of bed three times a night to pee!

Mahmood comes home tomorrow. We talked on the phone this morning— yes, I love having a phone, finally—and he said he would not be here for another four or five days. I started crying when we hung up and Bobby was so moved by my tears that he confided in me that Foo had confided in him that Mahmood had confided in Foo that he was coming home tomorrow, Valentine's Day, to surprise me. Thank Allah for brothers!

Speaking of Allah, my religious lessons are progressing well. Last evening I learned the prayers and rituals associated with being post-menstrual, post-coital and post-birthing. It's important to know the Muslim way. Pronouncing Arabic is intensely frustrating and I must do it over and over and over and still the guttural stuff escapes me.

Bobby is off on another adventure with Foo, who has been so good to him as they brainstorm and visit shops and factories for business ideas and contacts. Chu has taken him out twice to meet her interesting friends, tour a plantation and a couple of touristy handicraft places. Bobby is so desperate to get up to Thailand that I doubt he will last here until the end of the month. Mahmood doesn't think Bobby will find my conversion and the wedding that interesting, anyway. It will all be in Malay, but Bobby still thinks he should be there. We'll see.

With Mahmood gone, I've been catching up on my sleep and house-work, a temporary task, as Foo and Chu have begun the search for a servant. I have also been contemplating my state of mind. I am happy, genuinely happy. I feel right about myself, my pregnancy, my impending marriage, my new home and eating rice every day with my hands. As a Valentine's surprise for Mahmood, I spent two hours this morning contentedly mending a seam that tore in his sarong. I am so much in love and my life is working out so magically that I can hardly believe it.

Love, Patty

20 February

I have unearthed some family history. In 1967, P. Yusof's father sold Mahmood's father, Tunku Archibald Mohamed, four and a half acres to start the original Rawa resort. When P. Yusof's father died, the remaining twenty acres was split among his heirs. Two of his sons, Yusof and Yaya, leased their portions to Rawa Resort and, in 1985, two of their sisters sold small bits to Mahmood and Alang. Mahmood has a stretch of beach half way between the main resort and Omar's called Rawa Bay and Alang has the piece next to it. Omar bought a few acres at one end of the island and the rest of the land is unusable.

In 1989, the twenty-year lease came up for Yusof and Yaya's land. Yusof, not liking the children of Shirley (Mahmood's and Alang's younger half siblings), opted to lease his portion to Mahmood and Alang. Yaya, being a greedy bastard with only one and a half acres to his brother's four, tried to get a fortune for his signature from Mahmood and Alang, was rebuffed, then continued to go with the other siblings. Confusing, isn't it?

Since 30 June, 1989, 75 percent of the bungalows have been in Mahmood and Alang's names and they each have 10 percent of the whole resort. According to Mahmood, from the time Archie, the patriarch, died in 1980 and Shirley, the "Evil Stepmother," died in 1981, her six progeny have been unfair, negligent and rotten as they pocketed the profits, gave themselves high salaries and in every way tried to cut Mahmood and Alang out.

For a year and a half now, the case has been waiting to come up in a court that doesn't want to hear it. No one doubts that Mahmood and Alang will be victorious and the others will have to throw in the towel and pay them hundreds of thousands of dollars of resort income for these past eighteen months…if the case ever comes up.

Mahmood and Alang have an old school chum, Choo Ken Weng, a wealthy Chinese businessman. For 50 percent ownership of Rawa Resort, he is willing to pay off the children of Shirley (including Chu) and pump millions into modernizing the place.

Mahmood and Alang will each hold 25 percent and retain the land and leases in their names.

Different figures have come and gone to pay off the half siblings and the latest is two million, except Lorraine prematurely told the others it would be three million and, of course, that's what they're now demanding, except the island is not worth that in its present condition. And so it goes. We hang out, Hassan and Mele, another half brother and manager of the mainland office, empty the cash register, the others collect salaries and the tourists come and go.

2 March

The day after Mahmood returned from Brunei, he and Foo took off to do "stuff," they said with a wink. Mahmood returned a couple hours later behind the wheel of a shiny, blue Proton Saga, Malaysia's national car. He hadn't even mentioned he was thinking of buying one. I love it and having our own vehicle made the trip to Melacca so much easier. I intend to get my Malaysian driver's license this week, though I wonder how it will be to drive on the "wrong" side of the road.

Today we drove our new car to Singapore and had lunch with Mahmood's mother, Margaret, and her husband, Geof. They're an attractive, witty couple in great health. She's sixty-two and he's seventyish. We told them our news and they extended polite congratulations. There is no demonstrative warmth between Margaret and Mahmood, though they get along fine. I enjoyed the lunch, but there is something unsettling about her. It may have just been the elephant at the table, that huge unspoken question that fills my mind, *Why did you leave your babies and wait forty years to reestab-lish contact?* She won't bring up the past and Mahmood doesn't ask.

Oddly, Alang will have nothing to do with them and Chu thinks they are unfriendly snobs. According to Mahmood, Alang had been very pushy with them about a business deal and was angry when they rejected his pro-posal. And Chu's overbearing personality, when they met on Rawa, com-pelled them to openly snub her. Mahmood thinks that Alang has unresolved hostility towards their mother and Chu is simply jealous because *her* mother isn't rich or white like Margaret. Mahmood thinks both Margaret and Geof are wonderful.

Margaret and Geof just bought a three million-dollar castle/exclusive resort in Ireland and are on their way there to make the place profitable. Their hobby is buying resorts, shopping centers, and companies with potential and turning them around. They live most of the year on a huge ranch in Tasmania and breed racehorses. Mahmood says Geof is the former Walter Cronkite of Australian broadcasting and he's never met an Aussie who hasn't heard of him. They always spend a day or two in Singapore on their way to and from Europe, so we can expect to see them a couple times a year.

7 March

The day after we returned from Singapore, we grabbed Bobby and drove up to Kuala Lumpur for twenty-four hours. After checking into a hotel, Mahmood left us to meet with Alang for some Rawa business as they con-tinue their quest to wrest control. Then we put an excited Bobby on a bus for a twenty-plus-hour ride to Bangkok, enjoyed a dinner of divine French food and returned to the hotel for Scrabble. Pregnancy is not helping my game, to Mahmood's delight.

The next day, we returned to Johor Bahru, unpacked, repacked and gathered up Chu, who wanted to bring Sapphire and her new baby, a slow loris. Chu accepted our 'no' with a pout and the drive to Melacca was uneventful. Haji Ibrahim had made reservations for us at a little resort a few miles from town. We found it easily, got settled in, had an early dinner and I slept twelve hours.

The next morning, I breezed through the conversion with accolades. My Islamic tutor had taught me so well there was much more I wanted to recite, to further impress the Qadi and witnesses. Turning me into a Muslim took twenty minutes and the certificate, plus a laminated, wallet sized I.D. are being sent to me.

It was for the best that Bobby did not come as he would have gone stir crazy with all the sitting, waiting, red tape cutting and time consuming diplomacy in Malay. Hopefully, he's happily wrestling giant leeches on a trek in Thailand right now.

The marriage ceremony, in Haji's living room, was thirty minutes long and my part was thirty seconds. I had to say in English and then in Malay (using my cheat sheet) that, "I, Noor Faridah Abdullah, accept this marriage to Tunku Mahmood Shah, and I accept my being given to him by the Qadi, and I do accept the forty ringgit dowry." Yes, I sold myself to Mahmood for fifteen U.S. dollars (at the current rate of exchange)!

After my little speech, I was ignored. Mahmood sat on a gold-colored cushion, surrounded by four witnesses and the Qadi, being lectured on the attributes of a good husband. Chu translated for me and we were especially moved by this part: "Have extra understanding for her because she is a foreigner and newly converted to Islam and so very far from her home and family and she is totally dependent upon you, Tunku Mahmood, so don't screw up!" Then Mahmood had to promise to buy me a ring, some clothes and whatever else I needed. There was a prayer in Arabic and that was it.

Mahmood came over and stood by me, but there was no kissing, only hand holding. Hajjah Maimunah and another woman helped me serve tea and cakes. The custom is for the bride to see that everyone is served and has enough, so I awkwardly walked around for a bit with a tray and teapot.

Afterwards, I needed a rest and we went back to the resort, where I slept like a newly-legitimized baby for three hours while Mahmood and Chu rehashed the day. That evening, the three of us went out for a wonderful dinner. I had lobster thermidor, Mahmood had a perfect filet mignon, and Chu had oysters Rockefeller and duck. Ohhh, it was nice and we splurged on desserts. We were giggly, goofy and knackered from three days of drama and intrigue.

chapter four

Lullaby and Good Nights

24 May 1990

I am a contented wife with my bonny lying over the South China Sea away on business these many three weeks. He phones every day with endearing words and I respond in kind. The fetal female I feel daily is fine. Yes, a baby woman! The ultrasound confirmed the absence of a penis. The name Noor Mariam is at the top of our list.

I am hardly minding True Love privation, as the gods have blessed me with a hilariously entertaining life of late, featuring two brilliant actresses and a pair of trained prehensile mammals.

Chu has been staying with me since Mahmood left. She brought Sapphire, the monkey, and Maxamillion, the slow loris, with her. Sapphire is not permitted upstairs as we make each other tense. Max, on the other hand, is a tiny and cute primate about the size of a small rabbit. He lives cuddled in a baby blanket in a lidded basket when he isn't in a lap or on a shoulder. With his dark-ringed, round eyes darting from here to there and his sweet disposition, he comforts and amuses me.

My darling sister-in-law is an amazing cook and an even more amazing eater. She can polish off an entire baked chicken, with skin, bones sucked dry, plus a half dozen side dishes and a generous dessert. She begs me to tell her my favorite meals and what I crave and miss and then she works herself into a lather to make my dreams come true, though I tell her I'll eat anything and she need not go to any trouble. Problem is, she thrives on trouble and the more complicated the recipe or hard to find ingredients needed for it, the happier she is. Until last week I dreaded her forays into the kitchen because, of course, it's only fair that I do the dishes, the piles of dishes, and chop the vegetables, the piles of vegetables, and go with her to the markets and grocery shops and carry the bags, the heavy, unwieldy bags.

This all day, every day (minimal exaggeration) food-centered existence would have been intolerable but for the volumes of priceless anecdotal monologues which spilled from the fair Princess Maria's lips.

Her life has been tumultuous. At the tender age of six, she was wrenched, screaming, from her mother's breast and sent, with her three-year-old half brother, Mahmood, on a ship to Australia. They lived with their grandparents, who had no interest in them, and servants, who did the bare minimum, although one did rape her when she was eight or nine. Chu took over the care of Mahmood, who was an unhappy, defiant little boy. They did see their father on occasion, but never for more than a few minutes. After a couple years, the grandparents hopped on another ship and moved the household to England. Chu has wonderful memories of that voyage and horrible memories of England. It was cold and dank. The teachers were cruel racists and she and Mahmood were bullied mercilessly by their peers. Things became even worse when their father married a waitress he'd met in a pub and the woman became pregnant. Chu said she was an evil stepmother who used to beat Chu and made her do all the housework. Her stepmother especially hated Mahmood, because he was the eldest son and she conspired to turn the father against him. Listening to Chu talk, I gained a new perspective on Cinderella and Snow White. Those girls had it easy.

When Chu was thirteen, they moved back to Malaysia and a year later, she was being seduced regularly by her cousin, the present Sultan. Then there were years of parties, boyfriends and, finally, true love with Mohamed Ali's bodyguard, an American stuntman. This relationship was thwarted by the family. She wanted to go to college and/or get a job, but, until recently, the family was opposed.

Chu has a weight problem, is epileptic, diabetic and, in my opinion, manic-depressive. She has never seen a therapist as the stigma is huge here and there are only a few such professionals in the whole country. We've been playing patient and diagnostician. So far we have theorized she also has Obsessive Compulsive Disorder, Post Traumatic Stress Disorder, Compulsive Eating Disorder, Dysfunctional Interbred Royal Family Syndrome and a bunch of sexual stuff. She loves it when I analyze her and now she wants to get some self-help books. I warned her that they are addictive, but she is determined.

Foo's wife, Theresa, stopped by the other night. She had a potential servant in tow, an illegal Indonesian woman in her mid-twenties named Aminah. The girl spoke no English so Chu interviewed her and concluded that yes, she would do and could start in the morning. Aminah seemed agreeable and said, "Ya, boleh, boleh," Malay for "Yes, okay, okay." They negotiated a monthly salary of one hundred twenty U. S. dollars, with Sundays off—an excellent salary for an illegal, Chu assured me. She does get full room and board, but, still, it seems to me like a low wage.

Aminah did not show up the next morning and Chu and I figured we must have intimidated her, being a Royal and a white person—Yikes! We were so bummed, because we had gotten our hopes up and boo hoo for our lazy butts.

Then there was a knock at the door and there she was, with all her stuff. Chu and I nearly cried with joy and had to restrain ourselves from smothering her with hugs and kisses. Within half an hour she was hard at work and by the end of that day, the house and our lives were transformed.

I am finding the reality of having a servant a guilty pleasure. She cheerfully brings in the morning paper, brews my tea, prepares, serves and clears my breakfast, makes my bed and carefully folds my nightclothes. Chu is training her and doing an absurdly thorough job, I suspect. Chu tells me that Aminah, who Chu calls "the girl," has no experience and is dumb as a board sometimes, so over-training is necessary. My sister-in-law claims to have vast experience in Servant Making 101, so I defer to her superior talents, but I suspect Aminah is just playing dumb. I do worry about one of Chu's neurosis being piqued, though, because I know passive-aggressive behavior when I hear it, in any language. I'll hear laughter one moment and screaming the next as they go over the proper way to fold Madam's underwear!

Aminah needs to eat rice and fish in stinky sauces three times a day and the upstairs kitchen was grossly insufficient, sending the three of us off on a shopping spree. We bought a refrigerator and a stove, two unfamiliar appliances to Aminah. She'd used a gas burner before and an icebox, but never a stovetop, oven or magical contraption that got cold without having to buy a chunk of ice. We also bought another wok, which she uses for 100 percent of her cooking, aided by a couple of wooden utensils. Second in importance to the wok was a larger mortar and pestle, which gets used a few times daily. You haven't lived in a developing country until you've seen a woman sprawled out on the floor with a mortar between her legs, energetically grinding chilies, garlic, shallots, ginger, tamarind and stinky shrimp paste with a pestle. Chu is teaching her to cook the way Chu wants things to taste, using recipes Chu and Mahmood love. Apparently, Aminah's repertoire is small and unappetizing, dirt-poor villager fare being heavy on the chili and shrimp paste.

I suddenly have hours every day at my disposal to read and write and nap and renap. Chu is putting in ten and twelve hour days downstairs and I've never seen her happier. She instructs and yells and chatters nonstop while Aminah's singsong voice can be heard saying, "Ya, Tunku. No, Tunku. Aiiiiiyoooo, Tunku." Then come streams of very fast Indonesian, which is also Malay, though Chu says they're very different in idioms and pronunciation. I have learned one important expletive: "Aiiiiiyoooo" is actually Chinese for "Oh, shit!"

5 June

Last night was dark and rainy. Around nine o'clock, Chu realized that Max, our adorable slow loris, was gone. Aminah, being absentminded, had left her bedroom door ajar, oh horrors, and her windows open. Chu allowed Max to wander freely downstairs, expecting that all doors and windows would be shut.

The thunderous lamentations of a furious princess soon filled the house. Chu had Aminah cowering, crying and scrambling desperately around downstairs to determine if Max were indeed outdoors. Once that was determined, the two of them moved the tragicomedy out into the rain. Chu didn't stay out long, realizing she could stand in a doorway and scream without getting wet. She told Aminah, who had a small flashlight, that she could not come in until she found Max. I went downstairs hoping to lend moral support, but Chu only switched half her ravings to English, because, of course, I wanted to hear what a bloody useless, bloody stupid girl Aminah was. Chu went on about how I should fix her, but I just kept quiet. Sapphire was also upset, crying and rattling the bars of her cage.

At 11:00, Aminah found him, ten feet up in a tree in the neighbor's yard. Chu sent Aminah over to the house ask them to put their Rottweiller inside, but no one was home. Then Chu ordered Aminah to go into the neighbor's yard, climb the tree and grab Max. Aminah began to cry, because she was terrified of the dog biting her, Max biting her and falling out of the tree. Chu found the reserves to scream at her more vociferously, all the while switching over to English to tell me what a bloody coward, bloody fool Aminah was. Aminah soon mustered her courage and climbed over the fence separating our house from the neighbor's. Fortunately, the dog ignored her, the tree held up and Max crawled happily into her hand. I whispered some sympathetic words to her in broken Malay while Chu wasn't looking. Then we all went to bed.

4 August

Dearest Mother, whose glorious countenance will grace the contents of this home in forty-seven rotations of the earth. Be still, my pining heart.

Mahmood left for Brunei this morning, after just two weeks home. He reckons he'll be gone for at least a week and he hopes this will be his last business trip until after the baby arrives. Between trips there and quickies to Kuala Lampur, Rawa and Singapore, he's been away on business more than half the time this summer.

The takeover of the island resort is stalled. Hassan has been threatening sabotage if Mahmood and Alang continue their legal efforts to usurp authority. The other five half siblings are willing to accept a cash buyout if it looks like they might lose in court. Mahmood and Alang have affidavits out, but the Malaysian courts are notoriously slow and no hearing dates have been set. They are further burdened, because no judge wants to touch a Tunku vs. Tunku case, a lose-lose situation unless the Sultan's side is known. He's doesn't give a damn about the island, but the court can't be sure and getting beat up by the Sultan's henchmen is a real possibility. Mahmood wanted to send Chu to Rawa to keep an eye on things, but she said, "Absolutely not. Hassan will murder Sapphire."

Chu phoned yesterday from the hospital. She went in a few days ago with a virus that, because of her weight, diabetes and epilepsy, prompted the doctor to admit her. She didn't sound too worried about her health, but she was really concerned about calling us. Hearing Mahmood was gone loosened her up and we had a good, long chat. Last time she phoned, Mahmood was angry with her because she was calling or stopping by so often to ask for money. He was still annoyed with her, because she overstayed her welcome by a month after he had returned from Brunei in June. I feel badly for her, because she has no money of her own and is dependent on family members, Mahmood and Alang mostly, though she did call the palace and they'll pay for her hospitalization. Health insurance is unknown here.

Mahmood and I took our first walk through the baby section of the department store last evening. Such a huge and fascinating variety of products had us both awestruck and intimidated. Mother, I am so pleased you and Mahmood will go on that initial shopping spree, sparing me the stress. I feel sad to think of the reason this custom of not buying anything before the birth began. With so many babies dying in childbirth or shortly thereafter, it makes sense, especially in a poor country where a dollar is a lot of money.

Mahmood has really taken an interest in the *Mother's Journal* you sent. I think he may end up writing in it more than me. The page he wrote this morning made me cry. I get all caught up in trying to be profound, while he has the effortless gift of saying the most beautiful things so simply. I have never known a man like him. He is better at expressing his feelings than I am. He is genuine without pretence. I am amazed daily by my extraordinary luck/karma in finding him.

The house feels so empty without my darling, but after the first day I get used to the solitude. When Mahmood is gone, I fall into a routine of waking up and eating muesli, fruit and a Shaklee protein shake for breakfast, all things I do myself from the upstairs kitchen. Then I call Aminah up to tidy the room. Lunch is always a big chef salad she prepares downstairs. Teaching her to chop vegetables for a salad and then convincing her I really did intend to eat them raw was an amusing part of Chu's instruction on "How to Cook for White People." Dinner is usually Malay food she fixes for the two of us: Rice, a fried fish or two, stir fried vegetables in coconut milk with tofu or tempeh thrown in.

Taking care of me directly only consumes about a half-hour of her day. Otherwise, she's downstairs doing laundry, by hand, because she thinks washing machines don't do a good job. Yes, we did buy one and it just sits there. Once the baby comes, she may reconsider her stand. She also spends time in the garden she and Chu planted with chilies, tomatoes, papaya, long beans, herbs and other things I can't recall and/or spell. While she's outside, she chats with the neighbor's Indonesian servant. They have become great chums and often run errands together. I'm happy for her, as I know what it's like to be a fish out of water.

Being alone with Aminah so much has really motivated me to learn Malay with more vengeance. I have a book and a tape. Aminah is good about allowing me to practice on her and she enjoys teaching me the words for things around the house. Chu cautioned me, though, that she speaks "low class" village Malay and has an awful accent. I am careful to double-check every word with Chu, Mahmood or a dictionary, as I dare not be caught speaking proletarian Malay. Chu told me there is a version of the language spoken only by the royal families. It's used primarily in the palace and is heavy on the royal "We."

Aminah, on the other hand, is a hopeless student of English. I reckon she has not learned more than five words in three months of my trying to teach her. Prepare yourself for using sign language with her and having her not understand, do something completely unrelated and unwanted, thus driving you to distraction or laughter. I always strive for the latter!

I just answered the telephone and it was Chu. They're discharging her from the hospital this afternoon and she asked if she could stay with me for two days before she returns to her mother's house. I said sure, thrilled to have the company and unable to refuse her anything. She'll fill me in on all the family gossip, with wonderful exaggeration and fabricated embellishments. It's funny, because if there ever were a family who did not need their lily gilded, ever, it would be the Johor Royal Family.

Mahmood's daughter, Zahara, has a flight here on the sixteenth and he may be able to return with her. She is a typical eighteen year old, thrilled about having a new sister, but suspicious about meeting her new stepmother. She is leaving her ticket open in case she hates me and wants to go home after two days! Her mother does not want her to come, so it is very difficult to be sure how Zahara will react to me.

I got a letter from Zoe and her mother's latest obsession is that either the baby or I (or both) will be kidnapped and sold into white slavery or a harem. I wrote Zoe back, suggesting her mother lay off the tabloids for a while.

The doctor laughed last week when I told him I'd read that there was no reason for me to get an enema, an episiotomy and a shave on the delivery table. I think he was embarrassed. I'm only the second white woman he's had as a patient and the first sounds like she was a wimp. I am his first Tunku's wife and probably the only patient who's ever questioned, challenged and treated him like an equal. He has never had a patient who delivered her baby naturally! When we toured his maternity clinic above his office last week, we learned from one of the nurses that none of the new mothers breastfeed. None!

It is so cool, Mom, that you're able to take the Lamaze refresher course this month. With you as my coach, I'll pop that baby out with nary a whimper.

Check this out, Mom: I was born in 1960, when you were thirty, thirty years ago, and now it's 1990, you're sixty and I'm thirty, about to have a baby, who will be thirty when I'm sixty and you are ninety, in 2020!

I lovelovelove you, Patty.

8 October

Auntie Zoe,

The last couple weeks of my pregnancy went on and on and on. The doctor said the baby could come anytime after the 18th, so I lived in anticipation of that first contraction. My mother arrived on the 20th and we raced to take her here and there and show her as much as we could before the birthing day. In fact, we were out shopping early on the evening of the 28th and my contractions were five minutes apart. Blithely, we decided to continue shopping! So every five minutes I just grabbed the nearest person or counter for thirty seconds. The contractions were really more annoying than painful at that stage. My overnight bag was in the trunk and, on the way home, we stopped at the clinic and got me checked in. The nurse did an exam and I was dilated two centimeters, so we went home a few hours later. I was feeling pretty blasé until the contractions were three minutes apart and then, oh boy, I was soon delirious from the pain and exertion (this was 10:30 P.M.). Back at the clinic, the nurse checked me again and I was still only two centimeters. The cervix had to dilate to ten centimeters before I would be ready and she told us that wouldn't happen until at least 8 a.m. For the next two-and-a-half hours, the breathtaking waves of agony moved from three minutes apart to one gigantic tsunami of mind-blowing pain on top of another. Mahmood and Mother were in the room with me half-arguing in a nice way. He was saying, "She needs the doctor or a nurse or a shot or something!" Mother, in a calm and steady voice, was instructing me to, "Breathe deeply and relax, Patty-cake. You're doing so wonderfully." If I had known that the birth was imminent, I'd have found them and the pain tolerable, but the idea of another eight hours sent me over the edge. At 1 A.M., I agreed (nay, begged) to take the shot the nurse offered, which would give me an hour of relief. Well, two minutes later, my water burst and before you could say, "She's a coming," I was on the delivery table with Mom holding one hand and Mahmood holding the other. Oh, it hurt like a son-of-a-bitch, but it was over so fast and it was soooo incredible to feel her head and body moving through me and out that I wasn't really conscious of the pain.

Mahmood and my mother loved every minute of it. Neither had really watched a birth before and they were awestruck.

Mariam came out blue and grotesque, but a half hour later, when they brought her to my room all clean and wrapped snugly in a little white blanky, she was angelic. We stared and marveled and stroked her face and hair. The shot had kicked in by this time and I happily floated off to mama land.

I woke up at 5:00 A.M. and stumbled out to the nursery, wanting to make sure all this wasn't a wondrous but fictitious dream. Mariam was there, surrounded by a half-dozen babies, with a bottle in her mouth. I began to cry as I banged on the glass, alarming the girl who was feeding her. She brought her out to me. I took Mariam back to my room and nursed her for the first time.

All that day I felt as though I'd donated three pints of blood on an empty stomach. I was drained and dizzy and amazed and unsure. Me, a mother? This creature, mine?

That morning my wonderful husband handed me a small heart-shaped velvet box. Inside was a stunning emerald and diamond ring. It's for Mariam, really, but I'll wear it until she's of age.

My postnatal life, these past ten days, has been a sublime cycle of feeding my baby every one to three hours, night and day, and coping with lack-of-quality-sleep delirium. Thanks to Mother and Aminah's help, delirium is kind of cool and life seems effortless, though we do fight over who gets to change her diaper, bathe and dress her. Did you know that breast-fed babies have a fascinating thin, tan, odorless effluence? And, as for my knackered nether region, I'm in the midst of the period that never ends and I have to put medication on a couple of places where the skin was stretched and rubbed raw. I didn't tear or need an incision, to the amazement of my doctor and the experts who say almost all first time mothers need a scalpel.

Midday now on Tuesday, October 9th. I've just taken a bath and the babe is beginning to stir and make sucking noises. There's a chance my darling may be showing up any minute. He never tells me when he's coming in, but knowing the flight schedule from Brunei, I always make myself ready (perfumed and pretty) when he could come in with a big "surprise."

I love you, my dearest friend and demand that you write me and come here, because my Mommy is leaving soon and I will cry. More pathetic groveling to come.

With love, Patty

24 October

The Chinese astrologer came by this morning and delivered Mariam's horoscope. The man has an accuracy rate of 80 percent, so no sniggering, Mahmood says. He had been told nothing about her except sex, date and time of birth. Well, the stars augur well for our little girl. The astrologer prophesied that she would be a brilliant student, very beautiful, with great health and vast wealth. The biggest thing, though, was something this man had never seen before in his forty years of doing horoscopes. Her marriage house showed that she would marry a king or the equivalent. He came up with this without even knowing she was a princess!! He also said she would have brothers and sisters and only some brief moments of hardship and unhappiness. As Muslims, we aren't supposed to believe such things, but it's such fun to hear wonderful things about our daughter's future and dreams.

We are tentatively planning on going to the island next week for a few days or a few weeks. I am so looking forward to swimming and fishing and watching the sun set with Mariam attached to my breast, the darling parasite. We're worried we won't be able to fit everything needed in the car and may have to hire a taxi to follow!

5 November

Auntie Zoe,

Life is so good here on Rawa I am unable to find a combination of adjectives to do justice to an existence so flawlessly perfect. We think we shall stay another decade or two. There are eight quiet tourists here, twenty smiling workers and no evil half brother extraordinaire.

This is Aminah's first time on the island and she is happier than I am. The boys are all in love with her—a puppy, teasing love she encourages coyly. She wanders around with Mariam in her arms and a serene smile on her lips.

We sit on the jetty every evening and Mahmood tries to tempt a shark to bite the huge hook he has hidden in a cute little coral fish. Aminah and the boys fish every chance they get for anything that will take a hook and it's great fun to see what they come up with. Tonight we are going to try to catch squid for the first time. They've rigged a bright light up at the end of the jetty that can be shone into the water to attract the squid. Then one has to snag them with a lethal looking multi-hooked doodad and pull hard. As the squid comes out of the water, it starts spraying black ink in every direction and the liquid really travels. It's hilarious to watch and half the staff has big black inkstains on their t-shirts.

We are leaving Rawa tomorrow for two long weeks, one of which Mahmood will spend in Brunei. We are going to return and spend the month of December on the island in the throes of the monsoon rains and winds and wild tides. Aminah and I have a long list of supplies to gather while he is gone and, yes, it will be quite the little adventure. Your presence is vehemently requested. Imagine a sylvan month of Scrabble, rice and weather to write home about. More, more and more to come.

Love ya, Patty

Early December

I honestly am not sure what day of the week or day of the month this is. Ah, blissful ignorance. We have been on Rawa a few sunsets now and have recovered from our tumultuous trip across in huge waves. Mariam slept through it, I endeavored to keep breakfast in my stomach, Aminah practiced her prayers, Chu gossiped and Mahmood chatted with the boatman, who was smoking a pipe.

There are six workers here to maintain the place, do repairs, flirt with Aminah, coo over the baby, take care of us and clean up after the Monsoon storms. I caught two gorgeous purple, yellow and blue coral fish today that Mahmood will use for shark bait. Yesterday, a shark took four fish and straightened the large, steel hooks, so now he's trying double hooks. We have no idea how big he is, could even be a Great White!

Chu spends most of her time in the kitchen cooking, baking and creating piles of dirty dishes for Aminah or the guys to wash. Today she made us a steamed pudding and has an elaborate, labor-intensive (not hers) Malay meal planned for dinner. Mahmood and I are in food heaven, marital, parental and most idyllic-setting heaven, too. We lack for nothing, we are never apart for more than an hour and we never argue. Pinch me!

Last night, during a torrential rain coupled with high winds, a coconut tree fell on the generator building and we were without electricity and used kerosene lamps and candles. We only have the generator on from 7:00 P.M. to 7:00 A.M., anyway, so, beyond the staff's missing their television for a night, we survived and it's fixed now.

Walking the beach after these big storms is a jolly good time. There are a plethora of beautiful shells, pieces of coral, plastic bags, garbage and other treasures. I have found three plastic shovels, two little toys and a glass fishing net float from Vietnam. Only a few shopping days left until Christmas!

We set up another crib with a mosquito net here in the restaurant where we spend most of our waking, non-fishing hours. Now Mariam can nap while we're in the kitchen or eating or watching the rain come down sideways or playing that S game.

Mariam is thriving and has two new talents: clasping her hands together and drooling. Watching her perform these amazing feats sends us into rapturous clapping. Mahmood, Chu, Aminah and I stand around the crib for hours on end watching these new tricks and hoping to catch one of her elusive smiles. We are determined to get a video camera so we can share her brilliance with Grammy and all of Michigan.

29 December

Santa's deliveries were wonderful. I got a gorgeous jewelry box and a diamond ring (WOW) from my most perfect in every way True Love. I gave him two books on Scrabble, a book of Malay political cartoons and coupons for backrubs. We gave Chu stationery, scarves and chocolate. Aminah got a bunch of clothes from the Rawa shop and Mariam got a hot water bath and turkey-flavored breast-milk.

For the feast, we brought everything we could find in the grocery stores of Singapore and I can't say I missed a thing. Chu made a superlative oyster stuffing and Aminah mashed potatoes until smooth as a baby's bottom and I baked cornbread in a funky little oven that sits over a gas burner. Mahmood opened cans of cranberry sauce and carved the turkey and the boys looked on, curious about the strange customs of that Christian holiday.

We have been without electricity since Christmas Eve as the fuel oil for the generator ran out and Mersing won't send a boat, because Hassan is being a bloody Scrooge. We think one of the other half brothers schemes with him and we can just imagine them cackling over in the Mersing office. If they only knew how little we are bothered. There is an abundance of kerosene lamps and candles. The electric fans are not needed in the cool temperatures of monsoon season and Mahmood is letting the guys borrow his little battery-powered television to watch the Malay prime-time dramas. We do miss refrigeration but there is a well-stocked pantry and chilies, garlic, onion and limes growing out back. And there are fresh chicken eggs, fresh fish and fresh mother's milk for the baby.

Weather permitting, we are going to leave tomorrow on the scheduled boat to spend a few weeks at our house in Johor Bahru. If Mahmood tells the mainland he wants a boat, the brothers will see that one does not come. We will simply have everything ready to go in the morning and then relax until a boat arrives. The boatmen don't even know about the family feud so they'll happily take us and wonder why no one told them Tunku Mahmood needed a boat.

Two days later. Finally, the boat is on its way. I have a few minutes before our final packing frenzy commences. This has been one of the most wonderful months of my life. Mahmood and I are more deeply in love, Mariam is a magnificent source of miraculous joy and my life could not be any better.

28 January 1991

We have returned to Rawa, our island paradise, after three weeks in Johor. Mariam is on the floor beside me in her newest and greatest toy, a baby walker. She has mobility but unfortunately I just caught her chewing on an electrical cord. Not a hazard this time, as we have no power during daylight hours, but, still, a frightening habit to be sure.

Mahmood has a small black and white television we use to watch the evening newscasts in English and Malay. I wait for the broadcasts about Operation Desert Storm, praying no American lives will be lost. Malaysia officially is neutral, which means half the people support Kuwait, half support Saddam Hussein and everyone complains about the Americans, with whom I know they secretly count me. My own servant has a crush on Saddam, because she thinks he is so handsome and brave. She, like too many here, seriously believes the West will lose because Allah is on Saddam's side. The anti-Western feeling seems like it's growing and gives me uneasy feelings. I try not to think of where it could lead.

The Rawa boat is on the horizon, bearing fresh produce and wicked half brother Hassan. He knows Mahmood is here and we think he's going to grovel at Mahmood's feet in the hope he can convince him and Alang not to put barbwire around three quarters of the chalets. The barbwire is already here, Mahmood is determined not to relent and is furious with Alang, who was supposed to be here a week ago to back him up.

31 January

My stepdaughter Zahara arrived this morning and will stay until we leave. I will enjoy having her here and she adores Mariam, her only sibling.

Hassan is being good as gold. He hasn't spoken a word to Mahmood and sleeps in the staff dorm. He spends his days bossing around the twenty workers (who are here now as things gear up for the opening in three weeks) and pretending he wasn't ousted, he's still the manager and all is status quo. Strange chap.

For dinner last night we had canned sardines sautéed with chili, onion and garlic, fried squid with eggplant and rice. Tonight Aminah is preparing soybean skin, fungus, black mushrooms, glass noodles and other delectable Chinese weirdness in coconut milk with rice. Except for my breakfast meusli, I eat with my hands nearly all the time now and truly prefer fingers to forks.

2 February

My daughter monopolizes two-thirds of my time and my husband demands two-thirds. Fortunately, they overlap and anyway, I happily give them both nine tenths, because I am in maternal and marital bliss. Take now, for example. Mariam is in my lap and Mahmood is across the Scrabble board contemplating his next move while Aminah does laundry over in the Longhouse and Chu is in the kitchen preparing our lunch.

Zahara, on the other hand, is soooooo bored after five days on this island with nothing to do. No shopping, no friends, no fast food, no afternoon television she complains, and her rotten father won't let her leave until we do, so she sleeps in and mopes around all day. She can't believe we actually want to be here.

The barbwire goes up in two days, Hassan left without groveling and the half siblings are all in a real panic. They have been given an ultimatum: agree to accept seven hundred and fifty thousand dollars split seven ways (including Chu) and turn the company over immediately to Mahmood and Alang or go to court and have their illegitimacy exposed, be stripped of their titles and lose their inheritance, i.e. Rawa. As Alang and Lorraine are firmly ensconced in Kuala Lumpur and have no inclination to live on the island, Mahmood and I will run the place and live here full-time.

5 February

Apparently, all the half siblings are willing to sell, except for Hassan and Mele, who have the most to lose, because they've been living off the company in less than kosher ways and have no discernable job skills. However, Mahmood's dastardly half siblings also went to court and filed an injunction against the barbwire going up and disputing Mahmood's and Alang's right to half the land. Our lawyer figures he can fix things within two weeks, though this is slightly ominous, as they seem to have banded together and won't give in easily. Taking them to court over the illegitimacy would be a long, ugly drawn-out affair and avoiding it is a major goal.

Midnight, 14/15 February

Dear Mother,

Last week, we returned to Johor Bahru and Chu took Aminah, Mariam and me to visit an elderly former servant of the family. Her name is Patong and she was with Mahmood and Chu in Australia and England. She had dozens of old pictures, postcards and stories from the post-World War Two years. Mahmood was adorable, Chu was really thin and their grandparents were so stern-looking in the photos. Her stories were sweet, but dull, as her memory was poor and she spoke in platitudes.

Tomorrow, Chu is taking Mariam and me to the wedding of a relative on her mother's side. I'll wear traditional dress, be the only white person there, have a gorgeous baby in my arms and hope it will improve their picture of Americans.

Mahmood met with our landlord before he went to Brunei, because we were concerned about a notice he sent asking us to move out, as he wanted to sell the house. We found out he really didn't want to sell, it's just that he hadn't received our rent in six months! Mahmood gave the money to Foo every month, but apparently Foo used it for other things. He is now on our blacklist and the mystery of why he hasn't come by in weeks is solved. Mahmood paid the arrears and all is well.

Enough for now. The girls and I are off to the mall for a walkabout. Speaking of the mall, Aminah went up an escalator last week for the first time in her life. She was terrified and I was patient. "Please, ma'am," she begged, in Malay, of course, "Don't make me do it. I am so happy to take the stairs or elevator. People can die on those things. I am too scared, too scared." She stalled and giggled nervously and I bribed her with ice cream and, after an entertaining half-hour, she realized ma'am was not going to let her off the hook, so she went up, then down, then up and down with the baby in her arms. Oh, she was so proud of herself. She didn't even know escalators existed until six months ago!

Love, Patty

23 April

Mahmood's business has taken him away again, but yesterday he had a meeting with his attorney. The lawyer hasn't heard from the court on the date for the Rawa hearing and he asked Mahmood to go and put some pressure on the court registrar, as he's sure they're stalling. People in Johor are loath to handle any legal action with Tunku's, especially Tunku vs. Tunku, as they don't know whose side the Sultan may be on this week!

Speaking of His Majesty: Last week was Hari Raya, a big Muslim holiday, and Alang, Lorraine and their kids went to the palace to see him as they do every year. It's traditional for the royals to have an open house on the first day of Hari Raya, to receive friends and family personally. Anyway,

Sultan Iskandar Mahmood has always thrown open his doors on this day, sitting pompously on his throne while growling at supplicants. This year, however, his son, Crown Prince Yem, borrowed his helicopter without asking and forgot to clean the lipstick-covered cigarette butts from the ashtray when he returned it. Sultan Daddy was furious, beat Yem up, (he's thirty-two!) and refused to see anyone all last week. His rudeness was taken by his subjects as a major insult and sister-in-law Lorraine was bloody annoyed about their wasted trip.

We got a phone call two days back from Mahmood's mother Margaret and Geof who were in Singapore and wanted to see her grandbaby! We happily hopped across the border and spent most of yesterday with them. They had a suite and Mariam made herself right at home, crawling around and over all the furniture and bodies and thoroughly charming her grandparents in the process. They gushed over her beauty, strength, cheerfulness and genius, then gave her a darling stuffed bunny.

They're selling the castle in Ireland. Seems they had terrible luck finding decent staff and twice the IRA threatened them over silly stuff. They had a long list of grievances against the medieval politics and the omnipresent Catholic Church, although they love the castle and countryside. Profit on the sale should be a half million. They're keen to move back to Tasmania, where they lived before and have a slew of holdings.

1 June

Mahmood's Aunt Khatijah died yesterday. She had been in the hospital for years with complications from diabetes and a few days ago she caught pneumonia. Uncle Bakar phoned us yesterday morning, said she was deteriorating rapidly and ordered Mahmood and me to the hospital. We went and, in the half-hour we stood by the bed, her heartbeat dropped from seventy to forty beats. We'd have stayed until she died, but when Mahmood heard the Sultan was on his way over, we quickly left. She died a few minutes later. I met Uncle Osman, Uncle Rahman and his wife, a middle-aged British woman, and Jackie, one of Mahmood's half sisters, who was very talkative.

Muslims are always buried within twenty-four hours of death and we assumed the funeral would be today, but were surprised when the summons came at 5:00 P.M. to be at the Royal Mausoleum in an hour.

A week ago I'd bought some appropriate fabrics and we sent them to our tailor knowing there would be a funeral to attend soon and that the traditional dresses I had wouldn't work. As soon as we got back from the hospital, we phoned the tailor and she said she could get one of the dresses done by this morning. God is good, because in my sartorial panic I remembered Zahara had left some clothes downstairs and among them I found a dress that would work. I put on a scarf and with Mahmood turned out dapperly in his traditional outfit, we were on our way in twenty minutes.

We got to the mausoleum just as the Sultan pulled up with his two Rolls Royce escort cars and a dozen cops on motorcycles, so we waited in our car until he went in. His wacky Majesty was wearing red slacks and a golf shirt, a slap in the face to his dead cousin, Mahmood noted. Right behind him was the convoy with the body and most of the family who had been at Uncle Osman's house, where Khatijah had been prepared for burial. We joined the small crowd, took our shoes off at the door, separated to the boys and girls sides as we went in and sat on carpets spread over the marble floor. There were about forty people inside and another fifty or so friends and minor royalty outside.

I sat next to the Sultan's brother's widow who is a royal from another state. The Sultan had wanted this woman's son to marry one of his daughters and when the son refused, His Childish Majesty stripped him and his mother of many of their powers and perks. Her son, who Mahmood says is a normal, nice gentleman, (three adjectives rarely used to describe a male Johor Tunku) went on to marry a princess from Indonesia last fall. He wasn't in attendance and his mother only came to the funeral out of respect for Khatijah. We had a nice chat and she invited us to visit so she and her daughter-in-law, who's pregnant, could see the baby. They have a handsome palace across from Yem's stables and polo fields.

Khatijah never married, lived with her parents until they died and then lived alone. She was with Mahmood and Chu in Australia and England and Mahmood says she was an unhappy person who spent her days sewing and cooking. He thinks she had a screw loose, though she was very quiet most of the time. Khatijah, being the only daughter, inherited many millions of dollars in jewelry and cash and it was all swindled or stolen by family members, servants and others. She and Chu were close. In fact, Chu took me to visit her in the hospital a couple months back.

While Auntie Khatijah was dying in hospital, two women from the Religious Department were sent over to recite a prayer that is chanted to people on their deathbeds. As she was dying they whispered in her ears and reminded her to recite her declaration that she is Muslim as she passed over. As soon as she was dead, her body was taken to Uncle Osman's house where it was prepared for burial. She was thoroughly washed and then rubbed all over with scented oils. Then she was wrapped in seven yards of unsewn white cotton, with only the face uncovered, and transported to the Royal Mausoleum. Her body was put into an open casket covered in yellow cloth to denote she was royal. The body was placed sideways in the box so that she can always face Mecca and then the box was lowered into the grave. Workers had previously removed some of the marble flagstone floor and dug the grave underneath. All the dirt that had been removed was in bags and they were emptied on top of and around her casket until the grave was filled. Two flat stones, covered with yellow cloth and then tied up, were then placed at each end of the grave, the flat shape denoting a female. Then the grave was covered with yellow carpets.

At this time, eight Imams began to recite prayers to remind the dead person that everyone who lives will die and not to be afraid when the two Angels of Death come to take her soul away. The Imams tell her what to answer the Angels when they question her about what her religion is and who her prophet was and such. After a few more prayers, large silver trays covered with scented flower petals and silver jugs of holy water were passed around to members of the family to scatter over the new grave. With that, it was over. That evening, and for the following three nights, prayers are recited at Uncle Osman's house and food is served. Prayers will be said again on the seventh, fortieth and hundredth night, then yearly after that.

To be buried in the Royal Mausoleum is really wonderful, because every day the Imams' job is to pray for the departed souls. The place is very beautiful and was built by Mahmood's great-great grandfather, Sultan Abu Bakar, who was a friend of Queen Victoria's. The entire huge structure is built of marble and the interior floor is marble flagstones, some of which are removed for burial and then replaced with different colors to denote a grave. Auntie was buried right next to Mahmood's grandparents, who have elaborate, built up graves with canopies of yellow tapestry over them.

It was an eye opener for me. Now I know how Mahmood's family members are buried and how someday we also will be.

6 July

Dear Mom,

I've done it again. A few weeks ago I had a pain in my lower right belly which felt like I was ovulating. Then last week I felt suddenly teary-eyed, homesick and in a strange mood. The other day I said to Mahmood, "I think I may be pregnant."

Yesterday we went to town and bought a pregnancy test and then in the evening the test was done. Well, oh my God, the test was positive, so someone is likely going to be a grandma yet again.

Then again, that was only one small test and the kit was made in Malaysia, so it could be grossly inaccurate. I do think we had better confirm this little bundle by going to the doctor and getting a scan and a second opinion. So, for the time being, until all the tests are completed, you could say that my condition is slightly pregnant!

Now, if the news is true, it strikes Mahmood and me that someone from Sutherland Central would be requested and required to witness the birth of this new child sometime in the future. Of, course, that person must have experience with at least six children, be certified in the Lamaze birthing method and have witnessed the birth of Miss Mariam. I think you had better go through all the Sutherland files to find the right person and kindly inform us at your earliest convenience. If such a person cannot be found, we shall have to make the requirements less stringent.

Love and kisses, Patty

19 July

We just returned from forty-eight fabulous hours in Kuala Lumpur. We stayed at Alang and Lorraine's spacious home in the poshest neighborhood in town and it is a busy and bustling place! People and animals were in and out constantly and the telephones were never idle. With four dogs, four kids, three servants and a few lackeys of Alang living in the back, things hummed, to say the least. Mariam was in heaven. She screamed with delight whenever she saw a dog, commenced to chase it, reach out when she got close and then scurry off when it noticed her, laughing uproariously all the while. She was also fascinated by all the children and contentedly sat on the floor and watched their every move in wide-eyed wonder. Mishal, too, took away whatever she was playing with, to her generous delight, and was constantly asking, "Where's my Mariam?"

Our first evening in town was spent at the Polo Club meeting people and watching Alang play practice games. All the kids were there having riding lessons. We went out for a too-late dinner (10:00 P.M., I was famished).

The next morning we went to the United States Embassy to register Mariam and get Mahmood a visa. Our marriage certificate is in Arabic script and before they could do anything we had to get it translated. A lawyer friend of Alang's did it for us in twenty minutes. The counselor clerk said that Mariam, being an American citizen, must have an American Passport to enter the United States, but she shouldn't get it until she has her Malay Passport, because they could make trouble as Malaysia does not recognize dual citizenship. We'll get her Malay Passport here and then go to Singapore for the American one.

Mahmood got a multiple entry visa to be used whenever for the rest of his life and he can stay in the country as long as he wants. A phenomenal coup because the U.S. is so strict. We figure they give VIP status to Tunkus.

Mahmood, Lorraine and I met with the lawyer that afternoon (Alang was AWOL) to discuss strategy for the big family meeting going on right now in a conference room at the Tropical Inn hotel. The documents turning over Rawa to Mahmood, Alang and their Chinese partner are on the table for them to sign, as are the checks that they can take with them if all comply. The suspense is killing me. Chu flew in for the meeting this morning from Kuala Lumpur where she is living and working at a new job doing something travel-related. Spouses were not invited and Lorraine nearly blew a gasket, furious that she, clearly the brains in her family, had been excluded.

Mahmood told me he and most of the others would have walked out if she had followed through with her threat to crash the meeting. I'm assuming she didn't, as it's been three hours and no Mahmood. I know he is under stress. How I wish he would leave his gun at home. But he refuses. The only time it's not tucked in his belt is when it's under his pillow. I have begun to wonder what he is so afraid of. Having one's husband armed hardly contributes to the tranquility so important when one is pregnant.

Last week when I went for my scan, we were shocked to learn I was eight rather than three weeks pregnant, as we had assumed. Mariam nursed for the last time a month ago and I never had a period. Anyway, beyond getting up to pee twice in the night and eating like a horse, I'm normal. Well, Mariam can't bounce on my stomach like she used to and I cry at the death of a gnat.

Evening now and the meeting didn't turn out as we had hoped, but rather as we had expected. There was constant arguing, nitpicking and complaining. No one shut up for two minutes, order was never established and Chu drove everyone bonkers as she loudly tried to be the peacemaker. The bottom line is they all want more money. Mahmood thinks he can convince the Chinese partner to come up with another half million.

We're still talking about traveling to Michigan in September, but Mahmood feels he can't commit until something tangible manifests with the island and he also has to spend a week or more taking care of his business in Brunei before he can leave. Furthermore, cold weather terrifies him and I feel guilty glossing over how brisk Northern Michigan can get in late summer.

I want to go home so badly I cry to think about it. I haven't been home in over nineteen months…Ah, here come the tears. Winter is right around the corner and, with the baby due early spring, we're looking at a year or more unless we go now. I haven't suggested to Mahmood yet that Mariam and I go alone for a few weeks but am thinking maybe I should…and soon. I will in a week if things are still in limbo.

16 September

We're here! We're here! Just Mariam and me, but that's okay. My visit home is filled with good food and wonderful moments with my mother and siblings. It makes me wish I could transport my family to our idyllic island. How difficult it is to live so far from so many I love.

2 October

Zoe Darling,

I have been back in Malaysia a week, and the cloud is finally starting to lift some. I believe this malaise is just a reaction to leaving you all, exhaustion, pregnancy and normal feelings about missing you. Mariam and I had an absolutely jump-up-and-down superlative time while we were there and I didn't want it to end. Mariam thrived around so many loving people and doing such a variety of different things. Still, it had to end and this is where we belong and where I want to be. Yet the reality of the thousands of miles and too many months separating us is painful to accept.

Onwards, or rather backwards, as I want to tell you about our long and hellish trip back. Mariam was really fussy and would not sleep until Tokyo. She cried and ranted and demanded I escort her up and down the aisles of the packed plane more than a dozen times while she stopped at every row to chat with the other passengers, 90 percent of them non-English speaking Japanese. Her theatrics were annoyingly adorable, except when she tried to wake someone for a chat; then I panicked! We got home at 1:00 A.M. on the twenty-fifth for a total of thirty-two hours awake for yours truly. Is it any wonder I'm a bit of a basket case?

Mariam recognized Mahmood immediately and to my great pleasure she went happily to Aminah when we arrived in Johor Bahru. We both had a rough time with jet lag. We wanted to sleep all day and stay awake all night and the stress of trying to do the opposite made us unhappy, grumpy and heavy nappers.

On her birthday, the twenty-eighth, the three of us went to Singapore. We bought her some toys, walking shoes and a stroller. On the way home, while caught in heavy traffic, she got very sick and was vomiting, choking, dry heaving and crying. Poor baby made a mess of herself and the car seat. Nearly an hour passed before we could get out of the jam and over the border and to the doctor's. She was so miserable and Mahmood and I were on edge with concern. The doctor gave her medicine, but she was worse the next day. Her breathing was raspy and she was coughing so we went to a different doctor who said she had the croup, a virus that causes the throat to swell. He gave us a load of medicine and said if she wasn't significantly better in twenty-four hours, to admit her to the hospital. We really sweated those twenty-four hours and endeavored to get every drop of medicine down her, a three-person job! I had to fill the dropper up about six times while Mahmood and Aminah held her down. She screamed and cried and fought, which broke our hearts, because she was in such pain and every breath was a struggle for her. Well, she did improve some and now, five days later, she's up to almost all her old and dear tricks. This little drama was also no help at all in our readjustment to a change of twelve time zones and a latitude drop of forty-three degrees. Further, the air over Malaysia has been polluted and hazy for weeks from out-of-control forest fires on Borneo and Java and many people have been suffering from respiratory problems. Especially older people and children with weakened immune systems.

I saw my OB/GYN two days ago and he did a scan that confirmed without a doubt there is a male creature in my uterus. We all saw the penis quite clearly and, yes, we already have a name: Tunku Iskandar Shah Bin Tunku Mahmood Shah. Iskandar is pronounced just like it looks. It's a good old family name except the present Sultan of Johor is called Iskandar Mahmood. We almost rejected it for that reason, because Mahmood really does despise him, but we both like the name too much. There is some cosmic irony in the fact that the Sultan and Mahmood share half a name and our son will bear the other half. Maybe they are destined to make up. Don't tell Mahmood I wrote that last sentence as he is intractable in all his enmities and gets angry with me when I suggest forgiveness.

I love yah, darling, Patty

2 December

We arrived on the island yesterday afternoon. The ride over was quite rough and for the first time ever, I felt queasy. I didn't tell Mahmood, because he would have teased me mercilessly, as I like to brag I've never gotten seasick even a little bit.

We are all too gosh dai n happy to be here and Mariam is indefatigable. She ran around like a dervish the first two hours chasing dogs and cats and workers and wanting to go everywhere and climb everything and swim and fish and climb coconut trees! It took all three of us to keep her in sight and out of danger.

Mahmood woke up early this morning and has begun a "health program" with vengeance. No smoking, only whiskey because he believes it has fewer calories than beer, no rich curries or teatime cakes and lots of exercise. He walked up and down the beach vigorously at 7:00 A.M., ate muesli with me, lost at Scrabble and is now off planning his monsoon fishing strategy with a few of the workers.

The rain is coming down in buckets. Mariam is coloring at my feet here in the restaurant. All the tables and chairs are stacked up against one wall and the room is wonderfully barren. We did put up the hammock I brought from Michigan between two beams and it will do nicely, to say the least.

Mahmood just ran by on his way to the room for his gun. Most of the time his obsession with it makes me nervous, but today there is a legitimate reason. There is a huge monitor lizard in the trash pile behind the kitchen and I suspect Mahmood intends to get rid of him. They really are frightening when they get big, because they will eat chickens, puppies, cats and toddlers, if they can catch them. I must go check this out.

Wow! The lizard was a little over six feet and was half way in the chicken coop when we got there. Mahmood raised his gun and shot him. Afterward, I watched them drag it out onto the jetty and drop it in the sea. Mahmood is hoping it will attract some sharks.

The rain falls. The lights go on every night from 7:00 P.M. to midnight and I go to the toilet by candlelight after that for my three pregnancy pees.

There is a well-insulated freezer that keeps stuff pretty cold around the clock and it is stocked with leftover beef, French fries, vegetables and other yet to be discovered treasures. We also have access to a pantry packed with canned delicacies such as sardines, corned beef and orange juice.

Life is good...

chapter five

Birth of a Prince

19 January 1992

I knew my mother couldn't stay away. We've been off the phone twenty minutes and a big grin is still plastered on my face. The moment we hung up I ran downstairs to share the news with Aminah and Mariam, who clapped their hand with glee. March first is my due date. I hope she will stay with us as long as she can. I miss her terribly.

25 January

Matthew arrives in ninety-six hours. Be still, my beating heart! My husband is two days behind him, a good thing, as I don't want to share my favorite brother with anyone until I've sucked him dry of all friends-and-family news, from the major to the mundane. Also, he and Mahmood are going to get along like a house on fire and, once they hook up, odds are high I will struggle to get a word in edgewise.

The girls and I are going over to Chu's new house on the other side of town for the afternoon. She now lives near a great park with equipment that actually works and there are no rats scurrying around. She's been in this particular house for three months and hasn't asked us for money once, so we are hopeful. She's cheerful, calls or comes over nearly every day, cooks me wonderful food and Mariam adores her auntie and prehensile cousins, Sapphire and Maximillion.

For the first time in months, I turned the air conditioner on last night. The heat has been stifling these past few days and last night it kept me awake and sweating buckets until I relented and flicked the switch. Wonder if there is any relation between heat intolerance and anemia. Dr. Chia is worried about my iron count as it's still at 8.9 and anything below ten is potentially dangerous. Weird, because I'm neurotically conscientious about my eating and haven't missed a day of supplements. Otherwise, all is well. Off to Chu's now.

10 February

I am sitting in the gazebo on a warm, sunny, perfect Rawa Island day, with the waves lapping at the shore and my brother's profile just visible in the distance, as he sits on a boulder and writes. Our seventh day in paradise with no contractions or other signs that Iskandar intends to interrupt our idyll.

Mahmood is in the restaurant getting a lesson in playing the juice harp. This morning he and I took the kayak to Rawa Bay, our beach, to brainstorm about the resort we want to build there. He wouldn't let me paddle, silly boy!

Here comes Mariam in a swimsuit and Aminah in swimming costume, long shorts and a T-shirt. She's too shy to strip any further and it took me months to convince her Allah did not care if she wore shorts outside the house. I think I'll join them as the tide is up, it's after four o'clock and I'm restless. I religiously avoid the sun between ten and four and also endeavor to keep Mariam in the shade and/or hatted and slathered with sunblock. Aminah complies willingly because she doesn't want to get any blacker and Mahmood ignores my warnings because he wants to be darker. Funny, my ebony servant wants to look European and my European-looking husband wants to look ebony.

Evening now. Mahmood and Matthew are out on a boat fishing. They departed after a dinner of steamed coral trout (Mariam's favorite fish), sweet and sour prawns, cabbage and chili with baby prawns, mixed vegetables in oyster sauce and rice. Matthew loves the food and, as he is grossly underweight, we are endeavoring to feed him many thousands of calories three times daily. Mahmood unfortunately is drinking more than is good for him. They consumed several bottles of wine at dinner and took a case of beer on the boat with them. His drinking worries me, but though I've tried to speak with him about the subject, he simply refuses to discuss it.

19 February

Dear Auntie Zoe,

I should be writing birth announcements, composing epigrams to entertain the people who warrant notice that my uterus expelled a seven pound, ten-ounce, twenty inch long male child at 12:02 A.M. on 15 February, 1992.

We left Rawa on the 13th and the hour-plus boat ride to Mersing was longer, bumpier, wavier, windier and wilder than usual. I think it convinced the fetus he was being called forth and if there were any doubt in his mind, the pothole-strewn path from Mersing to Johor Bahru surely did the trick. For, by the time we got home that night, I knew something was up down below. Mild contractions and nausea contributed to a terrible night and the 14th dawned, pregnant with possibility.

Matthew went off to Singapore for the day with instructions on how to get to the clinic if we weren't home when he returned. Mahmood and I went shopping and out to lunch. I was a bit out of sorts, though fully functional and at three o'clock we went to the doctor's office for a routine appointment. I saw Dr. Chia's associate, Dr. Lim, who stuck her finger inside me and said, "Two centimeters, fully effaced, time to go upstairs for admittance." Cleverly, I had my overnight bag in the car and up we went.

After a couple of hours just sitting around, we went home for dinner and to see Mariam. The contractions got closer, so we went back to the clinic, watched the news and a documentary, Matthew showed up, the guys went out for a drink, came back and, a bit after 11:00 P.M., things started to heat up. OH, THE PAIN! It did come, every two minutes, again and again, but I didn't really mind it tooooo much. Matthew looked on, concerned as his sister doubled over, moaning and digging fingernails into her husband's arm, although he really was more interested in the NBA game on the television.

At 11:50, I felt a glorious rush of warm water down my leg and sent Matthew for the nurse. We walked to the delivery room; I climbed up on the table and got down to business. Agony, agony, here's the head, agony, agony, whoosh, there's the body, catch it, please!

Then Dr. Chia arrived. Annie, the wonderful, sweet-as-honey night nurse I fell in love with when Mariam was born, delivered Iskandar and she was so proud. Chia cut the cord, pulled out the placenta, gave me two stitches (darn) and apologized profusely. We didn't care. Iskandar was ugly and perfect. Annie whisked him away to be gussied up before you could say Tunku Iskandar Shah Bin Tunku Mahmood Shah.

I walked back to the room, none the worse for wear. Matthew and Mahmood had both intended to watch the birth, but, as it happened so fast, only Annie and I were in attendance.

Well, the guys stuck around for a bit to see Iskandar, saw him and left to get some sleep. I nursed, sent Iskandar to the nursery, tried to sleep, couldn't and asked for half a sleeping pill. I slept until 7:00, cleaned myself up, went and got the baby, brought him back to the room and was nursing him when the men and Mariam showed up. We hung out, got restless and conspired to sneak the baby and me out rather than wait for the doctor to show up, look us over and say go. So we escaped and were home by noon.

Now, five days later, five, exhausting, semi-sleepless, baby cries, mother nurses, sleeps an hour, repeat....

I am just beginning to realize I have a son! A prince with huge amounts of black hair, big, dark eyes and light brown skin. Mariam has adjusted to his existence well and likes to pet him, though she is angry with me and prefers Aminah's company. She is coming around, blessing me with her antics and hugs and help changing diapers.

Matthew has gone to Thailand for two weeks. Unfortunately, newborns are not a spectator sport! Mahmood hooked him up with a friend with a yacht on Phuket, a hedonistic island off the south coast. Mother will be in attendance when he returns and we'll all take off to Rawa for the month of March. It's Ramadhan, the fasting month and a prayerful time in the city. And I have much to be thankful for.

Love, Patty

26 April

Mahmood has been gone five days. He said not to be surprised if he stayed in Brunei a month or more this time. He says he's really motivated to generate some new business and make some new money! At least I won't have to worry about his drinking. In some ways I need a break from his needs…especially with a tiny baby around who demands so much attention. I cherish the solitude…no, solitude is not the word in a house with two little ones and a sister-in-law who, when she hears her brother is out of town, points her taxi in this direction every morning. But eventually she must leave and I find there are minutes in the evening when the babies are asleep and I am still awake to read paragraphs and write pages and chew my food slowly. Such luxury.

27 May

Auntie Zoe,

Mahmood has been gone nearly six weeks and hasn't set a date for his return yet. According to him, business is great and more is promised, but he says he has to stick around to get signatures on contracts or all is for naught. Unfortunately, I'm feeling uneasy about him and these long absences.

Iskandar is asleep and Mariam will be shortly, as the time for her nap is drawing near. I can hear her and Aminah chatting downstairs. I'm reading a book that is borderline, not good enough to engage me but still worth reading. I ran out of things to do around the house weeks ago and it's always either too hot or raining (the latter as I write) to be outside during the day. I can't think of anything to buy if we went out shopping and no one I want to visit or be visited by. There is no television (literally) to watch during the day and I can't decide what to have for lunch. Shall I go on? No, because this will pass quickly and, in fact, I'm already feeling more vigorous.

Now Iskandar is awake and cooing at the musical mobile I just wound up for him.

Mariam is entertaining him with her toys and filling his crib with them—she just came back for more.

I am slightly embarrassed to share this trite (in retrospect) anecdote with you. But, for prosperity and future guffaws, I shall.

Aminah went off to visit friends for the day yesterday and left me alone with my children. Now, mind you, Sunday is her day off and yesterday was Sunday, so she was well within her rights to leave us. Except that she hasn't taken more than a couple hours off since Iskandar was born and I've gotten used to having her close. She was gone for eight hours and that is a very, very long time!!

The day began with my taking the darlings over to Chu's for a visit. They both fussed, but were manageable, though exhausting. We made it home all right and then the "fun" really began. I must have peeked out the window fifty times in the hope I'd see Aminah returning...When one baby wasn't crying, the other was or both were. Mariam was into everything she shouldn't have been, forcing me to run around taking things away from her. When I'd finally get Iskandar quiet, she'd start up, upsetting him.

Truly, it was the longest afternoon/evening of my life. I was on the edge of tears and starving, unable to spare even a moment for a bite to eat. And on top of everything, I could not find "doggy," the stuffed dog that would have calmed Mariam down.

Aminah walked in, found "doggy," and had Mariam calmed down in two seconds! I was desperate to eat and sleep once she had taken Mariam downstairs, but Iskandar had other plans for me and he finally went to sleep at midnight. I was frazzled!

Aminah just took Mariam off to visit the friends she was with yesterday. They are all Indonesians who live in low cost housing or squat in shacks they make out of scrap lumber and plastic sheeting. I do worry a bit that someone will steal Mariam for ransom or to sell, which isn't so uncommon here. But Aminah is tough and Mariam is a Tunku. If anyone tried such a dastardly act, the wrath and manhunt would be enormous and Mahmood would personally and happily empty a couple of magazines into the culprits' heads. People here are more afraid of the Tunkus than they are of the police—and with good reason. There are rules and procedures the police must heed...but none for the Tunkus.

I will close with another example of why God was smart to keep me sterile until I lived in this place.

Please do not call Child Welfare for I really am not a wicked, neglectful mother. Just now, however, while obliviously writing about Mariam being stolen by pirates, my poor, innocent, darling baby boy rolled off the bed. I heard a thud, looked up and he was gone. I sprung to my feet and then the cacophony commenced. He let out the most pathetic, heart-wrenching, guilt-provoking scream. I scooped my poor, injured baby up into my shameful arms and he howled a good sixty seconds with tears streaming down his precious cheeks. I rocked him and soothed him and soon he was whimpering softly and ready to take the proffered breast. Before you could say, "Lock her up," he was asleep and I was searching for non-existent cuts and bruises. Only Allah knows the mental scars inflicted. To my credit, the floor is carpeted and his fall was less than two feet. Blankets on the floor from here on out, Your Honor.

Please burn this letter!

Love, Patty

8 October

Ah, I have five minutes to write this journal entry. I can already hear the loudspeakers of the mosques. Evening prayer is exactly at sunset and since we are further south than the capital, the sun sets here three minutes earlier. The television station is in Kuala Lumpur and they broadcast the call to prayer immediately preceding the news. The "call" is five minutes of beautiful chanting in Arabic with lovely scenes of mosques, happy people praying and lovely scenery on the screen. And then the news, sponsored by CNN International, censored and sterile, lest it upset or incite. The news broadcast is a highlight of my day, especially when Mahmood is out of town.

My long absent husband did telephone today to toss me a morsel of hope. He says the paperwork is moving along and he may be home in as soon as a week...or two. I'm becoming more concerned about these separations. The Sultan of Brunei is having a half a billion dollars or so celebration to commemorate his twenty-five years on the throne and the happiness of his people. For the next two weeks Brunei will be in the throes of pomp, flags waving and smiling bureaucrats sitting on their butts, to my husband's consternation.

Zahara is here and having another voice in the house helps. Now that I'm finally driving my car with great skill and confidence, the days pass more quickly as we shop and visit and go to the pediatrician and play chauffeur to a demanding Auntie Chu. Had I known how difficult saying no to her would be and how often she would need to be driven on important errands, I'd never have learned to drive on the wrong side of the road!

Last night she telephoned at 6:30 to tell us to come over for dinner at Uncle Bakar's, where she's house-sitting. She had cooked a feast for us and forgotten to phone earlier! Zahara, Aminah and I did not want to go for a dozen reasons and she got angry, as though we had no right to refuse her. I was tired, Aminah was already fixing dinner, Zahara was on her way to Singapore for the evening and the kids were grimy and grumpy. Chu rejected all those reasons and was downright rude. Argh, she can be so exasperating.

3 December

Dear Mother,

Mahmood is determined not to go to Michigan with the children and me in March and I can't penetrate his stubborn refusal to talk about it. He claims the weather is the main reason but when I say, "Fine, we'll go in June," he changes the subject and pours himself another drink.

In the past he's talked about being too shy to go to a place where there are different customs and no Asians. He says he fears people will laugh at his accent, stare at his brown skin and ridicule his Malaysian ways. He has awful memories of his early years in Australia and England, two Western countries, and I think thoughts of returning to the "West" triggers some heavy anxiety. Anyway, he talks about going when it's an intangible, but the moment going becomes real, he balks. I fear we may never get him to come with us.

I've been unable to shake a nasty cold for two weeks now. I let myself get too run-down and I haven't been eating right. I put off going to the doctor until today and was shocked when I got on his scale: 118 pounds. I haven't weighed less than 125 since I was thirteen and am now in the novel position of trying to gain weight. Iskandar is not helping as he selfishly sucks away every calorie I consume. Yes, he is still nursing quarts at nine-and-a-half months, with no sign of quitting as neither of us has the energy or desire to begin the long, arduous weaning ordeal. Malay's commonly nurse for three or more years and Aminah tells me village women always nurse baby boys for at least two years to insure they never forget their mother.

Mariam is magnificent, Aminah is amiable and I am ingesting copious calories. Note the spots on the page—that's coconut milk.

Love, Patty

12 December

Dear Zoe,

Aminah, the children and I left Johor Bahru and arrived on Rawa two days ago. We came across after dark, my first time in the boat at night. Aminah and I were both scared, while Mariam loved it and Iskandar snored. We had been trying to leave, but flooding on the Mersing road prevented our departure.

Unfortunately, I am beginning to realize there are more bumps in paradise. The Sultan, whose second son is on the Johor Bahru field hockey team, beat up the coach, putting him in the ICU. The Sultan did this because the coach dared to reprimand his son when he beat up a player from the opposing team after the Johor team lost. All of this has been on the front page of every newspaper for the last couple of weeks. The Prime Minister is trying to push through a constitutional amendment removing the immunity of the royal families, because he contends they have abused the privilege and the whole thing is archaic. He's playing with fire because the rural folk worship their royals and many would prefer that they were still in charge of the country. Even in Johor, where everyone knows the Sultan, the Crown Prince and most of the other royals are depraved idiots, they'd still defend them with their lives.

Mahmood didn't come to Rawa with us. He says he has too much to do and plans to come over with our guests on the 20th. Zoe, I don't want to complain but I can't admit this to anyone but you. I haven't added up the days, but I think Mahmood and I have spent more time apart than together this year. Hmm...I am loath to open my Pandora's box of suspicions, lest they consume me and destroy my happiness. I tell myself that as long as mothering remains magnificent and Rawa stays magical, I can swallow anything, including the South China Sea, but I fear I am becoming waterlogged.

Love, Patty

chapter six

True Confessions

6 January 1993

Dear Zoe,

I have tried to shield those I love from the details of the sad reality of the most personal parts of my life lately. Forgive me for finally confessing, but I am becoming more and more uneasy here. This excerpt from the *Sydney Morning Herald* may give you more insight as to why.

"Few Malaysians ever dared mention the time Sultan Mahmood Iskandar, of Johor, opened fire from one of his helicopters, killing a smuggler. Or the time the Sultan's caddy angered the man who was then Malaysia's king during a round of golf. The caddy died after allegedly being hit with a golf club.

"But a decades-old taboo against questioning or criticizing the nine hereditary rulers of Malaysia has been abandoned by nearly everyone, from the Prime Minister down. A flood of resentment toward the rulers, particularly Sultan Iskandar, has suddenly been unleashed...The nation's government controlled newspapers have launched into a spate of royalty bashing.

"Aside from being seriously rich and owning large tracts of land in Singapore, oil palm plantations in Johor, islands off the coast, five helicopters, a private jet and a fleet of luxury cars and motorbikes, Sultan Iskandar has taken full advantage of his impressive bloodline...

"The Federal Government will meet in special session of Parliament next month to table constitutional amendments aimed at stripping the rulers of their immunity from criminal prosecution."

That's a bit of what the long article had to say. Odds are high the constitution will be amended and odds are high it won't mean a thing beyond a symbolic victory for the Prime Minister. The police, the courts and even the government are intimidated and a little afraid of the royal families and their influence. The sultans are so wealthy and revered by the common folk that it behooves people not to cross them. My guess is this hullabaloo will die down soon, the constitution will be amended and nothing will change.

In three days, Mariam is off to Brunei to be with Mahmood's daughter again for another round of reckless spoiling. I want to say no, but Mahmood is gung-ho for her to go and Mariam wants to go and is genuinely excited. She is older now and will enjoy herself. Zahara mentioned parties at the palace and an amusement park called Jerudong.

The separation will give Iskandar his greatest wish: Mama and Aminah all to himself. Both Aminah and I have perpetually sore backs and bruised hips from carrying two children around. Neither child can bear for the other to be held alone and neither Aminah nor I can bear to say no.

I saw the travel agent yesterday and switched our flights from 23 March to the 18th. Hari Raya is on 25 and 26 March and Aminah is going home to Indonesia while we're gone and needs enough travel time…it would be a shame for her to miss being with her family on the biggest Muslim holiday of the year. You will have us now for eight weeks and five days. Hip hip hooray.

Iskandar is able to stand unsupported for a few seconds. It won't be long before he takes that first step. The thrill of these milestones in a baby's life is breathtaking and deeply fulfilling.

Love, Patty

26 February

Aminah, the children and I arrived on Rawa two days ago, leaving Mahmood in Johor Bahru to catch up on business, whatever that means. Unfortunately, I am becoming more suspicious as well as uneasy. While looking through his toiletry bag for nail clippers the last time he came home, I found condoms. We haven't used them since our courtship and, though I searched hard for an innocuous reason why he might have them, I couldn't find one. I have steeled myself to his infidelities. Having other women is part of the royals' natures. All his brothers and cousins are wildly promiscuous or want to be. Now I must accept that Mahmood is no different. They seem to think laws and morals were made for others, not Tunkus. Whether it be wise or foolish, I have made a vow to try really, really hard to carry on and be/act happy for the sake of the children. But it's very difficult. More than anything, I'm afraid. I am alone, far from home in a land where women have few rights and men have all. I am plagued with a free-floating terror.

My shopping is finished. I bought an assortment of gifts for my family and Zoe. Two huge suitcases are packed and waiting by the door in Johor Bahru and another is at the ready to fill with clothes and Pampers. I am counting the days and hours until we depart and I will see my family and friends again.

Mariam is wearing a pair of flippers and waddling around saying, "Quack quack, Mom. Look, Mom. Quack quack, Mom." Too precious by half, as Chu says. The workers are pushing Iskandar around in a wheelbarrow as they unload the boat. He shares the barrow with bags of rice and blocks of ice and reckons himself king of the world.

7 March

Mariam got very sick five days ago with vomiting and a high fever. I took her to Mersing; Dr. Linus said flu and gave me four different medicines. We went back to the island, I gave her the medicines and, within twenty minutes, she was having trouble breathing and minor convulsions. In a panic, I ran to Hassan and told him to take us to the mainland in his speedboat. "Yes, get her. Let's go," he offered.

Hassan turned us over to Mele at the Rawa office and, because it was after 6:00 P.M., Mele took us to Dr. Fatimah's house. She said Mariam had pneumonia and needed to be in a proper hospital immediately. I'd been trying to reach Mahmood since we left Rawa without success and stood there, knowing I was on my own and needed to make a decision. Mele, who was still with me, said, "I'll take you. Let's go." Five minutes later, we were in his car on our way to Johor Bahru.

Mariam was semi-conscious and struggling with each breath. Fatimah had assured me she was not in grave danger and would recover fully. My little girl slept in my lap and Mele and I chatted anxiously during the two-hour drive to the main private hospital.

I got her checked in, said thank you and goodbye to Mele and was finally able to reach Mahmood on the telephone. It was midnight. He was furious with me and ranted, "This is your fault. I told you not to give her cold milk in a bottle and now you see what happens? What is wrong with you? And you give them baths at night and then they get chilled. Now she has pneumonia, because you won't listen to me. You think you know everything, because you're American. But you don't know the Malay way and now Mariam is in hospital. See what you did." He was beyond reason, wouldn't let me talk and finally hung up on me after saying he would be at the hospital in an hour.

I was a mess, trembling and choking with shock, guilt and fury. They let me carry Mariam up to the room where we got her settled in, medicated and soon she was asleep in my arms.

When Mahmood showed up, he was quiet and detached. We barely spoke and then he left so I could get some sleep.

My breasts were dangerously engorged and Mariam was crying when I awoke. I calmed her down and then spent twenty minutes expressing milk into the bathroom sink. My fingers were cramping; my breasts hurt like hell and tears of frustration were streaming down my cheeks. I took a quick shower and went out to meet the doctor, who was chatting with a relaxed Mariam. He wanted to give an x-ray to confirm the pneumonia. Within a few minutes, I was pushing her to the elevators in a wheelchair.

Mahmood was in the room when we got back. He'd telephoned the island and Iskandar was fine. I began to cry and felt frantic in my desire to be with my son, to nurse him. Mahmood was sarcastic and told me not to be silly. Again he yelled that I was at fault for Mariam's sickness and that it was my own fault Iskandar couldn't have his milk. I bit my tongue. Lately, he seems more and more angry with me. I can't seem to do anything right.

The doctor returned, said the X ray did show pneumonia, recommended another twenty hours of Ventolin treatments and antibiotics in the hospital and said she could safely go back to the island afterwards.

Mahmood had brought some books, crayons and drawing pads for Mariam. After he left, my daughter and I spent a peaceful day reading, coloring, eating and napping. Twice I had to express milk and was in tears both times.

Mahmood came by in the evening for an hour, said he wouldn't be able to drive us to Mersing in the morning but would come and get us into a taxi.

Which he did and here I am, back on Rawa with Iskandar at my breast. The little Miss is recuperating splendidly and I'm still a little shaky, but nearly back to normal. This is the other side of Mahmood and I am thrown by it. He frightened and infuriated me. While we were waiting for the taxi that last morning, I tried to speak to him about it. He angrily cut me off. "Drop it," he snapped. I did.

It's sevenish in the evening and the sun will soon be setting. I have a glass of wine in front of me and Hassan, my new hero, is on the mainland so the workers are frolicking. A dozen of them are playing in the water; Mariam is on the shoulders of Plastic Man, a room boy, while he walks up the jetty and Iskandar is with Dem, the only worker he'll go to. There are only eight guests and I haven't seen an American in weeks.

I'm eating eggplant curry, long beans with fermented shrimp paste and fried fish for dinner tonight—staff food cooked in big pots and heavily laden with chilies. The children are easy to feed and will have mixed vegetables with their fried fish and rice.

Mahmood should be coming tomorrow and then hopefully, I can shake this anxiety about our relationship and get back on a normal footing with him.

I am making a list of what to pack in my carry-on bag and agonizing over each item, as it must be packed with genius and military precision. Trying to keep the children occupied for over twenty-six hours on airplanes and in airports is a daunting task. I can hope for a few hours when they will sleep, but odds are they won't both sleep at the same time!

I am so excited to be leaving in eleven days. Mahmood is unduly sensitive about our leaving and he takes my happiness as a personal affront, assuming I'm happy to be leaving him! I stroke his tender ego while reminding him he could be going with us, though secretly, I'm glad he's not. He is just too volatile and I am a nervous wreck trying to pacify him. He loses his patience with the children over the smallest things, is resentful of the time

I spend with them and then complains about the bad habits they're picking up from Aminah! He assumes one and three year olds should have the manners and self-control of grownups and blames Aminah and me when they don't. I can't help but think back to Chu's description of their early childhood with stoic, formal grandparents and sadistic servants...Mahmood's demons are huge and I shudder to think of them.

29 May

Our time in the United States was wonderful, as always, but I do not want to relive the nightmare of our first three days back in Malaysia except to say I did not sleep, I did not eat, I did not chastise Mahmood for his lack of support and I did not snap, by the grace of Allah.

On the morning of our fourth day back, we left for Rawa. For now, I am able to sit on the toilet without two children in my lap, eat two bites in succession, sleep more than an hour, play Scrabble with my crabby husband, write a letter and suffer through the jet lag recovery I put off for a week.

Mariam is entertaining the workers with her English. She spoke only Malay with them before we went to the States and now she prattles on in English to their amused confusion. I was awed by the speed at which she effortlessly switched over to English while in the States and am curious to see if the opposite manifests here. They get such a kick out of mimicking her and she finds their gentle teasing hilarious, so everyone is happy.

We can't swim in the sea due to a jellyfish invasion. For the first time in anyone's memory, they are coming in to die by the thousands. The sea and beach are literally thick with them at times. To be safe, we have to avoid the beach as the poison lingers long after the creature dies.

There is another peril and I wonder about a connection. The crude oil freighters find the seas around Malaysia the ideal place to clean their bilges of tar buildup. Rather than dispose of it in port where they must pay, they throw the tar over the side. We have a glut of tar blobs lately on the beach and avoiding them is difficult. The tar gets hot, soft and gooey during the day and getting it off the feet takes ten minutes of scrubbing.

These things are bad for tourism and the government in Kuala Lumpur is huffing and puffing and putting the fear of Allah into every freighter captain's breast, I reckon. Hopefully the problem will soon be solved, the winds will shift, the newspapers will lose interest and the beaches of Vietnam will be inundated instead of ours.

2) June

Mother Dearest,

The sky is a lovely shade of orange; the tide is low and for some odd and unprecedented reason, moths are fluttering around me. Local superstition is they portend good news…and it's true! Aminah finally is back in Johor Bahru. (Remember, I told you her sister was very ill and she had to stay and nurse her.) Aminah is cleaning the house and taking care of Mahmood who leaves for Brunei in a couple days, then she'll come here. Samsea, the local woman I hired, wants to stay on and that's just dandy, so I'm a two-servant woman now.

Mariam has been my sidekick; 95 percent of her waking hours she sleeps, eats, bathes and hangs out with me. I love every minute of her priceless company. Ah, but I will love it even more when Aminah returns. Then I can read, write and chat with the tourists for longer than five minutes.

Also in the good news department: we may soon be seeing some joy in the Rawa takeover. The accountants have finished the monumental task of going through the books and though they found ten thousand discrepancies, there were no monsters. Now the papers are being drawn up for all to sign to receive their checks. Mahmood and Alang are going to be included in the payout and a check for $200,000 may soon be in our hands. I dare not make my shopping list now, as something(s) may go astray.

I have a new and consuming hobby that is child-friendly, fun and functional. We string shells and bits of coral with holes in them onto heavyweight fishing line and drape our gazebo in the garlands. Mariam and I worked six or more hours a day on the gazebo, which took us two weeks to embellish. We're taking a two-day break now to catch up on correspondence, coloring and potty training before we begin the next gazebo.

My day begins at 7:00 A.M. with a child or two, a mug of coffee, a bucket and a walk on the beach. Broken shells and coral with holes are plentiful and once our bucket is full we go up to our gazebo (the tourists know or quickly learn not to disturb Madam's gazebo), have breakfast and get to work. Mariam is a skilled threader and Iskandar excels at handing the materials over. A fine avocation.

Yesterday I had to go to Mersing after I stepped on a rusty, ugly spike that pierced my big toe. I telephoned Dr. Linus and he said, "Get here now."

I got there (with the kids and Samsea in tow as we never pass up an oppor-tunity to go on the boat, experience civilization and buy a toy) and he gave me a tetanus shot.

Hard to believe we've been back from Michigan five weeks and on the island a month already. Unfortunately, Mahmood has come and gone only twice, but I am determined to stay until we take over and then live here permanently.

Here's Mariam with a bag of peanuts demanding that I open them for her, "Mama, I want some peanuts. Mama, I want some peanuts. MAMA, I WANT SOME PEANUTS!"

More good news; she's potty—or, rather, potty and sand—trained. She likes to poop and pee in the sand and then bury the evidence to be stepped on or rolled in later while she and her brother play. Yuck. I know she picked this up from watching the cats, silly/clever girl. Peanut-cracking time.

Love and kisses, Patty

22 July

Mariam and I went to bed at 11:00 P.M. after a delightful evening of conversation with Chu, who's been hanging out here, and some of the guests. Hassan had left that morning and Tom, the head manager was still on leave. Joe, the lazy waste of human flesh assistant manager was nowhere to be found, giving some of the workers license to sit at the bar, drink and have a ball.

At approximately 12:45 A.M., in my dream state, I thought Mariam had thrown an arm or leg over me. Suddenly I was wide-awake and there was a man on top of me, his erect Willie pressing through his jeans as he ground it painfully against my pelvis. I screamed and kicked him off me. (When the police were later taking my statement, I was embarrassed to say this in front of the innocent looking young cop, but he was more embarrassed than I was, especially when I had to help him with the spelling.) My assailant stumbled through the mosquito net, off the bed and out the door. I gave chase but stopped a few feet outside my door as I was only wearing a bra. I caught a glimpse of him rounding the corner and knew, without a shadow of doubt, who it was.

I closed and locked my door and lay back down on the bed, thunder-struck. I don't know how long I lay there, trying to calm down and get up the courage to walk down the hall to Aminah's room, but I'd estimate it was fifteen minutes.

Aminah was awake and when I told her the story, she knew immediately who it was, because the same jerk was harassing her earlier and had knocked on her door after she went to bed. A little later, she'd heard him under my window, softly calling my name.

Together, with a big flashlight and a stick, we went to find Faud, the head man. We filled him in, got Joe up and joined Chu, who was still in the gazebo.

I sat down, shaky and undone, though at the same time astonished and furious that one of the workers would have the balls and be so stupid as to come into my room where I was sleeping with Mariam beside me. She never woke up, thank you Allah.

They told me he was very drunk and probably had taken something else, as well. Furthermore, on three previous occasions that Joe knew of, he'd tried to get into women tourist's rooms. Two weeks earlier, Tom had fired him for climbing through the window of a woman's chalet. Hassan had rehired him the next day, the bloody idiot!

After endless discussion, I decided to telephone Mahmood and got him on the thirty-fifth ring. His response was: "First thing in the morning, get the police over there to arrest that asshole and we will prosecute him to the fullest extent of the law." Those words were music to my ears and I went back to bed. The suspect, Joe had ascertained, was sound asleep in his room.

I slept in snatches, woke up a couple times in a cold, terror-stricken sweat and welcomed the dawn when it finally came. I went out at 8:00 and Joe was already on the radio trying to reach the police, which he finally did. They arrived at 10:00.

In the meantime, Azmi, the culprit, was wandering around cool as a cucumber. When Faud confronted him, he said, "Nope, wasn't me."

There were eight men on the police boat, typical for half the force to come out for anything even remotely interesting, especially when they might see a woman in a bikini. My statement was taken, as were Aminah's, Joe's, Faud's and other staff members. Photos were taken of my room and the escape route. Then the shirt the culprit had worn was retrieved from his room and identified.

I balked when they told me I needed to go to Mersing for a medical exam. The only physical evidence was a slight tenderness and a small bruise on my pubic bone. I think he gently climbed on top of me, got excited and then started the grinding that woke me up. Anyway, I asked Maria, a Swedish woman I'd befriended over the weekend, to go with me to the hospital and we went on the police boat with all those cops and the suspect. I should have taken the Rawa speedboat, but was too flustered to think straight. It was a long half hour. The doctor examined me externally, but when we were in the car leaving he ran out and said he'd better do an internal exam, just in case! I wished it would all go away but I complied and even plucked a couple of the pubic hairs he requested.

From there, trying to get back to normalcy, Maria and I did some shopping. I bought the children presents, as they were both angry Mama dared go to Mersing without them. Then we crossed the street to Dr. Linus's office and he gave me some sedatives, sympathy and sleeping pills.

I was a physical and emotional wreck, functioning with no sleep and trying to stay civil through all the difficult questioning of the police.

We arrived back on the island at 7:30 P.M., ate and I went off to bed with Iskandar attached to my breast. Tired, I didn't take a pill and slept for a few hours like a log. Then I woke in a panicked sweat and lay there awake the rest of the night.

The next morning I was puttering around upstairs in the storeroom looking for hammock rope, found some and walked downstairs right into the police chief, who had been waiting patiently for me.

Apparently, Azmi had denied everything and had an alibi (he must have worked it out with his roommate before the police took him off). But the police hadn't bought this story. They interviewed the roommate whose story did not mesh with Azmi's.

Before he left, the chief took me aside. "We have an airtight case. Would you drop the charges if the boy were to confess and say sorry?"

"Never!" I said adamantly. "He deserves to be punished." The minimum sentence for an attempted rape is caning and five to ten years in prison.

Mahmood was in the midst of Rawa negotiations in Johor Bahru and could not leave to be with me. The staff, however, really rallied around me and the tourists who knew about my case have been concerned about me.

Yesterday, no police came and things were back to normal. Feeling better, I cleaned the gazebo, wrote my mother a long letter and collected shells. However, I was tormented by weird, sexual dreams last night, so I guess I'm not recovering as well as I think.

I've always felt completely safe on the island, rarely locked my door when Mahmood was gone and have always been treated with great respect. Unhappily, I shall never feel that sense of security again.

9 August

The boy has confessed. This will be, I hope, the end of the incident, at least for me.

A storm is brewing. The meteorological variety makes this land of two seasons intriguing. Whipping winds, glossy gray/black skies, the peal of thunder and translucent lightening, crashing waves and torrential rain are the stuff of dreams. For me, they have become dreams of Michigan.

I may see my husband this week. He said he'd try to get here, but he still had a few things to finish up in Brunei. That was six days ago. I've tried to stop keeping track of our separations, but they are daunting. This one has been seven weeks, at least.

Uncle Bakar showed up on the island. He moaned, bitched and complained for three hours. The poor guy tries to hard to be a good uncle, to be nice and please everyone (except for Chu, whom he loathes) to the point where no one is happy. Unfortunately, I haven't met a Tunku yet who can take criticism of any sort and I've learned to smile and keep my mouth shut. My husband is no exception. Then Uncle opened up to me like he's never opened up to anyone (his words) and told me things I'm not even supposed to tell Mahmood. Things about family weirdness which unnerved me. I can't even write them here.

Meanwhile, the takeover is at a critical stalemate. The six younger half siblings each are demanding $33,000 more, to be taken from Mahmood and Alang's share, because they feel it is unfair for my husband and his brother to get both the island and one-ninth of the payoff. Uncle Bakar said they'd be happy with half of Mahmood and Alang's portion and, if given, they all would sign promptly.

Chu is refusing to sign unless she has a piece of the action, such as a role in the new resort and/or shares in the company. Technically, she has every right to demand these things. She is one of the three "legal" heirs and should be included. She's been pushed aside and treated badly all her life and I, for one, feel sorry for her. However, Mahmood and Alang absolutely do not want her to have anything to do with the business.

The plot sickens. George, a Chinese man who will be head of the new management team, is here this week and has been picking my brain for answers, insights and advice about all the ins and outs of running the resort. I am uncomfortable being in this position, but he has been so nice and tells me my perspective is wonderful and invaluable. I pray I don't say something awful that could get me in deep trouble, i.e. upset Mahmood, who seems terribly agitated with me these days. About this I feel more and more anxious, yet have no one with whom to talk over my feelings, least of all my husband.

Next day. I must be incredibly stressed. This morning I was nursing Iskandar while peeing in the women's bathroom off the restaurant. I heard Mariam calling me, wiped, jumped up, washed my hands, grabbed the baby and went out to look for her. I was half way through the restaurant before I realized my breast was hanging out of my bathing suit. Two of the waiters, the bartender and I don't know how many guests saw me...I was soooooo embarrassed.

2 October

Dear Zoe,

Mahmood surprised us all with a twenty-four-hour visit. He tells me he's trying to make sense of and bring about a conclusion to this travesty of a takeover. He is wound so tightly and obsessed and angry with everyone, especially me, that I am worried. When will he be transformed back into the man I love?

The attempted rape case goes to trial in twenty-four days, barring the ever-inevitable postponement. I spent three hours with the police a few days back going over testimony and it's a cut-and-dried case of attempted rape. Except he has demanded a trial with jury. Why does a guy who gives a full confession plead innocent and request a trial? I suppose because the punishment is caning and prison.

Please forgive this downcast letter.

Love, Patty

chapter seven

Good Fortune and Bad

30 October 1993

Good fortune has shined on us. We own the island. We really, really do. I still haven't grasped the enormity of the situation. Our business partners have very big bucks and they want to spend four to six million dollars on renovation. Mahmood estimates we will be millionaires in three years. We won't be suffering in the meantime, as the company intends to compensate Mahmood, their Chairman of the Board, quite nicely. I'm lah-de-dah about the whole thing, because there is nothing the children or I presently lack and the thought of turning Rawa into a fancy, expensive resort makes me sad. I love it just the way it is.

Mahmood was finally able to fly to Brunei yesterday, after weeks of being stuck in Johor Bahru and Kuala Lumpur facilitating the take over. We spent last weekend together, but our marriage is not improving. Except for the first night, he was unpleasant and distant. Things between us still are shaky. Nevertheless, he promised that when he returns from Brunei in a couple of weeks or more, he'll come straight to the island and we will begin our new Rawaiin life. My fingers are crossed and the Scrabble board has been dusted.

Aminah and the children are in homemaker heaven, ensconced in Hassan's old rooms with attached bathroom and air conditioning. I helped the workers rip out a wall to double the size of Mahmood's and my room.

We've been cleaning up the other rooms (there are ten) and beautifying the common/play room. The island closes for the season in two weeks and soon afterwards construction will begin, preceded by architects, surveyors and their ilk. It should be a happening monsoon season.

19 November

We were in Johor Bahru for ten days packing up and doing my rushed Christmas shopping so I could get the boxes posted in time for delivery to Michigan. It was not fun. Half way through it all, Mahmood told me some new people have come on board and want to give him a check for one million dollars before Christmas in exchange for the thirty-year lease on 5 percent of our land. Mahmood is much more excited about this than I am and still has little patience with the children or me. I agonize as to the whys.

I've been having some serious stomach problems—the up-all-night-vomiting and doubled-over-in-screaming-pain variety. I figured it was an ulcer, as did the first doctor I consulted. He gave me medicines that did nothing and abstaining from coffee, alcohol, spices and citrus for two weeks also was ineffective. In the midst of this, Aminah, the kids and I returned to the island and I wandered around in pain worrying about my mortality for two days. I realized I was being stupid, so I packed up the gang and went back to Johor Bahru. I hadn't been able to reach Mahmood, so we decided to surprise him… Instead of being happy, as I'd imagined, he was furious.

It was mid-afternoon when we arrived and his car was parked out front, so I knew he was home. I sent the taxi away, then banged on the door for five minutes. I had my house key, but the security latch was in place and I couldn't open the door. I sent Aminah to the back of the house to throw pebbles against the window, assuming he was napping. No response. I was about to send Aminah to find a taxi to take us to a hotel, when the door opened. Mahmood had a sarong around his waist, his hair was disheveled and he had SIN written all over his face! He began yelling at the children and me, telling me to leave. I knew there was a woman in the house. I decided to move slowly, act ditzy and do exactly what he told me.

I followed him through the living room and into the bedroom. I was carrying Mariam and Aminah had Iskandar. Aminah put Iskandar on the bed and headed downstairs. Mahmood followed her in a rush and wild horses couldn't have dragged me from the bedroom during the next fifteen minutes. I talked quietly with the children and to calm them we sang nursery rhymes to drown out the marriage killers. Still, I heard muffled voices, someone running down the stairs, doors opening and closing. Disappointment and disgust washed over me and I knew with certainty that my feelings for my husband were forever diminished.

Mahmood did not have an easy time looking me in the eye later. When he reached for me that night, I complied but felt like vomiting afterwards.

2 November

I have new medicine that calms my stomach pain, but nothing seems to help with the other pain I'm feeling. Aminah, the children and I left for Rawa today. Mahmood gave me a distant peck on the cheek.

24 December

Mahmood was on the island with us for a week, but left for a Rawa Resort board meeting in Kuala Lumpur yesterday. Now he's stuck in Mersing (with three of our guests), because the sea is too high to come across. They hope to make the trip at 6:00 A.M. tomorrow, so the gift-ripping frenzy should commence mid morning.

25 December

The sea has not yet obeyed the petty wishes of mortal men, women and Santa-loving children. The weather is worse than yesterday and no boats are allowed out of the harbor. Mahmood tried to entice a few fishermen to take him across, but no one would budge so it must be bad. We are communicating with him by radio—*Over* and *Roger* and all that jazz. The children love it!

All festivities have been put off until he arrives. Mariam and I are sitting at a table in the restaurant by the Christmas tree. We are surrounded by presents while carols play in the background. She's wearing her taffeta "party" dress and both she and Iskandar are mellow as can be. They don't understand that today is the "day," because there is no hype and excitement. I feel subdued, but must pull myself together for the children's sake, decorate a tad more here and there, have the children draw a few more Yule tide pictures, further embellish our menu and enjoy the drama of "When will he come?"

27 December

Noon and the boat is on the horizon. The children are wound up, the adults are wound up, the ovens are cranked up and the tree is lit up. I only hope Mahmood is in a good mood.

6 January 1994

Dear Zoe,

I'm in the foyer of the restaurant struggling to find a comfortable position in a huge bamboo chair that should be hanging on the wall rather than taking up floor space. We have two of these behemoths and a matching couch, both of which are white elephants Hassan bought to help out a bankrupt buddy. Every once in a while I sit down in one, hoping for a miracle...excuse me while I move to a straight-back wooden chair.

The wait for our million dollars continues as the new partners do their arithmetic and consult with their lawyers. Unfortunately, Mahmood and I are not getting along so other things are on my mind. Nevertheless, motherhood continues to fulfill me.

Mariam calls me Daddy or Dad 90 percent of the time now. She started a couple weeks back when our friends were here and using the term. Mahmood is firmly Baba to her and now, to our great chagrin and amusement, I am Daddy. The more we try to break her of it, the more she perseveres. Soon Iskandar may follow suit. Yikes. Write soon!

Love, Patty

21 January

I am reeling… We came back to the city to do some errands and discovered that, sometime during the four weeks it sat vacant, the house was broken into. Above our bed is a gaping hole and I can see the sky peeking through. The room is a shambles, but luckily there was nothing of value in the entire place, as we'd long ago taken all the good stuff to Rawa. Definitely nothing worth hauling up through a hole in the fourteen-foot ceiling of a tall house. They did snag a cheap cassette player, the coins in the piggy bank and some costume jewelry.

Still, the idea of someone breaking in is horrifying. I'd thought the house was so safe with its iron gratings and big padlocks, never for a moment supposing someone could climb on the roof, remove a few brick tiles, break through the flimsy ceiling plaster and drop down on my head.

We telephoned the landlord, told him what had happened and said we'd be out of the house by the end of the month. Mahmood convinced me we could safely stay a couple nights and said he'd love the opportunity to use his gun if they did come back.

We cleaned up the mess enough to function, ran our errands, sorted stuff, packed boxes and hired a truck so we could move out in forty-eight hours.

24 January

It was a very long forty-eight hours for me. I had really awful nightmares both nights we stayed there. I woke up screaming once, twice I awakened in a cold sweat, too terrified to scream and a few other times I experienced the run-of-the-mill, half-hour-of-recovery, variety. Mahmood had no sympathy and, although I begged mightily not to stay the second night, we did.

I'm fine now that we're back on the island. The kids thought a hole in the ceiling was pretty cool and Aminah trusted her boss's gun implicitly. Only I was a nervous wreck watching Mahmood's trigger-happy state. What is happening to him?

All the house stuff is stored at the Mersing office and bits will be coming over on each boat. We won't know what is going to show up, so waiting on the jetty for the boat will have extra meaning as we slowly get the pieces of the puzzle that will make our Rawa home complete.

February 15

I had hoped the good fortune of getting to the island would bring further positive changes but Mahmood is an incensed, obsessed wreck. He's drinking more, chain-smoking and has a short and getting ever shorter fuse with the children and me. Mariam and Iskandar were squabbling over a kitten yesterday and he screamed at them and threatened to drown the kitten to teach them a lesson. When they begged him not to harm the kitten, he cruelly teased them and jumped down my throat when I asked him to stop. Incidents like this are happening on a regular basis now and all I can do is keep the children out of his sights and swallow my frustration. Nothing I do or say seems right. The other day I ventured to him and the children, "Would you like to walk on the beach, darlings?"

"What's wrong with you? The sand flies are bloody awful today. You want them to get infections?!" he interjected.

To change the subject I asked, "How about spaghetti for dinner tonight, kids?"

"Why are you always trying to make them hate rice? All you ever feed them is Western food. What's wrong with you? They are Malay children and need rice," he said curtly.

I sighed, "Fine, let's have fried fish and rice with vegetables."

The children don't know what to think. "Why is Baba so mean? Why is he always in a bad mood? Why does he get to call us stupid when you say that's not a nice word?" they inquire, when we're alone.

The very few times I've tried to talk to him about his behavior in the nicest, gentlest way I could muster, he came close to hitting me. His demons are vicious and dangerous. "We need to discuss the way you talk to the children. I know you don't mean to hurt their feelings, but sometimes you say…"

"Are you telling me I don't know how to talk to my own children? Bloody hell, who do you think you are? You think just because you're American and you went to college, you know everything…" and he's off on another tirade.

I wouldn't be surprised if Mahmood waved his gun around and threatened people. Mahmood claims it's sometimes necessary to scare and/or beat the shit out of people to get things done or done right. Last month, for example, we bought a huge bag of durian fruit from a street vendor, brought it home and discovered the guy had put some rotten fruit at the bottom. Mahmood was livid, ordered me to get in the car and we drove back. He confronted the guy, then knocked him out by whacking him with his pistol! I suggested on the way home that he might have overreacted. He went into an ugly tirade about all the people, especially Americans, who have ever done him an injustice and what he'd like to do to them. Then he glowered at me. I tried not to take it personally, but I could not help trembling all over. He poured himself a very stiff whiskey when we got home and was silent the rest of the evening.

22 February

Auntie Zoe,

In exactly fifty days I embark upon the journey back to the States with my two little ones. Mariam will be fine. She minds me pretty well, is quick to help out, knows how to use a spoon, can even put her clothes on and she's toilet trained.

Iskandar is a paragraph unto himself. Hide the hammers, sticks, sharp objects and chocolate. He is a boy obsessed when he wants something and a destructive madman when he gets it! He's crazy for anything with a blade or a point and when he has something lethal in his hands he swings it around and tries to cut and/or pierce everything in his sights. I wonder where he has seen this behavior which he now emulates. With as many times as he's managed to snag dangerous implements, it's a miracle there has been no bloodshed.

Mahmood, who has been in a continually bad mood, is in Kuala Lumpur at a board meeting to resolve the management crisis, i.e. get Rupinda, the manager, fired before he kills her. Mahmood hates this woman with a burning passion and I've found, as time has passed, he's very good at hating people. I've been staying out of his way lately as he's in a perpetually foul mood with no time for the children or normal familial interaction. All he does is bitch and sulk. Oddly, we still play three or four Scrabble games a day. This seems to be our one social activity. He also spends hours alone on the jetty fishing and his nights in solitary drinking. I get so frustrated and angry with him that I end up crying, because he's impossible to talk to and twists things around so skillfully that suddenly I'm the bad guy feeling guilty. I pray he comes home with tangible good news and a smile…

I'm going to leave you with one big question: Can this marriage be saved? Please write to me now, please.

Love, Patty

3 March

Aminah and I are on the boat headed toward a rendezvous with history. It is all because of that crazy assault against me last summer and the bi-monthly trial postponements of these past eight months. Today I am supposed to be testifying in a Malaysian court of law. I was tempted to drop the charges, but Mahmood won't hear of it. He's right; I must follow through.

Aminah is along as my star witness, leaving Mahmood and Zahara, who showed up a few days back, to baby-sit. With the staff there to play with the children, the day shouldn't be too hard on them. Zahara is nearly as useless as Mahmood around children and if it were only them, I know they'd be at each other's throats by noon!

Later—Azmi and his lawyer didn't show and what do you know, another postponement. Aminah and I shopped an hour and now we're waiting at the Rawa office for the tide to come up enough so boats can leave the harbor.

28 March

Dear Zoe,

Mahmood returns this afternoon from his forty-eight-hour foray in Johor Bahru. This is fasting month and the city is prayerful. I am too, mostly about my husband. He can't eat, drink or smoke in public and he's a chain smoker. And something else I never wanted to admit: he's a too-many-cocktails-an-evening drinker who's convinced he doesn't have a problem. He's sure of this, because he never has his first drink before 7:00 P.M. and everyone knows alcoholics drink all day long.

These days I'm always asleep or pretending to be asleep when he comes in every night around 1:00 A.M. Sometimes he stumbles and has a spot of trouble getting undressed and into bed. It is my misfortune to be awake on these nights, because his snoring eventually drives me to go sleep with the children in their room.

I haven't had a drink since December and don't miss my two evening glasses of wine. Perhaps though, abstinence has made me less tolerant of my husband's excesses.

I looked at my itinerary and we fly on the 14th rather than the 13th and arrive in Traverse City, Michigan at 6:05 P.M. Mahmood is definitely not going to join us later and, frankly, at this point, I'm relieved. He has been so difficult these past weeks that I am counting the hours until we leave here. Something is going on and he won't talk about it. Possibly nothing is going on and he's just a jerk. I forgave him everything during those many months of Rawa Resort take-over purgatory, believing he would undergo a transformation once he had the island. He did, for about three days.

Mahmood's dictatorial ways and cruel teasing are getting to the children. He can be so awful to them. His childhood demons come out more and more lately and they scare me...Anyway, soon the children and I will be flying eastward and we can talk about it when I see you.

Love and kisses, Patty

30 May

The children and I are in Michigan now, enjoying being spoiled by my mother and the company of family and friends who love and support us. All should be well, except for our being away from Mahmood. The problem is that I have had time here to think about our deteriorating relationship: his preoccupation with his gun, his alcoholism, his women and his treatment of me and the children. My sister-in-law, always concerned about me, called from Malaysia to tell me he had moved a girlfriend into our home within hours of my departure. Before this, I have pushed these truths away, not wanting to think about the consequences for the children and me if I admitted them. But I can't look away or repress them anymore. They fill my sleepless nights with pain and anguish.

16 June

Our return flight to Malaysia is in three weeks and I find myself wishing it would never come. At the very, very least, I want to extend our time in Michigan until fall. Not only will that give me more time to make a decision about my marriage, but I need more time in the safety and security of my loving family. I gather strength from them.

I telephoned the airline and flights are wide open in September. Now I must phone my husband to ask his permission. Somehow, I doubt he'll care much. He's only written to us twice and our weekly telephone conversations are stilted and uncomfortable.

I no longer know how I feel about him after his behavior during this past year: the drinking, his women and his frightening actions toward me and the children. I don't know if I even want to go back. The advice from my family is mixed. Mother says, "Go back in September and work out an equitable divorce. Tell him you'll raise the kids here and he can have them every summer."

The consensus from my siblings is for me to adjust. "You can fix the marriage," they pontificate. "Just accept him as he is, try to be more tolerant and lower your expectations."

Zoe, who knows the most about what has been going on, gives advice that scares me. "Screw him. He's a jerk. He treats you like shit, is a terrible father, has been unfaithful and he lies. Don't go back. Divorce him here, get a job, settle down and forget about him. If he wants to see the kids, he can fly here. He's an abuser and you can't trust him." She goes off on a tangent comparing him to the husbands of women at the Domestic Violence Shelter she manages. I listen to them all and agonize.

18 June

I telephoned Mahmood to ask if we could stay longer in Michigan. He said, "Sure, whatever. Stay until September. Goodbye."

Does he even want us back? Now what?

Perhaps I should write him a letter expressing my feelings and concerns. I will tell him I found the condoms and know about his infidelity and that he must confess, seek forgiveness and promise to be faithful. Or what? I know in my gut he won't confess and would rather die than ask forgiveness or promise me anything.

And will he listen this time if I suggest he ought to drink less (or not at all), because he is exhibiting alcoholic behaviors that are hurting the marriage and the children? I know in my heart he won't.

I wonder if there is a marriage counselor in Mersing. Probably not, but there most likely are dozens in Singapore. Would Mahmood agree to see one with me? For the children's sake he might. At least I must try.

chapter eight

The Same Differences

20 August 1994

My thoughts ricochet back and forth as I remain in Michigan with the children. I want to believe Mahmood could be different. I love Malaysia and our island home. I pity him his troubled childhood and unhappy marriage to Azizah. I understand his disappointment in Princess Zahara, their adult daughter, and her self-indulgent lifestyle. But I am beginning to realize it is his many character flaws and the depraved culture of the Malaysian royalty of which he is a part that caused most of these things and my present dilemma. My family has encouraged me to express my concerns to him over the phone. Today I did so and he flew into a threatening rage. He made irrational, cruel accusations from "You and the children are dead to me" to "Just send the boy back." He finished up with "You think I've been a bastard; you don't know what I can do to you. And don't think the fact that you are in America will prevent me from getting the children and you." I knew then our marriage was in desperate trouble and all my fears confirmed.

5 September

I have been hiding with the children for the past two weeks. My family and I have been distraught, afraid Mahmood was planning to send over some members of the Muslim extremist groups currently rising in

Malaysia to kidnap Mariam and Iskandar and kill me. And I know this threat could be real for these people hate Westerners and undoubtedly see me as an infidel. Two of my brothers and their wives fear he will go after their children and use them as hostages. Desperate and still in love with Mahmood, I telephoned him. He answered on the first ring.

"Mahmood, this is Patty. Please talk to me. I've been so scared since we talked before. I even called the sheriff because you said I was dead to you and I thought you might send someone over to kill me," I started, releasing a flood of pent-up words.

"Patty, Patty, relax. I was about to call you. I feel like a bloody fool for the crazy things I said before. I was out of my head. Please come back so we can work this out. I really miss you and Mariam and Iskandar. How are they?" he asked gently.

I was thunderstruck and excited but afraid to believe. "The kids are great. What are you saying, Mahmood? Do you want to work on the marriage? Are you willing to quit drinking, be faithful to me and work on our marital problems?"

"Just come back. We can work it out. I would never separate you and the children. They need their mother. And, you know, I always say I will never do to them what happened to me as a child. I love you. Come home to Rawa. I'll try to be a better husband and father. Give me another chance," he begged, sounding desperate and sincere.

I was weeping with relief. "Really? I didn't cancel our reservations. Okay, we'll come back. The fifteenth of September, I think..." I ran to find the tickets, laughing and crying and yelling to the children, "We're going home to Baba. He wants us to come home. He misses us."

"Here it is, 12:05 A.M. on 14/15 September. Oh, Mahmood, I am so relieved. You can't believe how miserable I've been," I babbled. I said, "I love you," and he responded, "I love you," and we said goodbye.

I was shocked and transformed by what he said in that telephone call. That gentle and loving voice begging me to come home. He promised everything would be fine and how I wanted to believe him. He said he was sorry about being irrational earlier, declared he loved us and would strive to be a better husband and father. He was so smooth and convincing, telling me everything I wanted to hear, I readily agreed to return.

On the appointed September day, the children and I left for Malaysia.

20 September

When I saw his face in the airport I knew immediately I had made the worst blunder of my life. From that day forward, Mariam, Iskandar and I endured an existence of unfathomable chaos. Mahmood, accompanied by sinister-looking bodyguards, confiscated the children's American passports and took us immediately to the island, thereby eliminating any hope we had of escape. We arrived on Rawa at dawn.

When Mahmood summoned me to his office later that day, my worst suspicions were confirmed. He sat at his desk fingering his gun and admitted he had lied to me over the telephone. He gloated over the success of his devious plan. He coldly informed me, "You will be sent back to America alone. If you cooperate, I will permit you to return and visit the children on occasion. Remember that anti-Western sentiment is growing here. If you make any trouble, I shall see to it that you never trouble me again." His face bore a cold trace of a smile. "I grew up without a mother," he spat. "The children don't need you." I pleaded with him until I was hoarse and hysterical to spare our babies the agony of being motherless, of being indelibly scarred as he had been at their age. He was impenetrable. Finally, he stood up. "You will be leaving in two weeks and should thank me for not sending you off tomorrow."

When I later tried to be tough and tell him of my right to stay with the children, he scoffed. "No force on earth can prevent me from doing as I please. Just remember," he threatened, "if you ever seek legal counsel or defy me again, the consequences will be tragic, not only for you but the children. Conversely," he added, "if you leave quietly, you may return to Malaysia next February and spend two weeks with Mariam and Iskandar and we will talk again. In the interim, I will keep them on Rawa under the care of Aminah and not divorce you." I wrote down these promises and a bit of what had transpired since my return in letters to his uncle and an esteemed family friend in the hope they might compel Mahmood to keep his word.

22 September

Mahmood is buying me a round-trip ticket so I can return in February for Iskandar's birthday, but he says I may stay only for a few weeks. He delivered this bombshell a few hours ago and the immobilizing shock has lessened enough for me to write without soaking the page in tears.

I begged, explained, pleaded, cried, tried to negotiate—all to no avail. Mahmood was a stone. He is unassailably, demonically convinced of his righteousness, complacently satisfied that everything is my fault and I must suffer the consequences. With Iskandar so young and attached to me, I fear that he will be irreversibly damaged. Mahmood disagreed with my tearful assertion that the children would be traumatized. "No, they'll be fine," he replied placidly. "I will care for them. They will lack for nothing." I felt nauseous at his words. That I am irrevocably at fault for causing this is his bottom line. If the children suffer, it's not his fault, it's mine. He twisted everything I said around to make me the bad guy, him the innocent victim and the children, sacrificial lambs, pawns, spoils to the victor. And oh, he is so good at it. And though not in the way he thinks I am, I confess I am guilty as charged. He is right, I am wrong. I am the one who mucked it up. The sin is mine. I returned to Malaysia.

For now, there are no other choices. I must accept reality, buck up and teach Mahmood, Aminah and Zahara how to care for the children…fruitless, to be sure, but necessary to at least try. Better I teach the children how to care for themselves.

I have to get my stuff organized, packed into boxes and shipped off this week. The quicker it's done the less it will upset the children and the odds of Mahmood changing his mind about financing it are also reduced. He is so volatile that I fear his threats of harming me may not be just heated words.

28 September

Last night Mariam asked me why Baba was so angry with me. And this morning she said she didn't like Aminah, because she's mean to animals. She kicks them, threatens cruel punishments and yells at them. "It's wrong, but it is the Malay way," I told Mariam, "and you have the right to tell Aminah to stop. She treats animals badly, because her mother and grandmother and her great-great-great-grandmother treated them badly. You can help her to overcome that habit, darling, by using gentleness and being a good animal-loving example."

Lately, Aminah has been trying to pull the children from my arms and cajole them to go with her. Mahmood must have spoken with her about my leaving, because she is behaving strangely. They might find the children developing some unpleasant acting-out behaviors once I'm gone, I shudder to imagine the response: Aminah laughing self-consciously while Mahmood smacks them.

29 September

I am in crisis. My shock, my fear, my tenuous grasp on reality is incapacitating. My hands are trembling and my vision is blurred from tears and lack of sleep. What Mahmood did last night is far beyond what I imagined him capable of doing.

Around midnight he banged on my door, demanding I get up and come to his room. When I entered he began a drunken tirade of unparalleled ferocity. He must have spent his evening at the bar obsessing over his resentments and my transgressions because he had such a long and ready list. He ranted about what an evil, white bitch I was, "You think I'm nothing but a stupid little brown boy, you white whore. I never should have trusted you and now you stand there and think you are so smart, but you will lose. The children don't need you and I know what you're doing, trying to turn them against me."

He carried on and on about my family, "You'll tell them all what a terrible bastard I am. No, you already told them this summer and now they all hate me and probably call me an ignorant, primitive brown boy. You Americans are all racist and your brothers are all laughing at me."

I was powerless in the face of his wrath, unable to defend myself as each attempt I made was twisted or ignored. While he was raving he picked up an ugly black vase and smashed it to the floor. It was from a set he gave me when we first set up house and I think it angered him I chose not to pack them. He went through one of my boxes and removed the baby book, a photo album and two of our many shared shirts, accusing me of theft. When I kept my mouth shut about the vase and asked to leave, he was further enraged, demanding that I talk, explain my sins, give him more ammunition. Finally I just walked out, trembling. I heard him rifling around in the room for a long time as I lay in my bed still shaking. I was unable to sleep until exhausted, I fell unconscious shortly after the roosters began crowing...A few hours later I awoke to face the terror of his wrath again.

I haven't been eating or sleeping due to the stress. This morning, though, I woke up ravenous. I ate a bowl of baby cereal from a tin here in the family house, which gave me enough strength to go make the children and myself pancakes in the restaurant kitchen.

I taught Aminah how to cook them, using bran and whole-wheat flour. She is a willing student and seems to understand when I explain the difference between healthy and unhealthy foods. I patiently lectured her on what to encourage the children to eat, what they should eat sparingly and so on. She was raised on white rice, palm oil and condensed milk, poor thing, and she's been drinking coffee since she was a baby!

Mahmood told me a short while ago I now would get only taxi fare to Kuala Lumpur and a one-way ticket home. Immediate departure. No boxes sent, no money, no return.

Midday. Children have had their lunch. They're bathed and are ready for me to tell stories before naps. Mahmood is in his room plotting. Will he send me away tomorrow? Will he soften some and give me a week? Has he forgotten his drunken diatribe altogether? We've not spoken since this morning and I don't want to see him. Mothering calls; blessedly, I can still answer.

30 September

Well, I have a reprieve. I don't leave until the 9th of October. I lay down with the kids and managed to sleep for an hour after my five-minute conversation with Mahmood. My relief in knowing I have nine days rather than one or two is intensely palpable. I swooned a bit when he told me.

1 October

Late last night he must have had second thoughts. He kicked a table across the room and smashed a few doors in. Had there been glass in the windows, he'd surely have shattered them. Aminah told me that Zahara told her he used to go into such rages often when she was young, breaking furniture and throwing things through glass windows. Needless to say, I slept poorly.

Mahmood, Zahara, Aminah and the children have just left for a daytrip to one of the other islands. I was planning to go and stood with the children until Aminah pulled me aside and said Mahmood didn't want me to go. I confronted him and asked why he had to use Aminah to tell me I wasn't invited. He gave me an evil look and said I had no business going. I maintained my composure until I got back to the room and here I sit, tears streaming, heart breaking.

I went over to the kitchen to make a salad and saw my friend Blue, the chef. He asked why I hadn't gone to Besar Island with the others so I told him.

He sympathized and said, "You shouldn't have come back." I got really choked up talking with him and am now unable to eat this great-looking salad. When I feel stronger I'll ask him to read to the children and play with them after I'm gone. He speaks the best English on the staff, is a lot of fun and makes great spaghetti. He bought the children kites on Mariam's birthday and will teach the kids to fly them.

Mariam has been wetting the bed nearly every night. After more than three months of being dry in the morning, this surely is her way of acting out. I'm going to have the mainland send over a box of Pampers. She protested when I told her. "Mom, four-year-olds don't wear Pampers. I'm big now and it's not fair." My poor darling, life is not fair.

2 October

Aminah and the kids are watching *The Grinch Who Stole Christmas* and my tears have been flowing as I anticipate the holiday season without them.

These next eight days are going to be long and beyond painful. Oh, I do need to buck up, self-pity serves no purpose. Right, then, I'll begin a list of stuff to do such as stop crying and get my boxes on a boat and over to Linus's place in Mersing. I can store them there for the time being. Having them here is fraught with potentialities as I fear Mahmood will go into another even more destructive rage. Ironically, he still expects me to play Scrabble with him every morning and at least one other time during the day. I think he must crave the normalcy of it.

3 October

The days are quickly, agonizingly passing and very soon now I will have to leave. I dragged my wretched body out of bed this morning at six and stumbled over to the restaurant to make a cup of coffee. No one is up. My neck and lower back throb; I'm famished, though I have no appetite, and I have chronic diarrhea. The physical stuff is minor, though, and can't hold a candle to the emotional toll of knowing my separation from my children will soon be at hand.

After these weeks of extraordinary turmoil, I am so emotionally drained and intimidated by Mahmood's vindictive and histrionic behavior, I see no alternative but to agree to his demands, for Mariam and Iskandar's sake. The psychological damage inflicted upon them these past weeks is incalculable. My daughter wets the bed and my son bites his fingernails and toenails compulsively. They become agitated when their father is near, will not let me out of their sight and talk often of violence, believing their father will hurt the three of us. I am half-convinced he'll shoot the children and/or myself to keep us apart. As Mahmood's anger and threats grow, I know the situation will worsen if I stay and that the danger, not only to me but to the children, is increasing.

There is one other option and it obsesses me: the three of us must escape. I have spent many sleepless nights planning a multitude of ways I could run off with my children. Yet I have meager resources, there is no one I can trust completely in Malaysia and no way I can get the children out of the country without passports. There is, I'm afraid, no logic in taking such an enormous risk, one that would most likely end in failure and worsen our position in the future. Therefore, I have to get away to a place where I can gather support so I can challenge Mahmood for my children and rescue them.

10 October

Resigned, I have begun to prepare Mariam and Iskandar for our imminent separation. I assured them their father loved us and his crazy behavior was just a sickness which would soon pass. My leaving for a little while would help him to get better and when I came home everything was sure to be wonderful again. I told them they needed to stay, because we had been together in Michigan without him and now it was his turn to be with them. I concocted a fairy tale suited to their tender ages, which I prayed would console and convince them. I vowed to write to them every day, send lots of presents and phone them often. Aminah, I promised, would protect and care for them just like a mommy until I returned. She and I once again have become very close in these turbulent weeks, our mutual love for the children and fear of Mahmood bridging the culture and language barriers. She is my friend and now must be my surrogate.

I tell myself the island itself will also nurture the children. It has been our idyllic home since they were infants. Together we have explored every inch of its twenty-five acres, made palaces of the bungalows, treasures of

the shells and corals, uncles and pirates of the young, gentle Malay workers
and playmates of the guests and their children. We often visited the grandfather spirit who lives in a cave at one end of the beach and I have convinced
my little prince and princess that he is their guardian angel whose powers
can carry their whispers to Michigan.

Before I must leave, I'm going up to the capital city, Kuala Lumpur, to
stay with Alang and Lorraine, who have quietly set up a meeting for me
with an attorney.

13 October

I am at Alang and Lorraine's house. I have an hour before I must return
to the island, the abyss. My head is swimming with an overload of weirdness after three days here. Alang thinks Mahmood will shoot me when I go
back. Lorraine tells me I should go straight to the United States and hire
commandos to rescue the kids. Prince Hassan has a friend who, he says,
will kill Mahmood for $2,000. By the way, Hassan told me that during our
marriage Mahmood slept with dozens of women, even seducing women
tourists on the island while I unknowingly was home with the children
sleeping. Mele, the Filipino servant, says praying to Jesus is the answer.
Chu wants me to get some of Mahmood's hair so she can put a spell on
him and the lawyer believes gentle negotiation will suffice. I am thoroughly confused.

My meeting yesterday with Puan Ani Salle, attorney-at-law, gave me
hope. Lorraine had filled her in on my situation, so she got right down to
business. Mothers, she assured me, have the exclusive right to custody under
Muslim law, barring madness, disability or apostasy. My being a former
Christian foreigner is irrelevant. Mahmood's being part of the Johor Royal
Family could hurt him in court because of their sordid reputation. He has
no right to send me away nor can he divorce me without my permission. I
should not file for divorce as it looks very bad for a woman to do so. I can
make a police statement and get a lawyer to file an injunction against any further harassment. Unfortunately, it must be done in Johor and the attorney
is not licensed there. She gave me the numbers of a few firms in Johor and
I called them all. Unfortunately, despite Puan Ani Salle's optimism, not one
would touch the case because of the royal family connection. I was thrown
back into despair. When I told her what I'd learned, Puan Ani's only advice

was to go back to my children, hang tough and try to work something out with Mahmood. I feel so very, very alone.

Had I used the airplane ticket Mahmood gave me, I'd be half way to Tokyo right now. The mad desire to go home is overwhelming at times—to run away from this wretched hell into the loving cocoon of family and friends. But no, I must return to my babies. They are my life now and forever. Truly, I feel as melodramatic as I sound. The taxi's here, time to go.

Later. Things are bad. I arrived in Mersing at 8:00 P.M. and the speedboat was not waiting for me on the jetty as I'd been promised by Devin in the Rawa office. There was no one around. Thank heavens Dr. Linus, my stalwart friend, was home when I telephoned. He came and got me and I'm at his guesthouse now. It appears Mahmood found out I was returning (I thought I could trust Devin; however, I don't sign his paycheck) and he called the speedboat back to the island.

Linus telephoned around for me, but as it's late no boatman wants to go across. Linus is in a difficult situation as is anyone here in Mersing I ask to help me. I'm the foreign wife, he's their prince. So I called Mahmood's half-brother, Prince Omar, who lives here in town and told him the story. He was really sweet, though noncommittal, and suggested I call Krishnan, the Chief of Police, and get his advice before I go. I did and he's on his way.

Much later. Krishnan has come and gone. He took a statement from me, suggested I be careful and wished me luck. If things get ugly, he assured me a police boat could be on Rawa in fifteen minutes. I'm glad he's Indian and not Malay, so he's willing to help despite the influence of the royal family. At least I hope he will. I am fading fast and must sleep. Linus' friend, Shakur will take me across in his tiny boat with a big motor at 7:00 A.M. I will try to be brave, but I am frightened.

15 October

The ride across on a blessedly calm sea was uneventful. Shakur dropped me at the jetty and rushed off. There was no sign of Mahmood as I set off determinedly for the family house. I wanted nothing more than to crawl into bed with my two little darlings.

Halfway there, Mahmood was suddenly beside me. "What the fuck are you doing here? Haven't you fucked up my life enough? So you think you're high and mighty now? You have no right to be here. Leave NOW!" I ignored him and kept walking. He continued to harass me, staying close on my heels as I went into the family house and the room where Aminah and the children were just waking up. He ordered her to go and pack a bag of clothes for the kids and him. She left to comply. I jumped into bed with the startled children. We kissed, hugged and chattered happily, but then Mahmood's unceasing tirade riveted our attention. Mariam began to cry and Iskandar had a terrified, confused look on his face as it began to register that their father was screaming at their mother—and them. I cried too, while trying to soothe them and drown out Mahmood's voice.

"You despicable bitch. Haven't you done enough already to fuck up my life? You only came back here because you and that evil whore Lorraine think you are all high and white and mighty. You're both foreign, bloody, lying, stupid, white. So, how do you think you can get away with this? What would you do if I just pulled those children out of that bed and threw them on a boat and took off? You have no right to be here, to see them, to fuck up my life. You don't give a shit about the children—you just came back to be an albatross around my neck." He went on and on for at least a half an hour. The words albatross, bitch, whore, white, despicable and a cornucopia of shocking profanity came up repeatedly.

The children and I huddled in the corner of the bed and stared through the mosquito net at the madman; his eyes bloodshot, his bloated, unshaven face purple with rage. Both children began to hyperventilate. I was on the edge of panic, mute and shivering with fear. I am trembling as I write this. I managed to find my voice at one point and told him to think of the effect he was having on the children. He was beyond reason, deranged and oblivious. At times he was incoherent. He repeated himself, contradicted himself, broke into fits of coughing…then suddenly he stopped and sat there, staring at us. I wiped the children's tears, stroked their hair and whispered calming words.

After a few minutes, the children quietly asked if we could go eat breakfast—a good sign—but I was afraid he'd grab them if we got out of the bed. "Let's wait and see what Baba does," I whispered. Another five minutes passed and I found the courage to get up and carry them past Mahmood, zombie-like and slack-jawed. He didn't even seem to notice.

As we walked over to the restaurant, Miriam began to ask questions. "Why is Baba so angry? Why does he hate us? Is he going to take us away?

Is he a monster? I was so scared I peed a little bit." Iskandar said, "I want a pancake." I told Mariam to wait and I'd explain it all to her during our breakfast. I was shaking, my mind consumed with the scene I feared was imminent: Mahmood dragging them, screaming, onto a boat.

We went to the kitchen and I asked one of the cooks to make pancakes. I got the kids juice and myself some coffee. We sat down and I began to talk, "Baba is very, very angry, but not with you. He will not hurt you, I promise, but, but...he might try to take you away from me and that is wrong. You have the right to say no to him and you can refuse to leave my side, my lap, no matter what happens. Hopefully, Baba will stop being angry and not try to take you away or send me away, but whatever happens I love you both to the moon, forever and always. Don't ever forget that."

My anxiety level was unbelievable. I don't know how I was able to function. My eyes were darting continuously to the path, leading up to the restaurant. I was anticipating "The Big Scene" at any moment and I was frantic. Fortuitously, Blue, the chef, walked by; he was the one person on the staff I felt I could count on. I called him over and explained what might happen. "I'll try to restrain the prince if necessary and stay within earshot," he promised. Then he told me, "Mahmood has a Malay girl in his room." Startled, because of the more sinister things I'd been imagining, I couldn't help but laugh, which broke the tension.

Just then Aminah showed up and said Mahmood wanted to see me. We talked about what was going on. She's freaked out by his behavior and so happy to have me home. She had half-heartedly packed a bag (per his orders), but told me she thinks he is bluffing about running off with the kids. "Don't worry, ma'am, Prince Mahmood is a big talker," she said. Oh, how I wanted to believe her, but I have felt his threats, I have heard how angry he becomes and I have seen the gun he has with him all the time.

Still, I know I must face him. When I felt ready, the children, who refused to stay with Aminah, followed me over to the family house. I sat down across the table from him in the common room. Iskandar climbed up in my lap and Mariam stood by my chair. He asked the kids to leave and they ignored him. "It's okay to go," I said gently and they finally crept away. It was obvious from Mahmood's first sentence that he was desperate and irrational.

He rambled without pausing and said the most bizarre, ludicrous things. He jumped from telling me he was taking the kids to the Middle East, to Australia, to a small village in Africa where the children would receive hours of religious training every day and not get enough food, to a dozen other ways he would screw up their lives if I stayed. He made it clear that they were his pawns and expendable, if necessary, in order to get even with me. I was speechless. Then I remembered Puan Ani and told him what she had said. He laughed without humor. "The law is mine. You have no rights, as you will see, and I will do as I like." He was too deranged to reason with.

The children returned and I asked for permission for us to leave. He didn't answer so we left. He went to his room and the rest of the day passed without further incident but with a surreal edge.

Meanwhile, the staff were being wonderfully supportive, telling me how much they'd always hated him! They told me he was drinking a lot (which, of course, I've long known) and acting strangely (ditto). He told Tom, the manager, I was not allowed to leave the island with the children. He was overheard talking with Azizah on the phone, about taking the kids to Brunei. But, despite their kind words, I know every one of them would follow his orders if Mahmood waved his fist in their face or threatened to fire them, so I just smiled and nodded.

I am hesitant to write about what I am really thinking for fear he will search the room and find my journal. I have stopped considering ways to escape with the children. I know now to attempt to do so would be impossible and insane without assistance. My hands are shaking as I try to write. I have never been so afraid.

October 16

The children and I slept together last night with the door securely locked. I had a nightmare about Mahmood breaking into the room, drunk, with his gun drawn. I woke up gasping for air and lay awake panicky for the rest of the night.

This morning the children and I went to telephone my mother from the office. Mahmood stormed into the room, grabbed the telephone out of my hand and threw it against the wall. I gathered the children in my arms and took them out. I am now "forbidden" from going into the office or using the telephones.

These five weeks have been awful and I have to believe things will get worse. A few minutes ago I left the children and went to the bathroom. Suddenly, I was in a panic to return to them. I have to hold onto my sanity, watch my back and always have the children with me. Earlier today Mariam went swimming with some guests and their children. Iskandar and I climbed the hill and walked the beach. We didn't see her. I began to get really anxious, but didn't say anything. Iskandar did, though. "I want Mariam. Where is she? Let's go find her now," he insisted. When I saw Mahmood placidly fishing off the end of the jetty, I calmed down and we went to take our showers. Still, when Mariam showed up a few minutes later, I cried with relief.

17 October

Iskandar woke up whimpering several times in the night and grabbed my hand. He gets so tense when he sees his father or when Mariam and I are out of his sight. He talks a lot about wanting to leave on a boat, bus or airplane. He is obsessed with fighting with his father and shows me how he would hit him. He wants me to carry him everywhere. If I ask him to walk, he clings to me frantically and cries.

Mahmood is being far too amiable. He's planning something. Aminah and Zahara spent a long time talking with him on the jetty this afternoon and both acted strangely afterwards. Zahara talked with Azizah on the telephone and then Mariam spoke with her. She got off the telephone, found Iskandar and me and began chattering excitedly: "Iskandar and I are going to Brunei. Azizah has thousands of toys for us. We get to go on the airplane." Iskandar joined her in a happy, laughing, singing-about-toys dance.

I know for a fact Mariam's Malaysian passport has expired and Iskandar doesn't have one yet. Childrens' passports must be renewed every two years and we used their American passports for our two trips. If Mahmood's plan is to take them to Brunei, he will need pictures taken, a trip or two to Immigration for a slew of paperwork and at least a week of waiting.

I have been consumed with what might happen at any moment. I've tried to anticipate every scenario, every option and every horror. I've been desperate to find that one simple solution/answer to fix everything. I am driving myself crazy analyzing and intellectualizing ad nauseam. Now I know his plan and it comes as a huge relief. Here is something tangible I can grasp onto and work with. I'm going to call for legal advice. I may be able to get an injunction against him taking the children to Brunei.

19 October

I reached Puan Ani but her words were hardly comforting. She said Mahmood has every legal right to take them to Brunei without my permission. Though she doubts he could prevent me from getting a Brunei visa, she wouldn't be too surprised if he did. She advised me to let him play his hand and be open to any deals. "He's trying to wear you down and he obviously has little regard for the effect his behavior is having on the children," she said. "You are no good to your children if you're in a hospital bed and I suspect things will get worse before they get better. Conserve your strength for a long battle." I hung up the phone, stumbled to my room and sobbed for nearly an hour until the children and Aminah returned from the beach.

20 October

Unfortunately, the children both have sun poisoning. Mariam more than the little guy. They felt really sick before bed, their burnt lips and shoulders hurt and Mariam has blisters. Blessedly, the sky is overcast today and, with monsoon season upon us, sunny days will be rare for the next three months. The children are listless and sore. We're going to spend the day painting and reading and eating their favorite foods, rice porridge with little prawns, mangoes and lime-juice. Aminah is remorseful and emphatically promises me it will not happen again. I forgave her, of course. We are all unhinged these days.

Mahmood is in Kuala Lumpur at a Rawa board meeting for three days. He returns tomorrow and I have a bad feeling about it. My time is running out. My options are diminishing rapidly. My mental and physical health is greatly compromised. "Life is a swirling, sucking eddy of despair with brief moments of false hope." An apropos quote, but its source escapes me.

As long as the children are here on the island with me, I try to feel there is hope. Hope for what, though? I feel my grasp on reality is slipping fast. I know the children are also in bad shape and getting worse. I feel so powerless. We shouldn't have come back, but we did.

Before Mahmood returns, I must decide whether or not I should put up a fight about him taking them to Brunei. On the plus side, Azizah and Zahara will shower them with love and presents and Mahmood has told Aminah to go back to Indonesia and get her passport so she can follow. Further, he will spend nearly all his time here on Rawa so the kids won't be exposed to his psychosis.

25 October

I'm going to make one last try to gain support here by writing to my spiritual father, the man who helped me become a Muslim.

Dear Haji Ibrahim,

I hope this missive finds you and Hajja Maimunah well. You have been my spiritual father for five years and now is the first time I have come to you for help. I pray you will heed my plea, in the name of Allah, for wise counsel and support in this most difficult time.

I will be returning to the United States alone on 2 November. Mahmood has given me an ultimatum I dare not refuse. My Malaysian visa runs out that day and Mahmood has refused to extend it. I could take a day trip to Singapore and return to the island on a tourist visa, but he has threatened grievous consequences if I do this. And so, after weeks of turmoil, I believe there is no other alternative but to leave. I say this for the sake of the children who have endured so much trauma in these past six weeks. You can only imagine how serious things are if I am willing to leave them and say it is preferable to staying. He has told me he will allow me to return in February for Iskandar's birthday and he says I may stay for two months at that time.

Mahmood has given me his word that he will not divorce me while I am away, but that we will go to the Qadi together when I return. He has also given me his word that, as long as I cooperate with his demands, he will allow me regular access to the children. For the sake of the children, I have agreed. I am desperately unhappy with this arrangement, but Mahmood is not of sound mind and I fear his wrath could be deadly if I defied him.

I am hoping against hope you might agree to intervene and speak with Mahmood about his behavior. I have written a similar letter to his Uncle Bakar. Mahmood respects you both very much, as do I.

Haji Ibrahim, I am only asking for a mother's right to raise her children. I am happy to stay in Malaysia. I am willing to embrace Islam, wear tudong, learn Arabic and do whatever, forever, for Mariam Nabila and Iskandar Shah. They are innocent and should not be deprived of their mother's love. Please, for their sakes, go to the island and talk with Mahmood.

I have explored every option and made countless overtures for peace with him, to no avail. Now, I must leave the country I love and my home. The children are crying and my heart is breaking. Thank you for your support.

Affectionately, Noor Faridah Patty

2 November

Unfortunately, my attempt was in vain. Haji Ibrahim advised me that we were both guests in Malaysia and must respect and accept things we do not always like and that Allah frowns on divorce. He could only offer to be my spiritual support in the event Mahmood and I met with the Qadi.

And so the end was at hand. Saying goodbye to the children was agonizing beyond words, beyond feelings. Iskandar was in Aminah's arms and Mariam was holding her hand as my boat pulled away from the jetty. We yelled tearful "I love yous" until our voices were lost in the surf. Mahmood stood off to one side, impassively watching. My last image was of him trying to take Iskandar from Aminah; Iskandar was beating on him with tiny fists. His feelings were mine. How I wished I could join my son in expressing my own frustration, anger and sorrow.

Bitter tears fell from my eyes. My husband Prince Mahmood was winning. He had the children. He had the police in his pocket and appeared to have the law and Allah there, too. He held the psychotic conviction that he was invincible and he carried a 9mm in his belt. Truth and justice seemed irrelevant; love did not conquer all. As a foreign, white, female convert fighting a native-born Muslim prince for my children, I was in desperate straits. And now I have been expelled from his country.

chapter nine

Lost Dreams
and Foolhardy Plans

20 November 1994

Childless and broken-hearted, I have returned to the United States. Once here, I went into a frenzy of telephone calls to Malaysian family and friends for news of the children and Mahmood. Everyone with whom I spoke offered support.

Now I have learned Mahmood has taken the children to Brunei to live with his first wife, Azizah, whom the children barely know. Mahmood returned to Malaysia and was living with a woman on Rawa, according to my island sources.

I telephoned Azizah immediately and she confessed to having the children. Mahmood had told her not to tell me and, though she was afraid of him, her empathy as a mother overruled her fear. She allowed me to speak with Mariam and Iskandar on the telephone, write to them and she willingly filled me in on their daily activities. She begged me never to tell Mahmood and I readily agreed. I felt that she would help me be with the children if she could. Yet, I also know she would not risk Mahmood's deadly wrath. I was mindful of these things and also Zahara's presence in the home. Though Zahara and her father did not get along, I assumed she hated me more. I knew I needed to gather more advice and support if I was to rescue my children. I spoke with a teacher friend in Brunei who offered to help me in any way she could. I received encouragement from Malaysian allies and my family in Michigan to fly to Brunei and attempt to see the children. If I showed up on Azizah and Zahara's doorstep unannounced, my presence and the children's joy might compel Azizah and Zahara to let me stay. To ask or tell them I was coming seemed too risky. I told myself I have a mother's right to be with my children. I sold my marital jewelry and with the money I bought a plane ticket and some traveler's checks.

2 December

On the airplane, somewhere between Tokyo and Brunei, I formulated a scenario for what lay ahead:

My plane lands in Bandar Seri Begawan at 2:45 P.M. I find Su, my teacher friend, who is waiting by the airport fountain as planned and we drive to Azizah's house, arriving at approximately 3:30. I go to the door and knock. Zahara answers and we hug. I call to the children, who come running, and we embrace ecstatically. I will probably cry, which is okay. I tell Azizah I have come for the children, that they belong with me in Michigan, and there is a car waiting to take us to the airport. Our plane leaves at 6:55, I tell her, so there is enough time to pack bags for the children. I thank her and Zahara profusely for caring for the children and we commiserate about Mahmood. They will likely express how angry this will make Mahmood and that they ought to call him. I must convince them not to be afraid. I will tell her to assure Mahmood he can visit the children any time and write and call. If she still wavers, I will say the law is on my side and the United States Government is backing me up. She will acquiesce. While we are talking, a servant is off with the children packing up their clothes and toys. I am sure Azizah will be sad and will want to hug the children and maybe ask to go to the airport with us. I must remember to be highly sympathetic to her needs and so I will agree to this. At all times I must maintain absolute resolve that we are leaving Brunei at 6:55 and there is no alternative.

If there is trouble and Azizah and Zahara are adamant against my taking the children, I will: 1. Show the American custody decree I had made up. 2. Have Su come in and help me speed up departure. 3. Tell them there are people at the American Embassy who will come over. 4. Offer to write a note to Mahmood absolving them of any blame.

This then was the plan of action, as I envisioned it.

Upon arriving In Brunei, I went directly to Azizah's house. Immediately my plan failed. Fearful of Mahmood's anger, she refused to open the door, telephoned Mahmood in Malaysia and the police. When the police arrived, they tried to arrest me for trespassing and harassment until I explained I was there to see my children who were behind the locked door. The police had Azizah open the door. The house was empty.

The telephone was thrust at me and I listened to my husband rave, "How dare you go to Brunei. You have no right to be there. You went over the top this time, thinking you could just go into my house and disturb my family. I tried to be nice to you, but all you care about is disrupting my life. You don't give a shit for the children and I vow you will really never see them again after this. They have already been taken to a secret location and I will deal with you when I come to Brunei in two days. Best you leave the country now, because I will make your life hell, you stupid bitch." I hung up the telephone and tried to explain things to the police. They took my passport, told me to file a police report and left.

Azizah explained the children had been out with Zahara when I came to the house and Mahmood, when she telephoned him, had his thugs take them away from Zahara. Azizah insisted I leave immediately and I followed her out of the house, forgetting my jacket in the rush. She then drove me to a horrid little hostel. On the way, she said, "You have put me and Zahara in big danger, because Mahmood thinks we invited you to Brunei. Why did you come here? Now Mahmood is so crazy angry, he's hidden the children from us, too. He threatened to kill you and kill me and maybe the children." I stared at her. She was as frightened as I was. She dropped me off in front of the hostel, but promised to call if she learned where the children were. I felt she wanted to be kind, but I knew her fears of Mahmood would probably keep her silent.

When I reached the United States Embassy officials, they said their hands were tied and the social workers I called said they were afraid to make waves. I spent time with Azizah's brother, Zainudin, who promised to help me one day, then would not return my calls the next. I came up against one brick wall after another, though everyone assured me I was right and Mahmood was wrong and my poor babies were suffering. I heard Mahmood was hiding the children with strangers; had already given them to the sultan for adoption; had removed them from the country; and had slandered my character so effectively no one would ever help me. Finally I learned the truth. Mariam and Iskandar were back in Azizah's house and Mahmood was back and forth between Rawa and Brunei, biding his time until I left.

I telephoned Puan Ani in Kuala Lumpur for advice. "Brunei is a warped little country where justice is irrelevant. People there prefer to do nothing than take a chance their action might not meet the approval of the sultan or the Muslim clerics who control the court. Don't waste any more time there. Go back to Michigan, get some rest and statements of support from the family, then return to Malaysia in January prepared for a long and difficult battle."

Up to that point, I had been sitting by the telephone in my cell-like room at the hostel living on hope, ordering in food and afraid to go out and miss a call. But it was all in vain.

4 December

I am in a state of shock. I came to Brunei to get my children out and have failed miserably. Mahmood is beyond furious that I came here and "disrupted" his life. Azizah is freaked out by his threats. All I want to do is curl up on this small, hard, ugly bed and cry, cry, cry. No, I also want to bang my head against this stained cement wall until that pain numbs my other pain.

I have no options worth pursuing. I desperately need help right now but don't know where to turn. I have every right to be in this country to seek my children, Mahmood's sentiments non-withstanding. I have hardly slept since I left the States a day and a half ago but I know I must get some rest and then strategize. I am a wreck, a zombie right now.

5 December

The ringing of the telephone woke me up. It was my mother saying she had just been on the telephone with Mahmood. His words were so cruel and his speech so virulent that she found herself doubled over with fury and agony. She tried to reason with him, tried to penetrate his obsessive, self-righteous ramblings, but the attempt only upset her so much she had to hang up. Oh, Allah, how awful. She said that Mahmood had also called my brothers Matthew and Paul and tried to convince them their sister was in big trouble and had better get out of Brunei or else. Mother gave me a pep talk about being strong and serious and not succumbing to self-blame and hopelessness.

I have passports and plane tickets for the children. Mahmood does not know this and, blessedly, I did not blurt it out at Azizah's. She could go through the jacket I inadvertently left at her house, though, and find my transfer card—one phone call to Royal Brunei Airlines and my secret would be out. It already may be out.

Mahmood, I learn, is coming to Brunei today or tomorrow. Will he let me see the children? Will he simply grab them and fly off? Will he not even bother to come, knowing I really do have no options? Are there people here who would help? Is the embassy able to give me names and advice? I must switch gears. I am a mother who has come to Brunei to see her babies, who were given to a woman who has no legal right to them. I flew here in the desperate hope I could be with them. Their father is a madman and must be stopped! Should I mention that he threatened to kill me when he arrives in Brunei? That he threatened to kill Azizah if it turns out she invited me to Brunei? Should I say he also threatened to give the children to the Sultan of Brunei or take them to Saudi Arabia or Africa or get rid of them? Is this man sane? Will he hang himself if he gets enough rope? Should I be terror-stricken?

I tell myself what I need to do is turn my focus towards how to see the children. I will gladly prostrate myself at Mahmood's feet if it will get me a few hours with my darlings. On that note, with fresh focus, I telephoned Azizah. She said, "Mahmood flies in tonight and will let you see them tomorrow at 5:00."

"Where are they?" I asked.

"I have no idea where the children are. He has hidden them with a friend, because he no longer trusts me." She seemed genuinely distressed and begged me to convince Mahmood she knew nothing about my coming.

I tried to calm her down. "The important thing," I reminded her and myself, "is that the children see their mother."

I heard agreement in her silence.

6 December

I decided to try to get help at the United States Embassy. I spoke with Marta Martinez, First Secretary, and learned that all the Americans who live here work for the sultan and would shun getting involved. "My hands are tied," she said, "as the Embassy policy is not to get involved in marital disputes." She did give me a list of lawyers and the offer of advice and support while I'm in the country.

I telephoned Ahmad Isa, a lawyer she recommended. He said he will send a car for me in the morning. He sounded very interested in my situation. His father is a special counsel to the sultan and, as Azizah's father is the former Prime Minister, he may help.

Azizah telephoned to say she would pick me up at 5:30 to see the children and Mahmood. I told her I had been to the embassy and spoken with a lawyer. "Mahmood is breaking the law and hurting the children. You must realize," I added, "he is also emotionally abusing the rest of us and we need to stand up to him."

She timidly said, "Yes, I know, I know," to everything I told her. I pity her almost as much as I pity myself.

Later—Mahmood telephoned me at the hostel. "I am going to allow you to spend one and a half hours in the company of the children, with me present." As soon as I arrived at Azizah's house, I could see my babies were distraught and unhappy. They clung to me, crying and begging me not to leave them again. My husband sat talking to Azizah, a few feet away from us. I tried to reconnect with my children, but Mahmood's hostile presence hovered over us so that we were afraid to say or do anything that might upset him. I whispered encouraging words of love to Mariam and Iskander and read them stories.

After half an hour, Mahmood called me over and ordered me to sit down. The children climbed up on my lap and clung to me. "This is the last time you will ever see them!" He spat out the words, then coldly instructed me to say goodbye to them and leave immediately. I tried to explain to him that what he was doing was inhuman and illegal. He scoffed "Go to the police, the chief Qadi, the sultan if you want. In fact, I am considering just giving the children to the Sultan of Brunei, who will gladly take and raise them."

"You can't do that; I'll fight you in every court," I said.

He ridiculed my options. "There is no one on earth who can stop me from doing as I please."

The children and I were crying and pleading with him not to separate us. He viciously pulled Iskandar out of my arms and grabbed Mariam's wrist. "Leave now," he hissed. "Take her," he shouted to Azizah. The children were screaming as Azizah urged me to leave, whispering, "You must go. He said he would kill you if you stay." I believed her, though I was tempted at that moment to risk it.

My mind was spinning frantically. This second goodbye was the most painful of my life, more even than saying goodbye on Rawa. This time Mahmood made damn sure the children and I knew without a doubt we would never see each other again. "Stay, Momma, stay Momma. Please stay. Please don't go, don't goooo," they cried.

I had to leave and I had to find words to make it easier for them and there were no words better than, "I love you. I will always love you. I will find a way to be with you, I promise."

Azizah was beside me as I stumbled out the door, the children's hysterical screaming following us down the stairs. Azizah's voice was shaking as she told me she had tried to reason with Mahmood, but he was too crazy and angry.

I was consumed with rage and agony. "He is a monster, a pig, a bastard. I hate him. I hate him. Oh, my babies, my babies. I want to die. I want to kill him." Over and over I chanted my fury, my pain. Azizah helped me into the car and offered me pills to relax. I was tempted but did not take them. *I have to keep my mind clear*, I told myself.

He was harming the children immeasurably and with no remorse. Earlier, when I challenged him on the monstrosity of his cruel behavior, he said nothing, only looked at me with an evil, self-righteous half smile. Could there be any doubt he is an unfit parent?

As I drove away in the cab that Azizah had called, I tried to concentrate on my next step. Surely, my first course of action should be to pursue a charge of abuse and have the children removed from his care. Would it be possible to get statements from Azizah and Zahara? Nope, and without backup I'll just seem like a vindictive bitch, something he will happily reinforce. Maybe the lawyers can come up with something to keep him in Brunei. I am sure he is planning to leave with the kids pronto. Is he searching for a place to take them where I cannot find them? Maybe to Sri Lanka and his friend's home. Maybe to Peter House in Kuching or his mother's farm in New Zealand or simply Rawa. I tell myself the world is too small and the children too noticeable for him to just disappear with them. Am I being optimistic about this? He could conceivably pull it off. I must convince the lawyers tomorrow that a madman who will stop at nothing is viciously abusing two gorgeous, wonderful, innocent small children. I half believe his words that he would kill the children and himself and/or me rather than give them up. If he were cornered he'd do most anything, really. In ten years I will still tremble when I recall having to leave that apartment. What has been imbedded in the psyches of my babies, I shudder to imagine.

I must get a lawyer. I must get help.

7 December

At my meeting with Mr. Ahmad Isa and Mr. Siva, they made copious notes and their demeanor was one of grave concern. The priorities we established are to get Azizah to work with me, to have her learn where Mahmood is keeping the children and to possibly get her elder brother to help get the children away from their father and into my care. The lawyers can't help me get the children out of the country, but there is a "good" chance I may be able to get temporary custody.

Azizah's brother, according to Ahmad, is very resourceful. He was formerly in the Special Forces and, word is, he despises Mahmood. They advised me to telephone him. Nothing can be accomplished, they asserted, without the support of Azizah's family. Her father is just too important an elder statesman and his nod is imperative before the police or court can choose sides.

I have been trying to telephone Azizah and her brother's office without any luck. I checked the local phonebook and there is a Zainudin Marshal listed—should I try it? I'm starting to feel overwrought with frustration and exhaustion. But I must not give into it. I have to accomplish something.

At 4:00 P.M. I phoned Zainudin's house and reached his first wife, Faridah, a Chinese Muslim convert, and we talked for twenty minutes. She lives next door to Azizah. The children are there and have been there. Mahmood is not staying at the house but is in and out regularly, Faridah said. "Azizah is a good person and wants to help you, but Mahmood controls her." She went on to say that Mahmood had informed the family I was a wacko and my intention was to take the children to America and convert them to Christianity. I quickly pacified her by stressing my love of Islam and enthusiastic willingness to raise them Muslim. "Don't worry," she laughed, "we all know Mahmood is a big liar."

Faridah had me in tears of relief as she shared these priceless jewels of information. To think she lives right next door to Azizah and is willing to tell me all that she sees out her window is a miracle. Unfortunately, it is a miracle tempered by a cyst on her ovary, which she will have removed tomorrow in the hospital. "My servant will be here most of the time and can spy for me, a job she'll relish," Faridah assured me.

After we hung up, I telephoned the secretary at the Embassy and Mr. Siva and gave them updates. No sooner had I hung up than the telephone rang. It was Faridah telling me Mahmood and his cronies had just pulled up next door and she'll keep me posted. I can't help crying and trembling.

8:00 P.M. A call from Chu came at 7:30. She has been talking with family members in Malaysia and promised me unanimous support if the battle-field moves back there. She knows Faridah and said she is a wonderful, sincere person and that Azizah's brother could be the savior I seek. This is good news and yet I remain numb.

8 December

I stumbled, still tired, out of bed at 7:00 A.M. I was awake half the night mulling over possible scenarios. I was struck (like a bolt of lightening!) by the conviction that I ought to be doing as Puan Ani in Kuala Lumpur advised me after Mahmood sent me from the island in October. "Go and be with your children," she had said. There is no divorce, no custody or visitation order, no law to prevent me from being with MY children RIGHT NOW. I could go to Azizah's house and demand to be let in and, if the police or Mahmood came, I could stay firm. A dozen different manifestations of this foolhardy plan played out while I lay on the thin mattress in my narrow, cell-like room.

I knew I was indulging in fantasies about rescuing the children. I felt guilty for teasing myself and up to now have resisted doing this for fear the tears would flow without ceasing or worse. They flowed anyway.

I am questioning God, Allah and the universe. I am driven to question my thinking, my purpose here. Is there some "Great Truth" I should be grasping? Is there a "Great Lesson" I must learn? Is God waiting for me to do, see, become, and know something PROFOUND before helping me? Is this a test, a quest of and for my soul, my character? Did I, somehow, create this reality? Yes, I fell in love with and married Mahmood. I brought Mariam and Iskandar into the world. I chose to end the marriage. I knew the risks and still returned to Malaysia in September. I let him defeat me there and send me away. Could I have stayed? Should I have stayed?

Mahmood is what he is, a twisted, sociopathic, unfit father. I also have my faults and there are many things I have done wrong in my life for which I have not sought forgiveness from Allah. I have not accepted my guilt, my responsibility and my blame. Forgive me, Allah, and please forgive Mahmood also, for his sins. I must let go of all anger, hatred and blame I feel toward him. Yes, I must embrace love, forgiveness and faith if I am to succeed. Faith in my mission, faith in myself, faith in those who are trying to help me, faith in Allah. Yes, I must have a deep, abiding faith that, if I am worthy, success will manifest.

I want to take Mahmood's children away from him. By what right do I judge him unworthy? I have no right. I want them to be with me in Michigan. He wants them to be with Azizah in Brunei. Is there room for compromise here? Is there more I could be doing? I have tried to reason with him, reach his heart, beg for a settlement that benefits the children, not us. Am I missing something here, some place in his consciousness I could appeal to? There was a time when he was so good to me, when we were happy together. I stayed in the relationship much longer than I should have. I swallowed too much. I gave too much; I tried to understand his warped character, empathize with his pain, accept his limitations. He is a victim of an unhappy, dysfunctional childhood and family and too many unfulfilling years with Azizah. He is now forty-nine years old and change is difficult, maybe impossible, for him.

I can accept his rage toward me and I forgive him for it. The children are all he has left, his only link to happiness in his life. They are innocent and beautiful and funny and they love him. So of course he is holding on to them like a cornered rat, for if he loses them he has nothing. If they are taken from him, he will die. He might kill himself or drown himself in Johnny Walker Black. He refuses to see he has already lost them by denying them their mother. I am sad and sorry for Mahmood's suffering, but I cannot allow the children to be sacrificed on the altar of compassion for him.

He is coming here at 5:00 to tell me "the whole story." Dear Allah, let this be something good I can hold on to. I only need the smallest morsel. Everything, everything, every damn thing I've believed in has crumbled to dust these past three months. This road leads to madness and I won't take it.

It's happening again; 6:00 and the telephone has not rung. If Mahmood hasn't telephoned, it can only mean he has no intentions of calling me. I am loath to admit this, but I can't deceive myself any longer. The reality I must confront is that I am not going to see my children for many weeks or months. The battle is going to be long and hard. I can't bear to think about it...

18 December

I am flying to Bangkok at 2:00, spending the night with a friend from Malaysia who lives there and then on to Michigan.

Somehow, I made it through the night, I thought the thoughts I had to think, faced the facts I had to face, felt the pain, cried the tears and lost control for a bit. I bruised my head and strained my voice banging and screaming in the shower, a great muffler. I went into the bowels of hell, danced with my demons, came back and got on the telephone to schedule the flights I needed, refused dinner and tried to sleep. I closed my eyes and saw my children's faces. I heard Iskandar howling "Mama, Mama, don't go, don't leave me." and saw Mariam, fetal-like, sucking her thumb, staring at me lifelessly and I began to fall into madness. I stumbled into the bathroom, splashed water on my face, then returned and lay back down. I bit my lip hard to distract the screams and pressed my eyes closed tightly against the tears and waited for sleep. I slept and woke up crying. I am sad and scared.

I have spent three weeks in Brunei futilely seeking help from Azizah's family, lawyers and the United States Embassy. It is a week before Christmas and I have finally admitted to myself that my rescue attempt was a dismal failure. It is time for me to go home to America and formulate a new plan, for I will never give up the fight for my children.

I leave in an hour. I have spent fifteen days and fifteen nights here. During that time, I spent less than two hours with my children and they were so close, just a couple of kilometers away. No, they were really no closer that they will be when I am 11,000 miles away. They are in me. Mahmood can never sever the umbilical cord that binds us. But 11,000 miles is a long, long way and damn these tears.

I am in the airport now waiting for the gate to open. I look around me, foolishly thinking maybe I will see the children running towards me. I can see the entrance from where I'm sitting and I can't take my eyes off the door. I tell myself I will not look, will not torture myself, will still this trembling and stop these endless tears from falling. But I cannot for I know there will be no reprieve, not today. I am leaving alone.

chapter ten

Futile Wishes, Dire Realities

24 January 1995

I cried every day the first week back in Michigan, less lately. Emotionally, I'm numb. I am reminded of the children a hundred times daily and I want to break down every time, but I resist and persevere. Sometimes I feel as though I am betraying them by not giving in to the agony of missing them. Guilt and anger are my constant companions.

Mahmood telephoned Lorraine and Alang's house looking for me a few days after I left Brunei. They assured me they gave him no information. He hasn't telephoned Michigan, which leads me to believe he thinks I'm still in Asia. Has he left Brunei? I wonder...

I am so worried about the children. I can't fathom how I manage to function without them. I hate having to go through the motions of life, when I desperately want only to sit in the corner of a padded room, screaming and banging my head against the wall.

Mariam and Iskandar don't have a rational explanation for what's happening. They don't know if I still love them or why I'm gone or if I'm coming back or how their father uses my absence to sever my relationship with them. On one level, they must know Mahmood is the cause and see Azizah as his accomplice. But they are so young and they have seen and heard too much over these last months. They must be horribly confused. But if they act out on the premise that their father is the cause of all the trouble, they will suffer. I can't think about this; it's too painful. The most difficult part for me is that I am powerless to help them right now. I pray that whatever they are enduring, they can recover from in the future. I tell myself leave it be, but I can't.

25 January

I spoke to my family this morning. "I must go back," I told them. "I have no choice." My brother Bobby, frightened for me, insists he'll come with me.

26 January

Dear Mother,

We are in the air between Tokyo and Singapore. Bobby is a mellow traveler and has been infinitely patient with my tears and babbling.

We had delays in Traverse City, Detroit and Minneapolis, leading to an unscheduled overnight in Seattle. The airline put us up in a hotel with generous meal vouchers and Bobby was able to sweet-talk them into giving us separate rooms. We slept well, had an uneventful flight to Tokyo and Northwest put us on a Singapore Airlines jet for this final leg. We've decided to go directly to Chu's house after we land for dinner and an update before we catch the 11:00 P.M. train to Kuala Lumpur. Hopefully, our meeting with the government minister is still on.

I go numb when I think about what struggles lie ahead for the children and me. I spent my month in Michigan planning for this week. Now, the reality of the abyss I must cross stops me cold. I am consumed by images of Mariam and Iskandar crying, "Please hurry, Mommy. Come now, please." How will I keep from breaking down at every turn, I wonder?

Love, Patty

4 February

Dear Zoe,

Two weeks have passed since I left the nurturing arms of family and friends. Bobby and I left Alang and Lorraine's house in Kuala Lumpur after two days. The highlight of our time there was my meeting with the Minister of Women's Welfare. She threw up her arms and said, laughing, "Why on earth did you marry a Tunku? They have no respect for the law. Why didn't you stay in the States with those children? Why don't you just kidnap them from Brunei? The Government and the courts can help, but it will take months or years. You must go back to Johor Bahru and go to the sultan. Keep it in the family if you want action." She advised me to go to the Religious Department in Johor Bahru first, see the status of my divorce and then start working on the family.

The next morning at 7:00 A.M., Bobby and I were on the forty-five-minute shuttle flight to Johor Bahru and I was at a desk in the Religious Department by 8:30. I was taken in to see the chief judge and the head of Women's Affairs and again I heard the same refrain, "Why did you marry a Tunku? Tunkus all think they are above the law. They are all crazy and have no respect for the courts. You must go to the sultan; maybe he can influence Tunku Mahmood. Be humble and get in good with the family."

There was no record of a divorce there so we headed over to Mahmood's half-sister Jackiah's house. I'd telephoned her from Kuala Lumpur to ask if we could stay with her. She and her husband, Johan, were wary of us for the first day, as I'd only met her briefly on a couple of occasions and never met him. We talked, talked and talked some more and it wasn't long before they realized I was sincere, innocent and in the right. They already knew Mahmood was an ass—Johan's word—and had no trouble accepting that he was an even bigger jerk than they had ever imagined.

The next day I went to visit Uncle Bakar with Jacky and spent nearly three hours with him. He is undergoing intensive chemotherapy as lung cancer has spread to his liver and he looks so much like my father did near the end. He is heavily drugged and rambled on to me about getting along with Mahmood, compromising, being patient and accepting Allah's will. I didn't want to let him know how futile such wishes are.

Chu was there and I saw two of the other uncles, Osman and Rahman. Uncle Rahman asked me where Mahmood was and I told him he was probably on Rawa. Then he asked me to bring the children over to his house as he wanted to photograph them. The moment was charged and you could've heard a pin drop as I replied, "I'd love to bring them over, but unfortunately they are in Brunei living with Azizah." Uncle Rahman was confused and the others stumbled to find a smooth transition out of the awkwardness. Unable to contain my tears any longer, I rushed out. Chu and Jackie soon joined me and then we left.

That afternoon, I telephoned Zsa Zsa, the sultan's favorite daughter and a good friend of Jacky's. She already knew quite a bit and wanted to know whether I had American passports for the children. I was afraid to tell her yes until she convinced me she was on my side and it was okay. Then she warned me not to tell anyone else. "Mahmood's behavior is most intolerable," she said slowly. "Stay at Jacky's and let her take care of things." I was crying with anxiety and fear of rejection while talking with her. Her support could be very important and I bawled with relief for twenty minutes afterwards.

She telephoned Jacky as soon as we got off the telephone and they talked a long time. Jacky told me, "Be patient and don't worry. Zsa Zsa is a woman of action."

It's 9:00 A.M. on a Saturday morning and everyone is in bed except two of the four servants and me. Mahmood is on Rawa with his sleazy Malay prostitute (Hassan's words) girlfriend and probably doesn't know I'm back in Malaysia. Alang and his children also are on Rawa, while Lorraine is in Oman, but Alang has no intention of telling him I am here and his children are oblivious.

I am going out in a little while to pick up the "official copies" of the children's birth certificates, which I ordered a few days ago. I can use them to get my permanent residency card and to have on hand for other uses. Rather than borrow the car and driver, I'll just call a taxi. Jacky and Johan have been so generous and I don't want to take even the smallest advantage.

Hassan just walked in and said he'd love to take me on this errand!

This week with "family" has been truly magical. They have forgiven me, without reproach, my five years of ignorance while under the spell of Mahmood. They want to help me, they like me, they respect my agony and empathize with my tears.

Jacky has made my religious education her mission in life and I am getting at least an hour every day of lessons. The family is committed to helping me be reunited with my children and assume I will want to raise them right here. I smile demurely and scream *NEVER!* to myself.

9 February

Bobby and I had a meeting yesterday with Zsa Zsa, the sultan's daughter. Zsa Zsa is my age, single, has four adopted preschoolers, lives with her father in the big, big palace on the hill and is his closest advisor. She is very well educated, opinionated, open-minded and she has her finger on the pulse of the family. According to her, the family's lifeblood is gossip; everyone knows or conspires to know everything there is to know about everyone else. She finds it obsessive and disgusting and admits she's as guilty of it as the others. She knows far more about Mahmood than I ever would have suspected and none of it is flattering.

The purpose of our meeting was for her to meet and grill me, I assume, because nothing else of note transpired. She did say she was working on things and had not spoken with her father about my situation, because she wanted to get him when he was in a good mood. She also had not contacted anyone in Brunei yet. But she is very busy so I am to stay at Jacky's and continue to fast, study Islam and be patient. Golly, I had gone into that meeting so full of hope for something tangible to grasp hold of. I'd fantasized that she would tell me my reunion with the children was imminent, so my disappointment was immense. Once again, I was stymied in my quest.

Strangely enough, Hassan has become my favorite ally. He showed up a few days ago with an incredible plan. He said he was going to get the crown prince here to talk to his great friends, the Sultan of Brunei's younger brothers about getting some thugs to snatch the children from Azizah and give them to me. I encouraged him to go for it. He's usually full of hot air, but you never know.

The other day he drove me to the Immigration offices and I broke down and cried while we were driving. He became so concerned and protective that I cried even harder. He invited me to come over and spend time at his house and said his wife Zurieda really wants me to visit and become her friend. They have a two-year-old boy, who is very much like Iskandar. "Being around your little boy is just too hard on me," I confessed to Hassan, who understood. He despises Mahmood and we have been sharing memories of our years on Rawa when we did not speak and discussing our different versions of incidents. I was so brainwashed by Mahmood that I never thought to question whether Hassan might, in fact, be an okay guy.

Hassan swears to me, though I have to believe he's exaggerating mightily, that Mahmood had hundreds of liaisons on Rawa while I was off in the family house, sleeping with the children. I knew Mahmood hung out at the

bar and often chatted with the tourists until quite late, but I never suspected that he was seducing everyone he could get his hands on, as Hassan
alleges. Hassan says he really felt sorry for me and wanted to tell me on
many occasions to go out to the beach or to a certain chalet and catch my
husband in the act. I'm glad he didn't. No, I wish he had.

13 February

I am trying to be comfortable with Bobby leaving. After all, he was by
my side in the beginning when I needed him most, but now I have support,
I am safe and I'm learning more about the religion. My "case" is in the hands
of those who can help. It may take them days or even weeks and I know
Bobby must go back to his own life in Michigan.

Sometimes the temptation to call Mahmood is very strong; I want to
try to reason with him and ask to see the children. Last night I sat by the
phone for a long time, fighting the compulsion to pick it up. Yet I know in
my gut it would be a fruitless and self-destructive call. He would be hostile
and I would look weak. Further, he would speak with such arrogant confidence about how this is all my fault and I had brought it all upon myself. I
know I would get disheartened and sick with fury and I can't let him destabilize me. The more I learn about him, however, the stronger I feel that he
does not deserve the children or any sympathy.

I have no plans beyond trying to speak to Tunku Zsa Zsa each day. My
earlier optimistic feelings about her helping me are fading. She is always too
busy or not around when I call. Tomorrow is Valentine's Day and Iskander's
third birthday. My tears are already flowing.

17 February

I am in the waiting room of Zain & Co., on the seventh floor of the
Datuk Zainul Building on Melaka Street in downtown Kuala Lumpur. I am
wearing a traditional Malay dress and have a scarf over my hair. I'm waiting
for my 2:30 appointment with Tuan Haji Suleiman, reputedly the premier
Muslim, Syariah Court lawyer in the country. He is a man who loves high-
profile, interesting cases. He is on television regularly and often quoted in
the newspapers. My heart stopping hope is that he will choose to represent
me…and will do so *pro bono*.

He's twenty minutes late and the secretary says he's not back from Friday prayers yet. Pious men go to the mosque every Friday for the noon prayer and sermon afterwards.

On my lap is a folder containing Mahmood's divorce affidavit. Once again, he lied to me and I believed him. I learned through the grapevine that he had divorced me in Melacca. After a few telephone calls, I spoke with his lawyer who said he had some documents on his desk for me. Unfortunately, he could not send them and I had to go there and sign for them. I went by taxi the day before I came here. Jacky orally translated Mahmood's divorce affidavit for me when I got back to the house. It's a pack of lies, but now he has legal custody of the children. My situation has gone from bad to grave.

18 February

Dear Bobby and all,

I just got off the telephone with Mother and made her week with the most promising and genuine development of this entire drama. I, Noor Faridah Sutherland, am being represented by the best Muslim lawyer in Malaysia. Tuan Haji Suleiman and his two women assistants, one who just passed the bar exam, are overwhelmingly supportive and motivated to expedite my getting custody of the children ASAP. Further, they are determined to expose Mahmood's criminal affidavit and have it overturned. In fact, during our two-hour meeting, Suleiman made telephone calls to Melacca to get more details and inform the relevant parties there that he was on the case. He is, in fact, willing to fly to Brunei as soon as we have a custody order and argue, in the religious court there, for the children's immediate return to Malaysia and into my custody. He knows people in Brunei and assures me justice will prevail.

He is working under the assumption that I will be staying in Malaysia with the children, though he appears supportive of my desire to return with them to the States. He said that, since Mahmood acquired most of the Rawa shares after we married, they would be part of the marital property for distribution. It is possible I may find myself as part owner of Rawa with a seat on the Board of Directors. Ah, too much to digest. All I want is my children.

My attempts to give Suleiman a retainer were dismissed, which leads me to believe he is taking the case *pro bono* unless there is a substantial amount of money from Mahmood forthcoming. He says the cost of my legal representation in this matter is Mahmood's responsibility.

Enclosed is a copy of Mahmood's divorce and custody orders and his supporting affidavit, translated for me this afternoon. I gave the lawyer my statement and the letters of support from the family, which he read. He was deeply impressed by our statements and told me I appeared to have a very wonderful family. Allah be praised!!!

Love, Patty

December 29, 1994
IN THE SYARIAH HIGH COURT AT MALACCA
IN THE STATE OF MALACCA, MALAYSIA
    BETWEEN TUNKU MAHMOOD SHAH BIN TUNKU MOHAMED—APPLICANT AND NOOR FARIDAH SUTHER-LAND BTE ABDULLAH—RESPONDENT
ORDER

This Divorce Application was heard before The Honorable Judge Tuan Haji Ibrahim Bin Lembut in the presence of Tuan Yusuf Rahmat, Syariah Lawyer for the Applicant and without the presence of the Respondent.

The Honorable Judge, having perused the Applicant's Affidavit and the Affidavit of his witness, hereby issues the following ORDER:

Divorce by one talaq is confirmed against the Respondent, without her presence, as of today, Thursday, 29th December 1994.

Custody of the following named children to be granted to the Applicant:

Tunku Mariam Nabila Bte Tunku Mahmood Shah   DOB 9/28/90
Tunku Iskandar Shah Bin Tunku Mahmood Shah   DOB 15/2/92

Eddah Maintenance (financial support) of RM1,500 ($600.00 U.S.) to Respondent for duration of divorce proceedings.

Mutaah (property settlement) of RM5,000 ($2,000.00 U.S.) upon finalization of divorce.

AFFIDAVIT

I, TUNKU MAHMOOD SHAH BIN TUNKU MOHAMMED, having a place of residence at Batu 15, Kampung Ayer Merbau, 77200, Bemban,

An aerial view of the island of Rawa. The long jetty can be seen in the center of the island, which lies in the South China Sea ten miles from Mersing, a coastal city in the Johor territory of Malaysia.

During their wedding ceremony, Mahmood sits next to Patty who recites a short paragraph in Malay. Mahmood's sister, two family friends and the man performing the ceremony look on.

Wearing traditional clothing, the newly married couple pose for their wedding portrait.

Chu — Mahmood's half sister,
Princess Maria — holds her
pet slow lorus, Maximillion.

Mahmood enjoys the
sunset from one of
the many gazebos on
Rawa's resort beach.

Patty holds the newest
addition to the family:
baby Mariam.

Patty, dressed in traditional
Muslim attire, and her baby.

Patty holds baby Iskandar while big sister Mariam splashes in the water.

A family portrait taken during a happy moment.

Wearing traditional garb, Mariam and her baby brother Iskandar sit in an oversized bamboo chair.

Patty with the children as the family's servant, Aminah, stands close by.

After escaping, the children adjust to American life in Michigan.

During a cultural presentation, Patty describes Muslim life in Malaysia to American school children.

Mariam and Iskandar display traditional clothing for their cultural presentation.

Mariam and Iskandar have fun in the snow during one of their first winters living in Michigan.

Jasin, Melaka and being a Muslim male of full age do solemnly swear and state as follows:

I am the Applicant in this matter.

All the facts deposed herein are true and are within my personal knowledge and/or documents within my access.

I married the Respondent on the 28th of February 1990 at the residence of Datuk Hj. Ibrahim Axford at Batu 15, Kampung Ayer Merbau, 77200, Bemban, Melaka. A copy of the marriage certificate is annexed hereto and marked as Exhibit 1.

It was a marriage based on mutual love.

We have two children as a result of the marriage.

After my marriage to the Respondent, I was made to understand that prior to our marriage, the Respondent did not have a credible background.

Be that as it may, regardless of her behavior as such, I, as a Muslim made every effort to save the marriage for my own benefit as well as that of my children.

I state that even after our marriage, the Respondent continued to practice a Western lifestyle and not that of a Muslim.

I state to this honorable Court that due to irreconcilable differences on several matters between the Respondent and myself, we can no longer go on living as man and wife.

On this ground and for the good of my children and me, I humbly crave leave of this Honorable Court to confirm the divorce by one "talaq."

I additionally state that the Respondent has never performed the compulsory practices of Islam, even after being constantly reminded of such responsibilities towards the Islamic religion.

On or about the month of April 1994, the Respondent took my children to the USA with my permission and when I contacted the Respondent in the month of June 1994, the Respondent stated that she would not return to Malaysia anymore and threatened to raise my children in the USA.

After being coaxed, the Respondent returned to Malaysia with the children.

I hereby state that my two children are now under my care and are living with me.

After returning from the USA, the Respondent left the children and me.

I have made efforts to contact the Respondent in order that she return and continue to live in my house together with my children. All my efforts have been in vain.

To this date, I am not aware of the whereabouts of the Respondent and have entirely failed to contact her.

I verily believe that the Respondent will not return to my children and me.

Based on the foregoing grounds, I crave leave of this Honorable Court to grant an order so that my children and I may avoid experiencing mental distress and of the children being totally devoid of any aspect of Islamic education.

I humbly pray that this Honorable Court grant the orders applied for within this application.

Sworn by

Tunku Mahmood Shah Bin Tunku Mohammed in Melaka on 29th of December 1994

22 February

Family dearest,

I spoke with Salwah, Tuan Haji's assistant, this afternoon. She said they are working on the papers and, once filed, we'll have to wait for the court in Melacca to set a hearing date. Because of the fasting month and three-day holiday following it, there will be at least a two-week wait. And so, more patience is on the agenda. Meanwhile, after divorcing me illegally, Mahmood will not allow me to see my little ones. He has told people he intends to torture me until I kill myself. If I become too big a nuisance he will have one of his Western-hating minions do the job execution-style. Even with the top Syariah divorce lawyer in Malaysia, my prospects as a Western female against a gun-wielding Muslim prince are looking dismal.

I love you all...Patty

chapter eleven

Yin and Yang

1 March 1995

Last night I had an exceedingly long and disturbing bad dream—no, it was a nightmare. My karma must be seriously unbalanced: good days, bad nights, yin and yang. I self-destructively drank two pots of tea with Lorraine before going to bed, a bloody stupid move. Then the caffeine-fueled bad dreams began. I dreamed Mahmood shot me, shot himself, shot Mariam and Iskandar. I dreamed Azizah telephoned and offered me a million dollars for the children and I said yes, took the money and then stole the children from her. I dreamed Mahmood dropped the children off here with a few bags, but for some reason, we couldn't leave no matter how hard we tried.

This morning Lorraine and I drove to Melacca. We made our way to the Religious High Court ruled by the all-powerful Islamic clerics and tried to get my affidavit registered and a court date set. The irony of yesterday being Mahmood's and my five-year wedding anniversary was not lost on me. How does one tangibly celebrate irony, though?

At the courthouse we were told, "Sorry, no registrar, no judge. Oh, Oh, so very sorry, wives of Tunkus, but nothing going on today so registrar and judge take day off." The secretary and his two coworkers were nervous; we were determined and there was a standoff. Once they realized we were not leaving, they endeavored to placate us by making phone calls, which they did until they reached the registrar, who promised to be in at

2:30. It was just 11:30 and Lorraine wanted to push the envelope further, but I reined her in and we left, saying we would return at 2:30.

I was in Malay dress and a scarf. It is fasting month so I can't eat or smoke in public. I dared not indulge, because to do so is rude and, being a white woman, a flashing neon sign surely would appear reading, "Stare at me. Cluck your tongues."

We did the only thing we could do: We went shopping. I bought an out-fit that transformed Noor Faridah into Patty, the tourist, who could eat, smoke and relax. After lunch in the same hotel where Mahmood, Chu and I celebrated that long-ago wedding, I re-imprisoned myself in traditional garb and we went back to the courthouse.

The registrar looked my affidavit over and asked a couple of questions: "Children are in Brunei? Tunku Mahmood drinks alcohol?"

Lorraine speaks Malay like a native and I let her do most of the talk-ing. We played tough cop, traumatized cop with this guy and successfully compelled him to keep moving the first hearing date backwards in the appointment book. Finally, he said the tenth of March was the absolute earliest, although the book was nearly empty and he had originally wanted to give me a day in late April. I signed the documents, saw them filed and we left.

3 March

Today is the first day of Hari Raya, Super Big International Muslim Holiday to celebrate the end of fasting month or rather the end of Gabriel giving Allah's scripture to Mohamed. The country has shut down for the next four days and I am happy/not happy. Happy because Lorraine and her four darling monsters have left for a week on Rawa and I have the house and Mele, my favorite servant, to myself. Unhappy because, because, because, because, because...

I ordered a big vase of flowers to be sent to my lawyers on the day they're back in the office next week. I need to court their attention. Next week will surely manifest noteworthy news as the authorities have yet to cancel the 10 March hearing and Lorraine will have news from Rawa, where Mahmood is living. That could be interesting, if he doesn't run away to avoid her. She's promised to observe and possibly provoke him.

8 March

Newsflash: Salwah just phoned to thank me for the flowers I sent and said March 10th for the hearing was definitely out of the question. The hearing couldn't even be scheduled until the judge returned next week from his holiday and maybe not for days or weeks after that. I cried and raved and she felt badly and promised to try to push things. I need to work out and sweat through this agony ridden black cloud that's settling in. I've been obsessing about seeing Mariam and Iskandar in March. It was feeling so real and I don't want to let go. I am such a fool to be optimistic and hopeful.

And so the long wait begins. I dare not dwell on my chance to succeed.

11 March

I am heading over to the Islamic Outreach Center in a few minutes for their Sunday classes, sermon and social hour. It's a place for converts, refugees and people interested in converting and is only a ten-minute walk from here. I am wearing a Malay dress with a scarf over my head, determined to learn, network and be humble. Maybe I'll get lucky and find inner peace.

Sunday evening. What a wonderful place and what a wonderful four hours I spent at the Outreach Center. The lecture for beginners was about going on the Haj. There were forty people there and only a handful were white. A short, skinny local professor in a Haji hat spoke in English, though there were little groups getting translations into Chinese, Malay, Tamil and a couple of other languages.

After the lecture, I was pulled aside by a Malay woman and taken into the office. She told me her name was Normah and she was a staff counselor. She hoped I'd be willing to share my story with her. I immediately broke down and went through a few dozen tissues as she gently stroked my fragile ego while taking copious notes. I told her about the case and the children and, most importantly, my frustrations. I vented my litany of issues; how my color and Christian past are being used against me and no one trusts my sincerity. "I do want to embrace Islam, but my cynicism, anger and depression inhibit my willingness to believe," I told her. She held my hand and said she understood and promised to counsel me further this week. I felt drained and cleansed afterwards. I learned that Islamic Outreach is a powerful organization with the ears and support of the Prime

Minister, a multi-million dollar budget and charity works around the country and around the world, especially in Bosnia. In fact, there are hundreds
of Bosnian refugees living in Malaysia and many are active in the Center.

I sat through another forty-five-minute lecture on piety and then wandered over to the other side of the building where they have a thrift shop.
I spent two hours there, tried on twenty Malay dresses and bought two
along with some scarves. I got to talking with a young British woman who
teaches English and she said there is a big demand for English teachers. She
also told me the American School is desperate for substitutes and the
money is good. Subbing would be ideal with my unpredictable life, so I will
telephone them in the morning. I can't legally work in the country, though,
and they might be sticklers about under-the-table employment, but it's
worth a try.

12 March

Monday morning at 9:00 A.M., an hour pregnant with potential. I
tremble in this moment with anxious, bated breath. There are more than
forty hours stretched out before me without a public holiday in sight.
Hours I can spend on the telephone entreating, persuading, networking...hoping.

I just telephoned my lawyers. Salwah is on leave and Tuan Haji is in
court all day.

19 March

Dear Brothers,

You asked me to write to you when I was down and not to burden
Mother. I really do try to spare her much of my ever-present wretched,
agonizing, deep, deep, deep unhappiness, though bits do leak out. I know
that she is consumed with the children and yes, I realize she is not sleeping
well. Please forgive my helplessness and unhappiness. If I have a shred of
good news, a hint of a positive development, a pleasant interlude to report,
I do embellish it and send it along. But platitudes and hollow anecdotes only
go so far. My life is a "swirling, sucking eddy of despair with brief moments
of false hope." And it's doesn't appear to be getting better anytime soon.

Pardon my profanity, but I am driven to write—no, to scream—
"ANOTHER DAMN FRIDAY NIGHT!" This is my thirtieth and least

loverly day in Kuala Lumpur. I now know the court will not schedule a hearing until mid-May or later.

Another week has passed without a shadow of progress. I'm a thousand miles away from my children and Allah only knows how many weeks will go by before I see them. I can't even say their names out loud today without choking on the words.

Love, Patty

1 April

Dear Mother,

I am glad March is over; it was a cursed month and it lingered. April portends springtime, rebirth and my thirty-fifth birthday in eighteen days. I am hopeful and optimistic that this month will be simply splendid. Even if it isn't, I shall endure.

Love, Patty

3 April

My optimism is fading as time inches by. I sent the following letter this morning.

ATTN: TUAN HAJI SULEIMAN

I am praying that through this fax I may successfully make contact with you. My inability to reach you by telephone these past two weeks has driven me to tears more than once. I realize you are a very busy man but, as you know, I am a very unhappy woman who finds herself at the beginning of another month with no apparent progress in her case.

This afternoon, your assistant told me that the registrar in Melacca has gone off to take a course and no hearings can be scheduled until after he returns in May. I am shocked and outraged. Surely there is something you can do about this travesty. I am more than willing to seek an audience with the Prime Minister, the sultan, the governor of Melacca or anyone else who can help us to expedite a hearing. I implore you to do something and/or advise me as to what I can do to insure that Mariam, Iskandar and I do not have to suffer through many more weeks of this unjust separation.

I spoke with Azizah in Brunei on the telephone this evening. She said the last time Mahmood saw the children was in December and she has been trying to reach him for two weeks, to no avail! In fact, no one has seen or heard from him in twelve days. It is madness to allow this man to get away with such blatantly reprehensible behavior.

Azizah was sympathetic when we spoke. She said the children were fine and she was taking good care of them for me. She agreed that Mahmood was wrong to give her the children and she encouraged me in my quest to get custody. Only her terror of Mahmood prevents her from giving me the children. She tells them I am away on business; yes, the most important business of their lives. Why don't we just move the case to Brunei? You said in our initial interview that you would be willing to take the fight there if necessary. Please consider doing so.

I have been attending classes and volunteering many hours as counselor and advocate at the Islamic Outreach Center. I am praying and reading the Koran. I have found solace and a blossoming faith in the light and love of Allah and His faithful. Islam is sustaining my spirit as I beg you to sustain my faith in justice.

Thank you, Noor Faridah

I am reeling from a monumental telephone conversation I just had with Azizah. She called to say she is taking the children to Singapore for two weeks and that I can see them there if I get permission from Mahmood first. Of course, I could just go to the front desk of the Royal Holiday Inn, where she always stays, and ask for their room number or park myself in the lobby until they go by.

There is something else I could do, something radical. I am sitting here feeling overwhelmed by the reality of what I could accomplish. I just don't know whether I ought to do it that way. I talked to Lorraine who advised me, "Darling, don't count on the bloody corrupt and moronic system here." She added, "And don't think you will get custody or even visitation any time soon. And even if you do, they will never let you take the children out of this country." She told me to seize this opportunity and meet Dee, a woman I'd met at the Polo Club. She had offered to help me get the children back.

I went to the Polo Club at 6:00 to see her. Dee, a hard-drinking, polo-playing, brilliant Texan, said yes, she'll help me. She has friends in Singapore. She'll fly down tomorrow to spend a couple days scoping the scene and making connections. I will be ready and she'll call me when the time is right to act. I have a ton of stuff to do from embassies to airlines and I'm trembling with fear and excitement. I am frantically reticent to write about it, so I won't. Dee understands my crazed mental state and she is a gentle, empathic angel. She will handle most of the leg and telephone work. She will protect herself and me from any legal or criminal repercussions and we agreed we will not hesitate to abort the plan if necessary.

26 April

It was not to be. Azizah and the children never went to Singapore, but Dee and I did. I am angry, embarrassed and seven hundred dollars poorer. We figure Mahmood changed his mind at the last minute and forbade Azizah to go. I just came through an ungodly stressful week for naught. I am stupid, stupid, stupid. In the future, I have promised myself, I will be much more prudent.

Dee and I returned to Kuala Lumpur this afternoon and here I sit with tears streaming down my cheeks. The shock has worn off and I feel despondent and sick to my stomach. I telephoned Salwah as soon as I walked into the house. "I've just spent a lot of money in a desperate quest to see or maybe even hold my children in my arms in Singapore," I told her. "But I failed." I vented for a few minutes and she was duly sympathetic. "I want a very proper, professional and attractive portfolio put together with all the relevant documents pertaining to my case," I added, "and please have the best of my family's statements translated into Malay for inclusion." I said I hope to present the portfolio to His Majesty, the Sultan of Brunei. "It's time to seek an audience with him and make a personal appeal." She agreed that it was worth pursuing and that the portfolio would be ready in a week.

30 April

It's almost May Day. Memories crowd my mind. A year ago Mariam wore a crown of flowers and a beautiful dress and danced around a Maypole festooned with ribbons on an idyllic spring day in northern Michigan. Iskandar wore an orange sunsuit and toddled ecstatically through the crowd of smiling Montessori families. Why do I torture myself with memories? Why do I torture my family with self-pitying melodrama? The only answer: I can't seem to stop remembering.

Today is a national holiday, Labor Day, and everything is closed. Tomorrow would have been my father's sixty-eighth birthday. I wonder what he would have done if he were still alive? I bet he would be here raising Cain to help his grandchildren. On second thought, if he were alive, I would never have come back last September, and, if I had, Daddy would have flown right over and knocked Mahmood's block off.

Tuan Haji and I are going to Melacca in a week. Salwah is writing up an affidavit and she assures me Tuan Haji is determined to get us a workable court order. I can only pray it's true.

14 May

My eminent attorney definitely seems to be enjoying himself, playing the famous big city lawyer in the sticks. He chatted with the judge for two hours while his law student/protegee and I argued politics in a coffee shop. Then I went up and sat demurely beside him, in Malay dress and scarf, of course, while he and the judge discussed my case for another hour. They wrote up a rough draft of the order; I signed and they signed.

The judge appeared sympathetic towards me, disgusted with Mahmood and frustrated by his inability to do more. Due to the bureaucracy and the multitude of archaic qualifications, he has been without another judge for months and it could be many more before one is assigned. As a result, the poor guy is handling all the petty lower court and appeals court cases. This also means he is unable to hear my Affidavit response to Mahmood's divorce and rule on custody without another judge to appeal it to. He claims to have done his best for us, considering, and Tuan Haji concurs.

Barring custody and free passage home, I got more than I could have hoped for: unlimited and reasonable visitation and an order for the children's immediate repatriation to Malaysia. Hassan has agreed to help the courier serve Mahmood with a copy of the order and once he has it we will wait a couple days before I fly over to see what he does.

Now that I have the order, Lorraine and I have been brainstorming how it might be used to get Mariam, Iskandar and me on an airplane to Michigan. There are a few options and a hundred variables. The odds of such a plan working are infinitely better than they were in December. Perhaps not—they may be infinitely worse as Mahmood has probably instituted some security measures with the police and borders. Am I too

paranoid? Not paranoid enough? I suppose I can't know until I find myself
on a plane heading home with the children or in a jail cell.

At the very rock-bottom least, something good will happen. I will see
the children. I am literally and figuratively unable to fathom what our
reunion will be like. I am numb and I am frightened. Can I cope? How have
other mothers done under similar circumstances?

18 May

I am flying to Brunei in forty-eight hours and, with the help of Ahmad
Isa and Siva, my lawyers from December, justice will be pursued.

Mahmood has ignored the Court Order and is back on Rawa. Will he
fly over when he learns I am there? Will he try and prevent me from seeing the children? Will he refuse to repatriate them to Malaysia? There are
multitudes of *ifs* but I shall try to handle the reality which manifests. Finally,
there is forward motion.

chapter twelve

Fleeting Reunion

21 May 1995

My lawyers have been successful in achieving a small miracle. My tears have been flowing since Lorraine and I climbed into her Landrover for the drive to the airport more than three hours ago. These are welcome tears of hopeful anticipation. I am really, hopefully going to see my children soon.

On the airplane to Brunei, I try to decide if I should telephone Azizah when I am settled in my hotel room. I could tell her I am in town and I have a court order giving me unlimited visitation and I would like her to bring the children to my hotel...with their passports and some clothes, because I intend to take them to Malaysia. No, I don't want to send her over the edge; better to move slowly.

We are about to land. The drama continues. Action is afoot!

My taxi driver, Ramli, was sent by the angels. He has such a kind face and gentle manner that I felt compelled to blurt out tearfully exactly why I was in Brunei. A larger surprise—he knows Azizah and Mahmood. He called them both playboys, drinkers and bad people. He's seen my children more than once out with Azizah or Zahara and wondered where they'd come from. He said the children should not be with them and that he wanted to help me. Allah be praised. He will come by at 7:00 in his private car and we will drive by Azizah's house and look around. I wouldn't be surprised if he does a bit of detective work in the meantime for me. He is a devout Muslim, happily married with five children and he believes doing good breeds good for him.

The same girl from my December visit was at the front desk of the hotel. She remembered me and asked if all was well. I said no. I'm in a big, beautiful room with blessed privacy. I'm going to shower now before Ramli comes. Will wonders never cease! There is a blow dryer in the bathroom. I haven't used one in months.

When Ramli arrived, I met him in the lobby and went out to his car. He drove me past Azizah's, pointed out Azizah's brother Zainudin and sister-in-law Faridah's place and also where Azizah's father lives. He thinks I should get Zainudin involved again and told me one of Azizah's other brothers is a taxi driver. I said I knew that and was warned to watch out for him. We drove around town and then he took me to a grocery store where I bought fruit and yogurt for my dinner. I only had a few Brunei dollars on me and used every cent. I must remember to change money first thing in the morning. Ramli brought me back to the hotel, gave me a pious pep talk, his cellphone and pager numbers and wished me luck tomorrow. Allah is so good to have sent him.

Thinking about the morning overwhelms me. "I will not be afraid. I will be confident that I will see my babies tomorrow," I say softly before I turn off the bedside lamp and crawl into bed.

22 May

I slept ten perfect hours and it's a little after 8:00 now. I telephoned Salwah to update her and learned Mahmood has not been served with the court order yet. Hassan never showed up. "No big deal," she told me, "you just carry on with Mr. Siva. Whether Mahmood has been served or not is really irrelevant, as the court order is still valid." But if Mahmood doesn't know about the order and does know I'm in Brunei, what is he thinking? What will he do now?

Siva telephoned to say he was unable to reach anyone at the Syariah Court and Ahmad Isa had not returned to the office. When he said, "We'll have to wait until tomorrow," I burst into tears and shared with him how desperate I am to see the children. "Do you think it would be okay if I telephoned Azizah?" I asked. He said try. I dialed her number, said "Hello, Azizah" when she answered and she quickly hung up. I suspect the family knows I am here and alarms are ringing. How will they react when they hear about the court order?

Siva telephoned again to say Ahmad never came in and he was leaving for the day. He gave me a pep talk and promised to telephone the moment he had a breakthrough in the morning. It's only one night. Surely, nothing is going to happen in the next sixteen hours. The children will have their dinner, their baths and go to bed. Azizah, however, may fear sending Mariam to school in the morning if she knows I am here.

My thoughts go back and forth. Could I have planned this better? There is no textbook. There are no experts to turn to for guidance. I made decisions with the information I had and I do not have the energy to berate and second-guess myself so I will stop this pointless mental debate.

I try to think of other things but cannot. I do have the right to be frightened about what Azizah and Mahmood are up to. I worry they may be up to something I could have prevented had I done this differently. I can rationalize justifying my obsessive analyzing, catastrophizing and these sweaty palms. Argh.

More disparate thoughts crowd my mind. The worst they can do is to fly the children out tonight. I will die if that proves true. Yet, in the end, doing that would hurt the children and help my case. Things may have to get worse before they get better and I can only pray the children are not suffering as a result of my presence here. I am doing the right thing and I must continue to do the right thing. Mahmood has not, is not and probably will not do the right thing. Having the moral high ground is a mixed blessing, meaningless in the moment yet everything at the end of the day.

Except for one-and-a-half hours in December, I have not seen my children nor heard their voices in nearly seven months. They have not seen me or heard my voice either. Have they seen a photo of me? Been told I love and miss them? Heard a good thing about me? Do they understand why we are apart? Allah only knows what lies they have been fed. Their confusion, anger and sadness must overwhelm them at times. How do they cope? Acting out? Wetting the bed? Iskandar biting his nails until he bleeds? Mariam compulsively sucking her thumb? In the shower I turn on the hottest water I can bear, sit down and scream, wail, bang my head and attempt to purge this agony.

23 May

Siva wanted me at his office at 1:30 and I arrived promptly. We went to the Syariah Court and, in the typical roundabout way, ended up in the office of the Chief Qadi. He will help...maybe. He's going to call Azizah and also speak with someone "In Power." We shall see.

Siva suggested we go to Azizah's house and I concurred. It was closed up tight without a sign of habitation. On his first knock on the front door, I heard my children's voices call out excitedly and then silence. He knocked a few more times. There was no response and we left. On the drive back into town we spoke honestly about rescuing the children. He was enthusiastic and said breaking in would be easy. "Why bother," I replied, "unless I have a couple of big guys and a fast car and can get to the Indonesian border which is just thirty-five miles down the road."

He smiled, "Yes, it is."

Siva brought me back to the hotel. I cleaned up and was about to walk into town for food when he telephoned, "Do you want to see your children?"

I caught my breath, "Yes, when?"

"Now," he replied. "I'll pick you up in a few minutes."

I zipped through emotional stages: shock, fear, exultation and manic preparation. I gathered books, a few clothes for them, some photos and shakily walked down to the car.

On the way over Siva told me the Qadi had called him to ask if I was in Brunei to fight for custody. "No," he told the man, "she only wants to see her children." The Qadi hung up and five minutes later called back to say Azizah would let me see the children for thirty minutes. "I telephoned Azizah and she suggested tomorrow morning," Siva related. "I said *now* and she said okay."

I shared my terrors about seeing them after so many months apart. Azizah had told him only thirty minutes, which really upset me. How was I going to separate myself from them so quickly? Won't they be traumatized to say goodbye after such a short period of time together? Still, I was going to see them. I thanked him, thanked the Qadi, thanked Allah and we were there.

I was trembling like a leaf as I walked across the parking lot and up the stairs.

Siva knocked and the door opened Mariam flew into my arms. I sat down on the floor with her in my lap and held her tightly. As I rocked her I said, "I love you. I missed you, my darling, my baby." I looked around for my little guy.

Azizah called for Iskandar, who came out of another room, but did not want to come close to me. I kneeled and held out my arms. Azizah pushed him to go to me and kiss me. He pecked me quickly on the cheek but would not let me hold him. Though my heart was breaking, I understood.

Mariam, during this time, was running around frantically, showing me her dresses, her shoes, her toys, her everything. I kept grabbing her for hugs and kisses. Iskandar loosened up when I showed him photos of my family. Then he also went on a show-Mommy-everything rampage.

While the children and I turned months into minutes, Siva was busy explaining the court order and my intentions to Azizah. She showed him Mahmood's divorce papers and his letter giving her guardianship of the children. Then she got Mahmood on the phone and he spoke with Siva. Mahmood's first comment, Siva related to me later, was that he'd spoken with the judge, knew all about the order and had no intention of complying, because there was no time limit. He went on to tell Siva that he had never denied me visitation, which compelled Siva to look heavenwards and say, "Hah, not according to my information!"

Mariam and Iskandar brought me every shoe and toy they owned. We were surrounded by stuff and they had calmed down enough to sit in my lap, read a book and chat. Mariam told me about school and jumped up for her school bag, books and pencils. Mariam is learning four languages. She had Chinese, Arabic, Malay and English workbooks.

Iskandar talked in complete sentences. They looked well taken care of, though Iskandar's nails were bitten to the quick and Mariam only took her thumb out of her mouth to talk.

After forty-five minutes, Azizah said it was time to go. "You can come back at 1:30 tomorrow and spend the afternoon." The children let me give them hugs, kisses and promises. I did not cry as we left.

After telling me of his conversation with and impression of Mahmood, Siva advised me, "Off the record, my gut feeling is that you should grab the children and run."

"That hasn't worked either," I said. "I'm between a rock and a hard place."

Siva understood, offering to work on Azizah with me. He told me that, as he has free time and a burning desire to help the children and me, he is willing to do most anything to resolve this. All kinds of ideas flooded my mind, including running to the border with the children, but I have no intention of taking such a chance only to fail again. Whatever I do must be carefully thought out and executed. Next time, I must succeed.

Siva dropped me off at the hotel and went back to his office to telephone the Qadi and Salwah. I reflected while waiting for the elevator that for the first time in months, I felt good. I told myself this slow re-acquaintance was a good way for the children and me to get to know each other again. As we spend time together, I will regain my confidence with them and will feel empowered to rescue them when the time is right.

Siva does not think Mahmood has any intention of coming to Brunei and I agree. We figure he must have gotten the impression from the judge in Melacca that he didn't have to comply with the court order for a long time. The judge may also have told him a custody hearing won't come up for months.

Back in my room, I sit down at the desk to make some telephone calls. I want to spread my joy. I am in a wonderful mood, yet it all feels so unreal. Was I truly with Mariam and Iskandar this afternoon? I just calculated that we were apart for 169 days. My purgatory has ended. I tell myself I will not leave Brunei without them.

24 May

I spent an hour at the United States Embassy this morning. They'll have the passports done in two days.

I spent another forty-five minutes with the children today. We read Dr. Seuss books, looked through a big stack of photographs I brought, pretended to nap all cuddled up close and played swimming and airplanes. I gave them a bath and, oddly, Iskandar refused to remove his swim trunks. Afterward, they both climbed into my lap wrapped up tightly in their towels and, for the next half hour, I rocked them, sang our favorite little songs and told them five thousand times how much I love and miss them and want to be with them. It took all my strength of character not to blame their father for my enforced absence. "I had to go to America and then to Johor and then to Kuala Lumpur," I explained, "because there was so much to do to help me get all the crazy business done so I could see you." A bureaucratic snafu seemed to be the most innocuous explanation and I played it to the hilt. Surprisingly, it satisfied them.

I stressed repeatedly, "I will see you every day now and soon all the business will be resolved and then we will be together again, always and forever." They were quiet as they pressed close to me and looked up at my tear-filled eyes.

As I was getting ready to leave, Iskandar became hysterical. He ran and got his shoes and was frantically trying to put them on as he screamed, "I go, too. Mommy, you take me now. I go with you, I go with you, I go with you." He wrenched himself from Azizah's grasp and wrapped his little arms around my legs. I picked him up. I pleaded with him not to worry, "I will be back tomorrow. I promise, my darling. Please be a good boy." I kissed him and walked out, with fists clenched and blinded by angry tears. By the time I was driving away in the taxi, they were out on the balcony, staring at me. I yelled "Stop!" to the driver, jumped out of the car and blew kisses and promises of tomorrow, tomorrow, tomorrow.

When I got back to the room, I sobbed, stroking the plastic cup and hairbrush Mariam gave me for my birthday. I berated myself for telling an innocent three-year-old to be a good boy. I should have begged to stay longer or refused to leave. Iskandar, Iskandar, you are always a good and wonderful boy.

25 May

I am sitting in the lobby restaurant of the Riverview Hotel, a half-block from Azizah's house. She did not show up for lunch with the children at 1:15 as we'd arranged in a morning telephone call, so I grabbed a taxi and went to her house. There was no answer when I knocked. I left a note on the door requesting that she page me at the hotel restaurant when they come in. Then I went back to the Riverview Hotel and called my lawyer.

Siva telephoned me back five minutes later. He had just spoken with Azizah, who was in tears. Zahara and the children are gone. Disappeared.

I was speechless while listening to Siva, then blurted out, "Oh my God, they must be on their way to Mahmood." Siva had no words of advice; he said good luck, keep in touch, he'll send me the portfolio. I thanked him profusely for all his help. We said goodbye and I sat there stunned. I feel trapped. I can't breathe. I don't want to breathe. I tell myself to breathe deeply and repeat positive affirmations until they sink in.

chapter thirteen

Vigils of Hope,
Vigils of Despair

31 May 1995

I returned to Malaysia and stayed in one of Princess Zsa Zsa's houses. Finally, Zahara and the children, along with Azizah, were located on Rawa. Despite advice to the contrary, I went to the island.

The boat dropped me off at the jetty and I trudged up the beach to the longhouse. I walked in and immediately Mahmood blocked my way. He began to yell at me, which brought the children out of their room. When they saw me, they ran into my arms.

"Go to your room now," he demanded of them.

"No, Baba, we want to stay with Mama," they replied defiantly.

I let go of the children and tried to disengage them as I saw he was becoming angrier and angrier. He came at us and grabbed the children, who clung to me with all their strength. They were screaming hysterically as he pulled at them. Crying, I begged him to leave us alone. The children held me so tightly that he could not break their grasp, though he gave Iskandar a nasty bruise trying. Frustrated, he backed away, said he was going to call the police and left.

We sat in a heap on the floor, trembling, stroking, kissing and glancing nervously at the entryway every few seconds. "Why is Baba so mean? My arms hurt. Are you okay, Mama? Will the police put you in jail? Where are you going to stay? Can you stay with us?"

When I stood up, Iskandar said, "Carry me." I scooped them both up, put one on each hip and we went to find a room boy to give me a bunga-low. Luckily, there was an empty one a stone's throw from the longhouse. The children helped me unpack. Excited and laughing, they found the toys and treasures in my bag. After an hour, we nervously went out to take a walk on the beach.

Ten minutes into our walk, Mahmood, with Azizah beside him, con-fronted us, "Mariam, Iskandar, come here. Time to go, now."

Again, they both responded, "No Baba, we want to stay with Mama." When he and Azizah came toward them, they started running down the beach, yelling, "Go away, Baba. We want Mama. Come on, Mama, run, run."

Mahmood went after Iskandar and Azizah chased Mariam. They caught them easily, though Iskandar put up quite a fight, and both cried loudly, "Mama, Mama. No, Baba, no Azizah, no, no no," as they were carried off. I stood and watched, screaming silently to myself.

He did it once more, when the children escaped after their baths and came to my room. Within five minutes, Mahmood, this time with the ser-vant, came and demanded the children join him. I begged Mariam and Iskandar to comply and they did, crying angrily as they were pulled across the yard. I felt sick and impotent as I sat on my bed and banged my head softly against the wall. They must have fed them in the family house, because I didn't see them again that day.

When I went into the restaurant for dinner, Azizah was sitting by her-self at a table. I walked over and joined her. She had a little plastic bag on the table in front of her with quite an assortment of tablets and capsules. She offered to give me a stress pill and another for sleeping, as she rifled through the bag. She informed me she was taking blood pressure, stress and "relax" pills and showed me what each one was. She had difficulty carrying a conversation and walking to the bathroom was a supreme effort for her as she stumbled from table to table. The whole restaurant went quiet and watched, alarmed to see her acting so unwell.

Mahmood, at this time, was sitting at the bar with his back to us. Azizah rambled on about how she didn't want or need to take my children as she could get half a dozen in Bosnia if she wanted. In the next breath, she said she would use her millions to buy Mariam and Iskandar houses. "I pity you, their mother. You must feel so much, the sadness all the time." She lowered her voice and, with an anxious glance toward Mahmood, leaned closer to me. "Mahmood crazy. I try, everyone try to talk to him. He never listen. I so pity Mariam and Iskandar. They want their mother but what to do? Mahmood say no, never. I make them happy. I give them all the toys and clothes like Versace and Baby Dior. I make the amah feed them rice and vegetable and take vitamin tablet every day. You don't worry. Tell your lawyer let me take them back to Brunei. I make them happy and maybe then Mahmood not have so much stress and you can see them. Okay?"

She went on and on in a monologue with no beginning, no end and points repeated a dozen times or more. She barely made it from one end of a sentence to another without losing her train of thought, changing the subject, hitting dead ends and always coming back to please, would I let her take them back to Brunei. The whole conversation was very bizarre and I felt sorry for her. I couldn't be angry. She loves my children, fears Mahmood and has a conscience. Exhausted, I went to my bungalow at 10:00 and tried to write the days events in my journal.

It's 11:00 P.M. now. Another day of unfathomable despair, touched with joy at seeing my children, has come to a close. How does Mahmood sleep?

1 June

The day started out pleasantly enough. Mariam came running into my room as I was getting up. She climbed under the covers with me and we hugged, kissed, laughed and exchanged a hundred endearments. We had a priceless hour before the amah came for her to bathe and change. I said go and she went unhappily. Shortly afterwards, I walked over to the house and she was in the room naked. I went in to help her pick out a dress. Suddenly, Mahmood appeared, shouting, "Get out of this room; it's a private room."

"No, I'm helping my daughter get something to wear," I replied. He grabbed my arm and pulled me out. I told him to go ahead and hit me. He wanted to but dared not and I left. Mariam ran out a little later and we played until Iskandar joined us and, blessedly, Mahmood and Azizah left us pretty much alone for a while. The amah came by to take them for lunch and we parted with smiling, "See you after. I love you, love you, love you."

The police arrived early in the afternoon. Mahmood and Inspector Zul, whom I'd met before, ignored me and went to the longhouse. A little later

Mariam came over to the gazebo where I was sitting. She was visibly upset as she spoke, "The police are here. Are they going to take you away?"

"No, my darling, don't worry," I reassured her as I shivered with trepidation.

Inspector Zul came over followed by Iskandar, who jumped in my lap. I was very nice and gave him a copy of the court order, my affidavit and a letter written to the judge on 20 March. I asked him to read them before we talked. He walked off with them and a little later one of the workers came and told me to join the inspector.

The children refused to stay behind so I took them along to the little office behind the dive shop. They found room on my lap, sat quietly and held on to me tightly. From the outset, I warned Zul to be sensitive to the children and not say anything that might upset them. Or me. An impossible request. As the interview progressed, the three of us became increasingly agitated and, when I cried, the children were so concerned they stroked my hair and found me a tissue.

Inspector Zul said, "Mahmood is planning to have you arrested for criminal trespassing."

"I am here as the guest of Alang and Lorraine," I explained to him, "but, more importantly, my children are here and I have the right to be with them and I will not leave them." He asked me to follow him to Mersing and sort things out from there. I said, "No, I will not leave. If you need to arrest me, do so, but I will not leave my babies unless it is in handcuffs." I quickly turned to the children and assured them that would never happen.

Poor Zul was suffering and I expressed my sympathy for him. I told him a little of what the children and I had endured the past two days and I stressed my fears, as a mother, about the people who were caring for my kids. Azizah is in bad health, Zahara is young and wild and Mahmood is violent, I explained to him, and even the servant is incompetent.

The inspector, after tousling Iskandar's hair, left to speak with Mahmood again. They sat for a half-hour while I talked with Lorraine. Iskandar sat in my lap biting his nails, while Mariam played with her cousins in the sand.

At 6:00 P.M., after the police left, Mahmood, Azizah and the amah came down to the beach where we were playing. When Mahmood yelled for the children to come, Iskandar started running in the opposite direction while

Mariam grabbed her swim ring and paddled out into the deep water to get away from Mahmood. He had to get wet to grab her. Iskandar escaped from Azizah and ran, hysterical, towards me. I held him to me and implored him to go take his bath and not worry. Mahmood gave Mariam to the amah and grabbed Iskandar from me. As he carried him off, Iskandar was pummeling him with his little fists and yelling, "I hate you, Baba. Let me go. Let me go." I stood, frozen and impotent, and watched, as did a couple dozen shocked guests of the resort.

2 June

Iskandar came to my bungalow this morning, followed by Mariam and we set off for the restaurant and breakfast. Mahmood caught us halfway, on the volleyball court. He grabbed the children by the wrists and pulled. They tried to fight him and, once again, with twenty people watching, he dragged them off screaming.

I was informed that there was frantic packing going on in the long-house. At about 9 A.M. the kids came over, dressed to leave. Mariam was excited about the adventure they were going on. Iskandar just sat quietly in my lap as I assured them of my love and said not to worry, we'd soon see each other again. The word "soon" caught in my throat. I comforted myself that 'soon' is a relative concept to a three-year-old.

I kissed the children good-bye and they left. I stood sobbing as they walked off and climbed into the speedboat. The staff and most of the guests were on the beach watching.

At 10:00 I got Salwah on the telephone and told her everything. She instructed me to get statements from anyone on the island who would write them. She'd spoken to Hassan and he agreed to sign a general state-ment of support. He also told her the entire family was with me and that he wanted to help in any way he could. After discussing the subject, we decided against my filing a police report in Mersing. "Be calm," she told me, "and relax. We will help you. You have so much support. Don't worry."

Lorraine and Salaam, the bartender, will write statements, as will Vlatka, a Croatian friend and a French woman named Beatrice. Tom and Joe, the managers, don't dare, nor do most of the workers, though they are all totally sympathetic.

The room boys moved me over to the longhouse as the resort is filling up today. I got myself settled in to the room where the kids slept and looked around. I found a bunch of my clothes and stuff in the room I'd used last fall. I took a few of the things but gave most to the workers. Most of the children's books, toys, clothes and stuffed animals are rotted, molding or water-damaged. I intend to clean, sort and beautify their space here.

3 June

Not a word on Mahmood's and the children's whereabouts. I have three written statements to send to Salwah.

Around noon I was called to the telephone. Azizah was on the line. She said that Mahmood sent her to Singapore in a taxi and she and Zahara flew back to Brunei last night. She said she had no idea where the children are. "Mahmood took them off and will not give me a clue. I am so worried; he was in a very bad mood. Please talk to your lawyers and let the children come back to Brunei. Not good, they stay with Mahmood," she said.

I told her that I was going to call her sister-in-law Faridah and ask her if it was true Mahmood had the kids. Azizah got angry and said, "Don't call my family. Why you call her?"

I replied "I don't believe you."

She said, "You will know soon enough." I heard Zahara yelling at her in the background and then she hung up.

I returned to the longhouse and have been doing laundry and organizing the kids clothes. There are two big bags full of things too small for them that I will send to Mersing on Monday to be given away. The rooms were untouched in eight months. I snuck into Mahmood's rooms and they looked as though I had never been gone, though there were no pictures of me or any of my personal things lying around. The posters, photos, paintings and other Michigan memorabilia were as I'd left them. All the birthday, Christmas and anniversary gifts I'd given Mahmood. My shelves of books. I had no desire to take anything and I left without leaving a fingerprint. Poor Mahmood. Why does he torture himself? To feed his hate, maybe.

Suddenly it's 5:30 P.M. and I am fighting depression. It is dawning on me with ever increasing evidence and assurance that this case can only be resolved in an extralegal manner. My mind goes back and forth over my choices. Should I get to the States as soon as possible? Can Hassan help me find people I can trust? Doubtful. Allah, I need help.

I telephoned my mother and now feel guilty, because I told her too much. I know I upset her and then I sounded stupid as I tried to reassure her things were really not so bad.

Where are my children? My need to know, good or bad, is debilitating. I punish myself with blame. Had I not shown up on Rawa and refused to leave, they'd still be there, playing happily. By winning the right to bring them back to Malaysia and see them, I've disrupted their lives. I lose, they lose and Mahmood is still in control. Is taking them the only way to resolve this debacle? I'm a basket case. I don't trust my competence or my courage. Mahmood is a sociopath. He has no qualms about violating the law and damaging two little lives in his quest for revenge.

4 June

Took the boat into Mersing to file a police report. There is a woman lawyer here in town who will help with the wording and translation. I'll go see her now and hopefully be done in time to catch the 2:00 back to Rawa.

I telephoned Salwah from the Mersing lawyer's office after I finished with the police report. Salwah told me she called Zsa Zsa wanting to make a plea to intervene. Alas, not in. Salwah has been unable to reach Mahmood's lawyer about setting up a visitation or the judge about starting contempt of court proceedings. Tuan Haji is, as usual, in court and cannot be reached. Salwah promised she'll fax Inspector Zul a formal request for a copy of the police report to include in our next affidavit. Yusof Rahmat had faxed her that Mahmood was not allowing me to see the children for thirty days while he found a house in Johor Bahru and that he rejected our proposal to give me half of every month with them. He won't agree to anything nor comply with whatever we propose nor respect any court order or ruling. Yusof told Salwah that Mahmood had the kids with him. So that means they were in Melacca yesterday. At least I know that much.

6 June

Alang just confronted me. "You have to go. Mahmood called me and demanded that I kick you off the island."

I argued with him, stating, "I do have the right to be on Rawa and here are a few darn good reasons: My lawyers want me to stay, this is my marital home, we all agree that Mahmood is an ass who should be stopped and the best way to do that is to ignore his threats." Not wanting him to interrupt, I hurried on, "I'm willing to pay for overseas calls and food. I can help out in the office. I'll tend bar a couple of hours a day." I said a lot more than that and, of course, now I can come up with yet a dozen more points. I did ask him to let me stay through the end of the week, at the very least, and he agreed. I began to cry, "I am a very unhappy person who only wants her babies and then will go away."

I have a reprieve to think and plan. Lying on my bed now, I am miserable and in a heightened state of brain-dead strategizing.

11 June

The police are back. One of the workers came over and told me they were here. I got myself showered and dressed and am now waiting to see them. I heard last night that Mahmood and the children were in Mersing. Anxiety is creeping up and through me.

Shall I surmise? He wants to bring the kids to Rawa and needs to get me off the island before he does. He may have gone back to the police to try again with the criminal-trespassing charge. I respect Inspector Zul, who was here last week and is here again.

I've been waiting in the gazebo a half-hour and haven't been approached. The six officers who came with Zul are sitting in another gazebo staring at the women tourists. Why on earth are there six? I bet everyone in the station wanted to come and they drew straws for every seat on the boat. A royal scandal. What is better fodder?

Finally, Zul walked over. He said he needed to revisit the details of Mahmood's two days here and his treatment of the children and me. I recalled things as best I could and then we moved along to why I stayed on. I explained to him I was staying under advisement of my lawyers to protect my marital property and to expedite hearings on a financial settlement and visitation.

He asked four questions and then prepared to write down my answers. "Are you going to leave today, 11 June, as you agreed to do on 6 June, when you spoke on this matter to Tunku Alang?"

Being unable to answer, I went to find Alang and ask him what he knew about Mahmood's plans and what his advice to me was. He said that Mahmood was going to come to Rawa with the children early yesterday evening and then he never showed up to take the speedboat over to the island. Alang hadn't spoken to him since early yesterday and didn't really know much. He went on about wanting to sit Mahmood down and convince him to rent a house for the kids and me and provide us with maintenance and a car. Only three thousand dollars a month, he said, and it would solve everything. His expenses, he complained, were often twenty thousand dollars or more a month. Mahmood was alone with the kids, no servants. He had heeded Alang's advice and sent Azizah and company packing. "Mahmood can't take care of those children," he told me. I agreed and said that Mahmood might be willing to listen now that his case has been destroyed and he will lose custody anyway, in the end. Why did I say that? Has his case been destroyed? Will he lose custody in the end? Do I believe these things? Sometimes yes and sometimes no.

"I'll leave Rawa tomorrow," I said to Zul when I returned to the gazebo.

"Why are you waiting another day?" Zul asked. He said I could go with him on the police boat, but I insisted on not leaving until tomorrow.

Next question: "Do you have any intentions of returning to Rawa?"

"I don't know," I responded truthfully.

"Under any circumstances, do you plan on coming back to Rawa?" he asked, rephrasing the previous question slightly.

Again I responded, "I don't know." Odd, those two questions.

"Is there anything else you would like to say?" Zul asked, pen poised over his notebook.

The question I'd been waiting for! "Yes, my only concern is for the welfare of the children. I will do anything to protect them and to insure their right and need to be with their mother and be happy." He wrote down what I said, word for word, in English.

Zul drew a sketch of the family house and asked me about every room. When we came to Mahmood's room, I said it was where Mahmood and his girlfriend stayed.

"The Chinese girl?" Zul asked.

"No, the Malay one," I retorted and we both smiled.

The interview was over. I tried to get Zul to share with me what Mahmood was up to, but he wouldn't or couldn't answer. He said, "The case will be sent to my superiors and they will decide whether criminal charges are warranted."

Zul and his six curious escorts had lunch and finally left. I sat down to eat, discovered Zul's mobile phone on the table and ran frantically to the jetty where I flagged them down. I handed him his cell phone, went back and ate quickly before something else happened. I returned to my room for a nap and lay down on my bed, regretting the things I did not say. When I finally fell asleep, I dreamed about the children.

12 June

I was so exhausted I slept through the night and am consumed with anxiety this morning. I tried to call Tuan Haji at 7:45 and they said he wasn't in yet, that he went straight to court this morning. I may be able to speak with him when he comes in at noon. He may telephone me because I did leave an SOS message.

12:30 and I'm trying to reach Tuan Haji by telephoning his office every fifteen minutes. If I can't reach him, I will stay until tomorrow. I will tell the police my lawyers told me not to leave.

Salwah telephoned and told me she had put together two nice portfolios in English for Phillip French, First Secretary at the United States Embassy, and sent them over to him. She arranged a conference call and for two hours we brainstormed with him about what the embassy could do for my case. Our dream was to convince him to ask the ambassador to put pressure on the Malaysian government to intervene in Melacca on my behalf. Unfortunately, the ambassador left two weeks ago and they won't be replacing him until September.

Philip was frank with us. Any move the United States government made on my behalf is rife with risk. Malaysia's Prime Minister is unpredictable and would expect something in return for helping. He does, however, despise the royalty, especially the Johor royal family, and the opportunity for him to use my case to further his vendetta against them could be an ace in my deck.

Would Uncle Sam's involvement be productive or could his "meddling" hurt me? Philip is unsure. He's attending a reception in several days and will make some casual inquiries with powerful folks. In the meantime, he'll speak with friends, his network and Wendy, the acting Ambassador, but he is not hopeful.

14 June

Another day, another crisis. Alang confronted me and said, "Why are you still on Rawa?" he asked. Not giving me time to answer, he rushed on, "Go pack up your things and leave immediately. No, you may not call your lawyers and no, I am not going to listen to another word from you. I am fed up and I want you gone before the police come here with an arrest warrant and handcuffs." I have never heard him so worked up. Up in my room I gathered a few last things and packed in a daze. Then I telephoned my lawyer. "The police have been to the island three times to harass me at the behest of Mahmood and now this," I wept. "You must do something." Tuan Haji promised he would do his best.

16 June

I am in Mersing, disgusted and distraught, staying at an inexpensive hotel. I can't think about going home, although I am desperate to see my family. I must stay here until I get a date to go to court and see the judge.

5 July

It took weeks—endless weeks—but Tuan Haji, Salwah and I are really going to Melacca on 8 July to see the judge. I wasn't allowing myself to think about or believe it might happen, and now, Allah be praised, I can safely smile.

8 July

Salwah and the big, red, chauffeur-driven Mercedes came for me this morning and waited outside the wrong hotel. For fifteen minutes we each wondered where the other was, but finally she called her office and got the correct address. We set off to pick up Tuan Haji in heavy morning traffic. He climbed into the front seat, turned to us with a curt "Good morning," and then turned back, opened his newspaper and ignored us.

Salwah and I talked nonstop for the next two hours about everything. Her mother died two years ago from breast cancer, she went to law school in England and she is like a mother to her teenaged brother. Each time we talk I like her more.

We arrived in Melacca exactly on time, left the driver drinking tea in the coffee shop below and walked up the rickety stairs to the temporary court where Judge Lembut was waiting. I humbly sat against the back wall on a bench in the mock Judges Chamber, an ugly room with only his over-flowing desk, a few chairs and my rock-hard bench. Tuan Haji, dressed to impress in fancy sarong, traditional silk shirt and funky Haji hat, stayed standing and began to orate, while Salwah sat down, a pile of documents in her lap. Judge Lembut, in a black robe, was confused at first by our need for another visitation order and inquired why the first was inadequate. Tuan Haji quickly filled him in as the judge looked over our latest affidavit. Then the negotiations began. I understood about 50 percent of the conversation; just enough to put tears in my eyes a few times.

Afterwards, when Salwah explained to me exactly what we had gotten, I cried with despair. The judge eliminated our request for exclusive custody half of every month, but he did agree to six hours of visitation, undisturbed by Mahmood or his representatives, every day on Rawa or wherever else the kids are.

A half-dozen major problems immediately came to my mind. Mahmood could refuse to allow me on the island or he could make me hire a boat every day to come over from the mainland, which would be an expensive proposition. He could allow me to stay on the island, but make me pay full price for a chalet and my food. He could forbid the children to spend one minute more than six hours with me and keep them locked up in the longhouse so we don't see each other beyond that time. He could make my life hell and, more importantly, the children would be caught in the middle and would suffer. To expect Mahmood's compliance with this order would be foolhardy and cause so much turmoil for the children and me as to be not worth it. When I told these things to Tuan Haji, he chastised me for being such a pessimist. I burst into tears.

Salwah told me, "The judge is very angry with Mahmood and sympa-thetic towards the children and you. Unfortunately, if Mahmood continues in his refusal to comply with court orders, there is nothing that can be done." I sighed, having heard it all before. "The judge also wants to wait until his new courthouse is finished before scheduling the custody hearing,"

she went on, "because, of course, a VIP case should be heard in a nice place."
Tuan Haji became livid at this, Salwah added, and tried unsuccessfully to
convince his judgeship that we did not care about the location, only about
two suffering children who need their mother now. But the judge's wishes
prevailed, as he is determined that ours will be the first case to be heard in
his new courthouse, scheduled for completion in October.

We got the affidavit affirmed. We got promises the court order would
be ready in four days. Promises, promises...

13 July

Not surprisingly, Mahmood is ignoring the judge's order and refusing
me access to the children. I spoke with the Assistant Director of the Social
Welfare Department. She had lunch with Phillip French yesterday and they
discussed whether she could intervene on behalf of my children. He gave
her one of the portfolios Salwah had assembled. I pleaded with the woman
to help, to read the portfolio, to move quickly. She has a friend who may
be able to speak with the Sultan of Johor and she will try that avenue ini-
tially, rather than begin an abuse investigation and cause a scene. I cried as
I shared with her my agony over having the means but not the heart to trau-
matize the children by asserting my visitation rights. She asked me to give
her a few days.

14 July

I found out Azizah is alone on Rawa with the children! I telephoned
Salwah and got her approval to test the not-yet-stamped, new court order,
then I informed Inspector Zul. I chartered a boat to leave for the island at
9:00 A.M. Then I packed my bag.

Lorraine drove to Mersing, we had breakfast together and she took me
to the dock. She did this without Alang's knowledge. He's convinced terrible things are going to happen and he does not want his wife implicated or
shot by an enraged Mahmood.

I arrived on Rawa a quivering wreck and soon discovered that Azizah
and the children were not on the island. Exhausted, I lay down on
Mariam's bed and slept for two hours. One of the workers woke me with
a message from Mahmood demanding that I leave the island. The second
message from Mahmood said to come to Mersing and see the children.

The third message informed me there would be no food and no accom-modation for me on the island. The fourth message was from Inspector Tan at the Mersing station, telling me the children were there, I must leave the island and Mahmood would allow me to see them in Mersing this after-noon. I protested wearily, but agreed to return on the next boat.

I arrived in Mersing alone and both Mahmood and Inspector Tan were waiting for me in the Rawa Resort office on the dock. I told the inspector about the new court order and telephoned Salwah to fax it over to the office. Mahmood pontificated, ad nauseam, about what a great guy he was and how I could see the children "if I would only do things right." Despite my best efforts to stay calm, I became angry and sarcastic. Stupidly, I wept. Inspector Tan was trying to stay neutral and, after a half-hour of waiting in vain for Salwah's fax to come through, we went to the police station. I drove with Mahmood and confidently asserted, in his van full of toys and kids stuff, that I'd have custody in a month. He glowered at me and said nothing.

We sat for an hour in Tan's office while waiting for the police chief to finish up with a VIP guest. Then, once we were in the chief's office, the three men bullshitted for another half-hour, because the copy of the court order had yet to be faxed over from the Rawa Resort office. After it was received, another twenty minutes passed while they read it over and over and concluded it was not valid, because it lacked an official stamp.

Mahmood shouted, "Even if it were stamped, you will not be permit-ted to stay on Rawa or to use the Rawa boats to see the children. You will have to charter a boat if you want to go over and I will bring the kids to Mersing only twice a month!"

Finally, unable to get a word in, I politely asked for a private audience with the police chief and he agreed, guiding me into an empty office. "Mahmood is slippery and smooth," I said. "In front of others he is pleasant and agreeable, but turns evil with me when we are alone together." I explained some of our history, showed the chief Mahmood's divorce paper and my response to it and shared with him the judge's frustration with enforcement barriers. The chief read everything and seemed to listen intensely. I finished by saying, for the hundredth time to the hundredth per-son, that all I wanted was to be with my children.

We returned to the chief's office and Mahmood began his sob story about his ex-wife who is like a squatter on the island, shows up unannounced and uninvited, disturbs him and the children and doesn't realize that two or three hours twice a month is reasonable visitation.

Surprise, surprise... The chief of police agreed with Mahmood. The chief took me aside and said, "He sounds like a reasonable man and, of course, though you both love your children, Mahmood does seem to know what is best for them. And isn't he a wonderful guy to allow you to see the children this very evening?"

I swallowed hard and replied, "Yes, and allow me to see them again in the morning and every morning while we wait for the stamp on the new court order." I was ignored, though miraculously it was decided I'd get two hours this evening at Linus's and another two in the morning before they returned to Rawa.

There was nothing more that I could do. I told them I'd be staying at the Mersing Inn and asked Mahmood please to give me a half-hour to get checked in and then I'd walk over to Linus's house.

And so it came to pass that I was with my babies after forty-one days apart. Iskandar was asleep when I arrived, giving me nearly an hour alone with Mariam. She was frightened when she first saw me coming up the stairs and she looked at Mahmood for his reaction. When she saw it might be okay, she ran to me but kept looking over at him nervously. I had my big bag of toys, books and photos with me and, after doing an inventory, she settled down in my lap for a talk and a story.

After carefully making sure no one was in earshot, she said, "Baba is a bad man. He hits me and he hurts me. He hits Iskandar." She asked me if I was hungry, because she'd overheard Mahmood telling his island bodyguard not to allow me to eat. I assured her I was okay and had gotten a tuna sandwich. Meanwhile, Mahmood, Azizah and Linus were in the kitchen talking and eating.

When Azizah woke Iskandar, he went right to me, was intensely affectionate and we had a flawless time together. When the servant took them in for their bath, he became very upset until I went in and watched. After their baths I rocked them, wrapped tightly in towels, and reminded them over and over and over that I loved them to the moon and would always come back and thought of them constantly and spent all my time thinking about and trying to be with them. Mariam seemed able to understand what was unspoken. Iskandar did not and begged to go with me, begged me not to leave, begged me to hug him tighter. When Mahmood came in and said it was time for me to leave, Iskandar just walked off, looking hopeless. Then he turned and ran back for a hug and then another with far too much sadness in his eyes. I cried all the way back to my room, dazed, dejected and miserable. After a while, I pulled myself together and telephoned my mother to tell her about the children and our visit.

16 July

This morning my frayed emotions were at the surface as I showered, dressed and got organized to see the children. Their overwhelming joy at my arrival made me burst into tears. I regained control and we got down to the serious business of play, hugs, stories, kisses and a million ways to say I love you. The time passed much too quickly. As I was preparing to go, Iskandar climbed on my back and chanted, "I'm going with you. I go too." I simply don't have words for my pain, their pain and confusion, our hell.

Both last night and this morning, Mariam struggled with what to call me. Sometimes she used Patty or Auntie, as if that was what she were *supposed* to call me. When she slipped and called me Mama, she looked behind her and became nervous. I quietly told her "I am your Mama, always your Mama, and you should feel okay to call me that, though you don't have to if it will cause problems or worry." She nodded, relieved. Iskandar hasn't been as affected and he used Mama without hesitation.

They stood at the top of the stairs crying when I left.

21 July

Dear Zoe,

Another awful turn. The last court order has failed and devastated me. It was so beautiful on paper and Tuan Haji and Salwah's pleasure with it was contagious. Salwah was so enthusiastic that she inadvertently screwed everything up. She gave me permission to go to Mersing and show Mahmood and the police the court order before it was finalized. We are convinced Mahmood took the opportunity to call the judge and demand he delay or rescind it. I've just been informed that, apparently, the judge has done both! Tuan Haji scolded Salwah for letting me go to Mersing and for releasing the order prematurely. I wouldn't have seen the children if she'd done the correct thing, though...and so it goes.

Love, Patty

31 July

Today was sublime. I spent over six hours with my darlings. We loved deeply and we played hard. Mariam was a little chatterbox. She informed me that Azizah and Zahara hated me, said terrible things about me, called my mother a witch and wouldn't let them call me Mama. "Baba is not so bad as them," she assured me. She asked many questions about America, my lawyers, how passports worked, where I lived and why Baba didn't love me.

Iskandar only wanted to play with my makeup. He meticulously rubbed lip-gloss on his cheeks, used half the powder in my compact and kept sneaking into my bag for more eyeliner and mascara. "Am I beautiful?" he asked a dozen times. Mariam soon joined him and then they pleaded to make me up too. I said sure and we did have fun. They both ran to show Mahmood their faces and they even tried to pull me into the kitchen so he could see my makeup job!

Mahmood, Linus and two strangers cooked a huge meal, fed the children and ignored me. I shared the children's food. Mariam was really concerned about whether I ate. We spent time looking out the window at the street theatre. When they discovered I'd stayed at the hotel right across the street, they wanted to know which window and if they could visit me there and what was the room like. They wanted it to be where I lived.

Their behavior, however, was abominable. Iskandar spit out food, threw things indiscriminately and had loud, crying tantrums if Mariam or I said no. There was no evidence either of them were being taught manners or appropriate behavior at all. Just how much they have changed for the worse became depressingly apparent to me over the course of the day. I felt angry and overwhelmed by their degeneration and how they were drifting further and further from me. Mariam has forgotten her ABC's, numbers and the nursery rhymes she once knew.

When I returned to my hotel room, I telephoned Salwah for a long conversation about what to do next. We went around and around and ended up nowhere. If Mahmood gives me only a few hours every two weeks then so be it until we can see the judge again. In October, maybe. I was on the edge of hysteria as I told her that I didn't think I could live with a few hours every month. She stumbled for words of solace. I said, "Never mind," and hung up. How to tell her that it's not the few hours with the children I can't live with but the time between the hours.

3 August

The police came at 11:00 this morning and subjected me to yet another interview, this time a record three hours. Then Alang called, overwrought with the police harassment of me, him, the staff and the business, and begged me, in less than pleasant terms, to please go away for a while and spare us all these insane Mahmoodian maneuvers. To his great relief, I agreed. My lawyers told me to stay unless it became too difficult to do so. I believe that time has come to pass. I am accomplishing little here, except for my periodic visits with the children. There must be more I can do, but everything here is at a standstill.

It is 6:00 P.M. and I am about to write the words that will set me free of this madness and yet will signal my failure. The time is past due for me to go back to Michigan and work to get my children from there. I will go this weekend if I can get a flight.

I am not dropping the custody case. Mahmood would immediately assume something was up and have the children guarded by extremist fanatics with AKs if I did. The story here will be that I need to attend my brother's wedding. The court in Melacca has not returned a call, fax or letter in nearly a month now and if I tell Salwah to stop harassing them, they might do something bizarre like actually schedule a hearing.

4 August

Brothers and all who dare,

Look, guys, we have no alternative. The time has come to focus our energies on mobilizing a rescue. The right person for the assignment is out there somewhere. I have people here on the hunt for someone, but so far we have had no luck for a variety of reasons. All agree a rescue is absolutely doable and all agree I should get cracking. Please, please, please start asking around. America is full of professional child-rescuers who could help us. Put out feelers and get a few numbers and then, when the time is right, we can call people and talk turkey.

I spoke with Mother earlier and got the feeling from her you all think a rescue is too dangerous. I am joined by many others here who believe not rescuing the children is more dangerous. If someone's death is a fear factor, mine is the most likely. Mahmood still thinks he is going to win and the day he stops believing that or gets fed up with my hanging around, is the day he makes a telephone call and I say "bye bye world." Mahmood is not going to give the children up.

For a long time I thought he would let me see them if I got visitation rights, would let me have them if I won custody, would listen to friends and family if approached in the right way. I believed he would soften, would cooperate, would at some point realize he should begin to act in the best interests of the children. Well, nine and a half months have passed since the children and I mistakenly returned to Malaysia and Mahmood's disregard for the children's needs has only become more entrenched.

I am coming home but only for a respite and to rally your support.

Love, Patty.

9 August

These are my last few minutes on the ground in Malaysia as I wait for the airplane to take off... For how long? With every deranged and exhausted cell in my body, I know I do not want to return to this place ever again, though for Mariam and Iskandar, I would gladly relive my recent hell a hundred times over. And I may have to.

Mariam and Iskandar, I have not let you down. I have not let you down. Until we are reunited, I will be working every minute to bring you home with me. Bear with me for a few weeks or a few months or however long it takes. Know that I will never, ever give up...

I can do nothing here to make our permanent reunion a reality. I am not giving up my vigil, but the insanity of the law's irrelevance, my lawyer's powerlessness and Mahmood's delusory omnipotence have weakened me. To struggle on with only failure in sight is foolhardy. But I am not beaten; I shall never give up the fight. Still, I know if I am to succeed, I need to return home, gain support and formulate the right plan to rescue us all.

chapter fourteen

Concrete Pipe Dreams

10 August 1995

I wandered aimlessly through the transit lounge of Singapore's Changi Airport for two hours. What was I going to do when I got home? I agonized for awhile and then told myself that thinking so far ahead and so far away from my babies is too upsetting. I decided to go through the motions, zombie-like, until I arrive in Michigan and then, after some rest, I shall make concrete plans. Right now, I know nothing. No, that isn't true. I know one thing. I will get my children somehow.

Finally, they called my flight. On board, I slept fourteen of the last nineteen hours. We are landing in Detroit in less than an hour. What an extraordinary difference being back in America makes. I feel better. I do believe I am experiencing excitement and something akin to hope.

14 August

I am in Mother's kitchen drinking a cup of her weak coffee at eight in the morning. All the windows are open to a gorgeous summer morning. This is my fourth day home. Yesterday, I hiked through the woods and fields, took a nap on top of a hill, explored an old barn and swam in Lake Michigan. I felt my first authentic respite, even though it was only momentary, in a long, long time. But when I returned from my nature break to reality, my tension came back as well.

23 August

For the past ten days I have been plagued by severe anxiety and my weight's dropped to 112 pounds. Finally, this morning I made an appointment with Marilyn Singer, friend and MSW. We met for lunch and made the decision to work through my problems together. Marilyn assured me, "You are simply marvelous. You're a heroine to have endured so much." Everywhere I turn, people think I'm special, which is so untrue. I am just a mother who knows she needs her children and they need her.

Late in the day, I telephoned Rawa and reached Mahmood. "How are the children?" I asked him.

"Where are you?" he demanded.

"In Michigan," I replied. "How are the kids?"

"They're fine," he mumbled.

I told him I wanted to set up times when I could telephone and speak with them.

"They are asleep," he said and hung up.

It is a profound relief, at least, to know they are on the island.

6 September

I began a frenzied quest to organize and fund the children's rescue. I made countless telephone calls and sent off dozens of appeals for help to philanthropists and media personalities. I found a private investigator who agreed to take the job but estimated that it would cost an unaffordable $100,000 plus... So much for that possibility.

I intensified my search and prepared a letter which I have sent to anyone I think will be able to help me.

Dear _____,

I need to rescue my three-year-old son, Prince Iskandar Shah and four-year-old daughter, Princess Mariam Nabila, from a small island off the East Coast of Malaysia. I have spent the past year in Kuala Lumpur, Brunei, Johor and the United States struggling desperately, through every possible legal and diplomatic means, to free them from their despotic, vengeful father, Prince Mahmood, estranged cousin of the Sultan of Johor.

I recently returned to Michigan from Malaysia, after many tumultuous months, convinced the only way to be reunited with my children is to find someone to rescue them. I found a professional who is willing to do it, has

performed over two dozen successful child rescues and comes highly recommended, but he is expensive.

I am committed to doing whatever it takes to raise the money to rescue my children and ensure their security once they are here. I have extensive legal documentation of the authenticity of my plea. I am hoping you
are interested in knowing more as I am confident I can convince you of the
efficacy of helping to finance this noble endeavor.

Sincerely, Patty Sutherland

14 September

I sent a letter to Ross Perot, who telephoned this morning and spoke
with my mother for twenty minutes. Although he was very sympathetic to
my plight, he said he couldn't help because Mahmood has legal custody in
Malaysia and he'd be sued for the rest of his life. Mother said he talked so
fast she couldn't get a word in edgewise and he went on about why "all
these nice American girls marry fellows from over there and end up getting
themselves in so much trouble."

In the midst of all my efforts, a fax from Salwah arrived:

"We are pleased to inform you that your initial application to overturn
Tunku Mahmood's custody, dated 28 February, 1995 has been set down for
trial on Wednesday, 11 October, 1995 at 9:30 A.M. Kindly inform us whether
you will be available on that date to be present in court."

Encouraged but wary I wrote her back:

Dear Salwah,

Assalam Walikum. Enclosed is a letter from my family doctor. I suspect
Mahmood is going to allege in court that I came to the United States for
reasons other than my fragile health, frustrations with the case and my
inability to see the children as well as my brother's wedding.

I heard through the grapevine that Lorraine's cousin, Edwin, went to
Mahmood with a contrived story in an effort to make some money.
Apparently, Mahmood was happy to pay Edwin to file a police report alleging that I approached Edwin to kidnap my children. Would you please
phone the police chief in Mersing and find out the status of the case and
whether there is any possibility I could be served with a warrant for arrest
for conspiracy to kidnap when I arrive in the country?

I will be arriving in Singapore at midnight on Monday, 9 October and will take the first commuter flight up to Kuala Lumpur on Tuesday morning, giving me eighteen hours to clear my jet lag and settle in before going to court!

What is our itinerary for going to Melacca? Will the children be in court? What if Mahmood does not show up? Could you put in a request for a long reunion visitation or ask the judge to give me an overnight with the children? Salwah, I am a nervous wreck about all this and the more information you can give me beforehand the easier I will sleep these next few nights.

Looking forward to seeing you in a week and receiving your answers very soon, please. Noor Faridah

9 October

In Michigan the time is 2:00 A.M. In Malaysia the time is 2:00 P.M. and here in Tokyo it is 3:00 P.M. and I have three hours until my flight leaves for Singapore. I am tempted to make a collect call to Salwah but would she accept the charges? She did not respond with detailed answers to the questions in my fax from Michigan.

Question after question plagues me. Will I see my children in forty-three-and-a-half hours? What does Judge Lembut have in store for us? Dare I anticipate seeing them soon? Will Mahmood show up in court? Might something be accomplished? I sigh heavily. No, no, I have no expectations.

11 October

I am in the coffee shop of the Shangri La Hotel at 5:45 A.M. with forty-five minutes to savor before Salwah and the car arrives for our trip to Melacca. Tuan Haji is already there attending a seminar and will meet us at the courthouse.

Salwah managed to speak with the chief of police in Mersing yesterday. The chief told her the investigation against me on conspiracy to kidnap was still open and he could not divulge any details about a warrant, etc. Once the police learn I am back in the country, they will undoubtedly come to see me. I am trying not to worry.

Salwah spoke with Mahmood's lawyer, Yusof Rahmat, yesterday. He said he's been unable to reach Mahmood in over a month! Mahmood has not signed the last two affidavits and, though he probably knows about the hearing today, odds are high he will not show. My guess is that Mahmood will blow off the court case, thinking he can get me through the police investigation. I am hoping if he doesn't appear, his absence will work in my favor and we can get a solid ex-parte court order.

12 October

My hopes are high!

Yesterday, Salwah picked me up at my hotel and we set out for Melacca. When the car pulled up in front of the huge, new, gleaming Syariah Courthouse, the enormity of the day hit me. I shook with trepidation.

Mahmood's lawyer, my lawyer, Tuan Haji, and Judge Lembut were there. Salwah and I were sent to a small, stifling room for an hour of looking at my photographs and children's books while the men conversed. I'd brought the kid stuff on the off chance Mariam and Iskandar might be there.

At ten thirty we were called into the courtroom and five minutes later we were sent to the Judge's Chamber, a large, opulent room. Yusof Rahmat opened the proceeding by showing letters and stressing how hard he'd been trying to reach Mahmood for over a month. He sounded a bit desperate.

Tuan Haji began his plea to the judge by reminding him of Mahmood's divorce affidavit and his claim I'd abandoned the children. An obvious fabrication, refuted by my presence in the room. He noted that all the claims in Mahmood's affidavit for his divorce and custody were lies and Haji Ibrahim, his only witness, was easily discredited. Tuan Haji pointed to me and spoke a bit about what the children and I had gone through this past year. He reminded the judge that I have diligently appeared in court, worked hard, studied Islam and piously believed in Islamic Law as the path to justice. He told the judge, "There is not a single reason to deny Puan Noor Faridah custody of her children today." Then he added vehemently, "And we cannot accept another useless ex-parte order nor can this case continue another ten months. It is blatantly obvious," Tuan Haji continued, "Mahmood has no respect for the court and no interest in the welfare of the children and we demand the initial order of custody be overturned immediately and my client be given the children."

I caught very little of what was going on. Salwah explained it all to me afterwards.

The judge said he agreed with Haji, but felt he could not make a ruling without giving Mahmood one last opportunity to appear in court and respond to our case. So the three men went through their calendars and, though Yusof Rahmat begged for a month or more, the judge said no, even two weeks was too long and 10:00 A.M. on the twenty-first was chosen. If Mahmood does not appear on that date, then the judge says he will rule in my favor. Further, the judge wants an interpreter provided for me at the hearing so I can testify. I am beginning to feel optimistic that justice is attainable here, but I am still filled with anxiety.

Ten days to the new hearing! I am floored, shocked, thrilled and scared. Salwah chided me gently not to get my hopes up but admitted, with a smile, "The situation looks promising."

19 October

I have been checking in with Salwah twice daily and obsessing semi-constantly for eight days and nights about Mahmood's next move. I've written pages and pages of 'what if this' and 'what about that' and 'then what' potentialities. I have welcomed the dawn more than once, having sat up all night pondering my immediate future in neurotic detail.

At five this afternoon, Salwah told me that Mahmood has turned in an affidavit stating he will appear in court on 21 October and give oral testimony, thus eliminating my last remnants of calm before the hearing.

Tuan Haji told Salwah to advise me not to worry. He is confident that he can destroy any evidence in cross-examination and he wonders if Mahmood will even show up. His absence could be a delaying tactic, as the judge would be hesitant to rule until Mahmood's affidavit was presented and would have to postpone the hearing if Mahmood was a no-show. Why does Mahmood want to delay, I wonder, unless he has nothing for the court right now but is working on another plan? Perhaps he wants to find out where I'm living so he can have me eliminated, as he threatened to do. I go around and around, telling myself most of what I worry about is probably meaningless. But I'm anxious nonetheless. My palms sweat and my heart races.

21 October

Finally the day is here. I slept badly. As Tuan Haji, Salwah and I pulled in to the parking lot of the courthouse, I saw Mahmood's van and had a

panic attack. Trembling, sweating, gasping for air, I clutched Salwah's arm
for support and we walked in, a few paces behind Tuan Haji.

Mahmood, Haji Ibrahim, Hajjah Maimunah and Plastic Man, one of the
Rawa workers, stood outside the courtroom. Why was Hajjah here?
Mahmood looked wretched. He was fatter and his face looked swollen. His
eyes, yellow, sunken and beady, glowered at me.

Finally we went inside. Judge Lembut entered the main courtroom and
we all rose. My first formal proceeding had begun. For the first time, I
looked around and saw a room the size of a small gymnasium with plush,
mauve carpet.

Yusof Rahmat opened and I couldn't follow what he was saying. Tuan
Haji immediately started rifling through his dozen law books and challeng-
ing Rahmat. After twenty minutes of this, the judge left the room for a
short recess. Salwah explained to me that Rahmat was hoping for a delay by
asserting this case should be heard in Appellate Court.

"It's a ludicrous ploy," whispered Tuan Haji. I can only hope he is right.

Judge Lembut returned and ruled there were no grounds for moving
the case and asked Rahmat to proceed. He wanted to put me on the stand
and Tuan Haji protested they had no right. Where was the affidavit and oral
testimony they promised the court, he demanded? Flustered, Rahmat
pulled out a police report and read a short statement alleging I was with
many men before I met Mahmood, had been tested for VD, took drugs,
never followed the religion of Islam and was an all around rotter. "Also," he
finished, with a final flourish of Edwin's police report, "she intends to kidnap the children and take them to America."

All this time the interpreter beside me was writing the salient points
down in English. She looked shocked by Rahmat's charges. As their allegations were read, she quickly expressed sympathy towards me. "It is too
much, too contrived, too petty and none of it is backed up with a shred of
evidence," she said in a low voice. I nodded but bit my lip to keep it from
quivering.

Then Mahmood took the stand. He and his lawyer had obviously done
little to no practicing beforehand. This was typical of Mahmood's lazy, royal
ego once again getting in the way of common sense. Rahmat became exas-
perated, shuffling papers and asking inane questions. He began asking
Mahmood questions about my past, but the judge quickly put a stop to the

subject, stating "Anything prior to her conversion and marriage is inadmissible and irrelevant as all converts come in to Islam with a clean slate."

Rahmat moved on to questioning Mahmood about our marriage. According to Mahmood, I went around in a bikini all day. How many hours? From nine in the morning until six at night. I lay on the beach. I sat in public places, drank wine and read books in a bikini. The servant did all the housework and childcare. I neither fasted nor prayed and rejected all Mahmood's attempts to teach me about Islam.

Then they focused on the children having United States passports. Mahmood alleged that I'd deceived him by saying they couldn't visit the States without them. I sighed when Salwah told me, "This is such rubbish. It's a simple matter to get verification from the embassy."

The judge appeared bored as the afternoon dragged on towards two o'clock. He finally halted the travesty, instructing the parties to go through their calendars to find dates for future hearings. Then he left the room. The lawyers bantered and bounced days around and settled upon 31 October and 16 November.

A few minutes later, Judge Lembut returned and all agreed on the dates. At my insistent prodding, Tuan Haji then asked for visitation. The judge agreed that visitation should commence tomorrow. Mahmood became quite agitated and confessed the children were in Brunei.

Judge Lembut was livid and boomed, "Bring them back immediately!"

Mahmood replied, "It will be very difficult to get a flight."

Tuan Haji scoffed, "Three different airlines fly into Brunei every day."

The judge gave Mahmood until the twenty-sixth and then the argument began about where to put the children so we could be together. Judge Lembut suggested somewhere in Melacca, but when it became clear his order was for me to stay with the children, not just visit for a few hours, the tide suddenly shifted to the danger of my stealing them. Rahmat began blustering about why this would be a danger to the children. Tuan Haji scoffed at him, mentioning that Mahmood had stolen the children twice and taken them to Brunei. He suggested the court hold my passport. I searched through my bag, but I hadn't brought it so Tuan Haji assured the judge he'd get it from me before visitation commenced and bring it to court on the thirty-first.

Dr. Linus's guesthouse was chosen as the venue and I was permitted to go and stay with my babies from the twenty-sixth to the thirtieth. Breakfast, lunch, dinner, baths, stories, bedtime and sleeping. I get short of breath imagining it, but honestly, I don't see it happening. If Mahmood fails to retrieve them from Brunei, claiming there are no flights, what can I do? He could easily delay their return until it's too late. He could fly them back on the thirtieth or claim one of the children is sick and can't travel or they may simply disappear without a trace.

23 October

Today is Deepavali, a Hindu holiday of thanks. Everything is closed and only Indian programs are on television. I'm staying with Lorraine and Alang.

If Mahmood complies with the order, I'll take the night bus to Mersing on 25 October, return on the thirtieth and prepare for court on the thirty-first. I am smiling cynically to myself as I write a plan that is too pat, too easy and too susceptible to Mahmood's deviousness.

I am trying not to get caught up in the fantasy I desperately want to manifest. My intense desire is unnerving. I get short of breath. I can literally feel, hear and smell my babies. I close my eyes and see the three of us playing and laughing. Blessedly, Mariam and Iskandar are oblivious to what I endure, to the real lengths of our time apart, to the turmoil they are in the midst of and how depraved their father is.

I telephoned Salwah at eleven o'clock and she said, "No word. Try me again at three." I called again at five minute to three.

THE CHILDREN ARE THERE!

25 October

I am off tonight. Our visit is scheduled for 9:30 A.M. on Friday, 27 October at Linus's guesthouse in downtown Mersing. The courier came for my passport and Salwah will phone Linus's place and ask them to listen for my knock between four and six in the morning.

I am nervous and immensely excited to see and hold my babies after three months. Dear Allah, may the separation after this time together be a short one. I am going to leave this journal behind and anything else even remotely incriminating. Easy to imagine Mahmood will have the police search my stuff if he can wrangle it.

27 October

I arrived before dawn after a wretched bus ride. My knees ached, neck hurt and I couldn't get comfortable although I had two seats to myself on a nearly full bus.

I felt surprisingly calm as I walked to Linus's guesthouse through dark and empty streets. The door was locked, knocking elicited nothing, and so I walked on to the decrepit little Chinese hotel I'd stayed at before and got a bed. I did a quick toiletry when I awoke at eight-thirty, walked to Linus's again and now, after an hour of waiting, I am stymied.

The only evidence my children were/are here is a little raisin box on the table and two plastic toys. There are no shoes at the top of the stairs, no bags, no sounds except a fan whirring in one of the rooms. Patience is the operative word here as my humble dream is to bathe and breakfast with my children.

Nope, I'm finally told, they're not here but will arrive at eleven. A Dutch fellow just came out of the room with the fan on and brought me up to date. Mahmood took them to the island for the night. This guy's name is Mike and his girlfriend, who just came out, is Jet. They've been in Mersing a few weeks, know Mahmood well and spent ten days on Rawa last month as his guests.

28 October

I had twenty-four hours with the children. Mahmood twisted the knife yet again. Oh, I tried to argue with him, but not for long or with much vehemence. I lost and so I walked away, back to the children, to give them a year of loving in a day.

When my darlings saw me they shouted with glee, ran into my arms and we were inseparable from that moment onwards. Iskandar was like a starved little animal—starved for affection, that is. He gave me five hundred hugs, a thousand kisses and he even said, "I love you" a few times, a rare treat from his lips. There was surprisingly little conflict between them as we played and talked. They are so nice to one another and look out for each other so vigilantly, it's almost sad.

At one point, Mariam reminded me she was keeping our secret about my being her real mother. I told her concealment was unnecessary, but she wanted her secret intact!

Mahmood would not let me take them across the street to buy food and toys. He said I might have some people in the street to snatch them! I invited him to come along, noting that he was carrying his pistol, but he refused. So, while the children cried, I went across alone. I bought viewmasters, puzzles, pajamas and food for dinner and breakfast. While paying, I glanced across the street and saw the children leaning out the window, excitedly waving at me. I waved back, tears welling in my eyes.

I felt blessed to have the opportunity to telephone my mother and let her speak with the children. Mariam dwelled on it afterwards and Iskandar smiled. We went through the photos again and talked about each one. Their faces lit up with happy memories as they asked a multitude of questions.

Bedtime was both treat and torment. I deeply felt the year of bedtimes I'd missed, cuddled up close, reading them stories while stroking their heads. After Iskandar fell asleep, Mariam and I talked. She told me Baba never read her stories and that she cried whenever she looked at my picture. She clung to me and we cried together over life's unfairness. Then I gave her an upbeat pep talk and she fell asleep with a smile on her lips.

Mahmood sat in the other room chain-smoking, gun in belt, scowl on face while the children and I ignored him and spent most of our time in the bedroom.

Fortunately, there has not been a uniform in sight, leading me to believe the police aren't after me. Still, I'm glad I didn't take any chances and this little notebook I'm now writing in will slide nicely between the pages of my journal. Mariam had given me her necklace to wear soon after they arrived and, when I went to return it to her this morning, she asked me to keep it. "Hide it in your bag," she said, "So Baba won't know."

Now I'm holed up in the bedroom where a few hours ago love and laughter filled the air. I sit here alone and hope the children aren't too traumatized by yet another separation. They left quietly this morning. Mariam had one last cry in my arms as she tried to prolong the moment. But when Mahmood called her she went without protest, as did Iskandar. This was the first time they haven't clung to me, crying and begging for a reprieve. They now realize the three of us are helpless—Mahmood runs the show.

I called Salwah. She feels custody will probably be mine, although there are the hurdles of a visa and a work permit to surmount. According to Salwah, we must show Judge Lembut I can and will stay in Malaysia. Unfortunately, the immigration laws in this country are a mess and there are few options. I can, though, apply for permanent residency, get turned down, and use that rejection as an impetus to raise some hell. Salwah thinks I ought to go for it.

I am in a suspiciously good mood. Tomorrow is in Allah's hands. I must let go and trust that truth and righteousness will prevail. I can only do my best. I have two superb lawyers committed to my case and whatever happens, they won't abandon the children and me.

31 October

The day began with a pleasant forty-five minutes drinking coffee with Salwah at the Shangri La while we waited for Tuan Haji and his wife to join us. She is an AIDS educator/activist and was giving a presentation at a conference in Melacca. Together, we make our way to the courthouse.

First thing, Mahmood took the stand and Rahmat commenced his earlier, aborted questioning. This time they'd rehearsed, though not much. More was said about me in bikinis, my aversion to housework or childcare and what a great father Mahmood is. He asserted that Mariam and Iskandar are children of the East and should not be exposed to Western elements. Salwah did a superb job of interpreting the testimony for me.

As soon as Rahmat was finished, Tuan Haji stood up to cross-examine. Rahmat immediately stood back up and asked to postpone, claiming Tuan Haji needed an affidavit to cross-examine. The ploy failed and came off as a desperate attempt to spare Mahmood the humiliation of Tuan Haji's questioning. Mahmood looked like he was in the mood for murder. I sat with a Mona Lisa smile on my face, relishing my moment of vindication—hollow as it was.

Time was running out and Tuan Haji spent the last few minutes demanding Mahmood tell him why Noor Faridah should not be given custody immediately. Mahmood's face was purple with rage, his fists were clenched, but he remained mute.

"Not answering is akin to agreement," Tuan Haji said and sat down.

The next hearing dates were discussed, 16, 17 November and 5, 11 December were decided upon and the conversation moved to visitation.

The judge said, "As before." Then Tuan Haji told him of Mahmood's violations and an angry Judge Lembut ordered that the children be left with the mother, undisturbed, from 3 to 15 November.

3 November

The children are not in Mersing. I will wait until tomorrow. The fear that the children are at Linus's waiting for me while I'm in Kuala Lumpur and, that they are confused and angry while Mahmood is laughing, consumes me. Yet he has not telephoned Rahmat to learn I was going to Mersing today or Mahmood would have phoned Salwah. Still, I am plagued by doubts.

4 November

Mahmood is not on Rawa or in Mersing. He has not checked in with Rahmat. Damn, I am despairing and full of guilt as though this were my fault. I tell myself the children are fine and Mahmood is simply irrational as always.

6 November

Nothing.

I spoke with Linus and he has no clues. Where are my children? Has Mahmood finally run off with them? Should I call Azizah or Siva? Each day that passes without the children surfacing means what? I am afraid to formulate an answer.

9 November

Mahmood has outdone himself in maliciousness. He called Rahmat who called Salwah who called me to report that I could see the children on the twelfth—a Sunday. In the four weeks I have been back in Malaysia, the judge has granted me twenty days of visitation and Mahmood has deigned to give me twenty-four hours.

I pleaded with my lawyers. "Salwah, forget about visitation between now and the sixteenth. The issue has to be custody. Fax the judge this afternoon and explain to him that, under the circumstances, Noor Faridah feels it is too traumatizing for her and especially the children to continue this fiasco. She fears the effects of this inconsistent visitation on the children.

Without a guarantee of quality time at regular intervals, there is no logic in continuing court ordered visitation at this time. Either give something enforceable or don't bother."

I said this to Salwah and so much more. Her only counsel: patience.

chapter fifteen

Deportation
and Other Threats

9 November 1995

Khalid, an old friend, saw Mahmood in the bank today and reported their conversation to me.

"Is she still here?" Mahmood asked.

"Of course she is," Khalid replied.

"Why?" queried Mahmood.

"Because she wants to see her children and is trying to get visitation," said Khalid.

"But doesn't her visa run out soon? It's nearly three months," wondered Mahmood.

"She has plenty of time left on her visa," scoffed Khalid. "And she should have no trouble renewing it. When are you going to let her see the children?"

"On the twenty-third of November," Mahmood answered.

"Well, maybe if you let her see them sooner, she'll leave sooner," hinted Khalid.

"Really?" Mahmood mused. Khalid said his evil little eyes grew wide.

When Khalid told me about their meeting, I became excited thinking Mahmood might bring the children after school today. Thinking he might leave them with me until evening or even overnight. Thinking I could, no *should* take the opportunity to get them to the United States Embassy, I packed a bag, just in case. Then I counted the minutes, my stomach knotted.

I telephoned the embassy and asked Hugh Williams, the new First Secretary, what I should do if we came there after business hours. He said, "Tell the guard you want to see the Marine and tell the Marine you want to talk to the Duty Officer, because you're seeking asylum."

I clarified, "All I need to do to seek asylum with my children and be safe is tell the guard I need to see the Marine and that will get us through the gate where we'll be helped to return to the States?"

"Yes," he said.

A nagging question answered and a wonderful answer, to boot.

The hours passed and I began to suspect Mariam and Iskandar wouldn't show. My emotions rose and fell. I decided to concentrate on moving the ball forward.

I telephone the Prime Minister's secretary and said, "I'm checking in to discern whether you've looked at my documents and have done anything."

He laughed out loud!

"Why are you laughing?" I admonished. "This is serious. Nothing is happening with the courts. Every day I get angrier and more disheartened. I understand this is a controversial case involving an American and a Johor Tunku and anti-Western feelings are growing and for over a year no one has wanted to touch it. But something must be done before this blows up!"

He admitted that he only glanced at the documents and had decided it was a matter for the Religious Department.

"Have you sent the documents over yet?" I asked.

"No, but I'm going to," he replied.

"Can you give me the name and number of a contact person there so I may follow up in a few days?" I inquired.

"Uh, uh, the Religious Department..." he stammered.

I cut in, "Please just send them over immediately and tell them to take this situation seriously and do something fast!"

"Alright, I'll see what I can do," he said.

8 November

I am frightened by Mahmood's sociopathic bent. Salwah phoned to report that a fax had been received from Yusof Rahmat stating visitation would be from 10:00 to 11:00 A.M. on the twenty-third. He said no to any future dates for visitation.

I was duly devastated, cried, walked around in a daze and heard an infuriated voice in my head screaming, *He's going to get away with this. He will. He
will. HE WILL.*

12 November

Despite my fears, the judge sanctioned thirteen days visitation. Mariam
and Iskandar arrived at ten-thirty this morning.

I am worried about the children's state of mind. Iskandar told me,
"Baba said there are lots of kidnappers around and they will try to catch me.
He told me to stay close to him all the time. I'm scared. If they get me, how
will you find me?" Then Mariam complained, "Baba smacks me sometimes.
Baba smacks Iskandar all the time. Sometimes Iskandar spills a drink and
Baba gets very angry and hurts him."

Mahmood went out to buy the children breakfast. I asked him to bring
me back something and he hissed, "Do it yourself."

Iskandar's teeth are corroded from never being brushed and the children are not keeping up with their lessons as when we studied together.

Except for this, our reunion was sublime; the hours flew. "American
Mom. American Mom, I want to do like that," said Mariam, as we played
airplane on the floor. Too soon, Mahmood ordered, "Time to go," and we
parted, whispering, "See you tomorrow," as we hugged goodbye.

They left forty-five minutes ago and I am happily knackered after nine
hours of hard play. Oh, I love my children. Damn him.

16 November

We were back in court this morning. Tuan Haji cross-examined Mahmood. My interpreter was a sweet Chinese girl who asked if she could visit
me in Michigan.

My lawyers told me today will be Mahmood's downfall. I felt nothing
when they said that. Now, however, I do have feelings: fear, trepidation and
disbelief.

The first thing Tuan Haji did, once he had Mahmood on the stand, was
to clarify unequivocally that Mariam was conceived before marriage. A letter from my obstetrician and Mahmood's acquiescence to its validity were
the segue he needed to bring up the reality I loathe to face, but which,
according to my lawyer, is proof under Malaysian law that I should have

custody of Mariam. Under Syariah Law, the mother has absolute right to guardianship of a child conceived before wedlock. Guardianship is beyond custody and entails the right to take the child to the mother's home country and deny the father access. The law dates back to early Islam and was implemented to spare girls from incest, as the father could technically marry her, and to protect "legal" sons from an illegitimate son hoping to inherit. Although a doctor can now determine paternity, Syariah law is immutable. Mariam is legally mine and my heart breaks to consider separating the children. I know in my gut I can't let it happen but Tuan Haji says we are duty-bound to submit this affidavit and it could get me both children in the end.

Tuan Haji showed Mahmood the affidavit on the subject. "Do you have any objections to our submitting it?" Mahmood was silent. And so the session went on and on, punctuated by small delays whenever Mahmood's attorney could cause them.

Tuan Haji then went back to last summer and fall, provoking Mahmood with difficult questions. He was forced to respond to the letter I wrote to Haji Ibrahim and Haji Ibrahim's letter to me. Tuan Haji read out loud a supportive letter from Chu to my mother. Then he asked, "Is it true Noor Faridah has the support of most of your family? Why did you marry in Melacca? Why did you divorce her on 29 December? Let's go through your affidavit point by point. Tunku Mahmood, why did you do this, say that, tell the court all these lies? Is it true you ignored every rule, every law, and every right of your wife, because you knew she would get custody if you did things properly?" Tuan Haji had to tread these waters carefully, because the judge who gave Mahmood his illegal divorce and the lawyer who represented him were in the room.

The interpreter kept whispering to me, "Is that true?" as she listened in shock. She forgot to translate so often I had to keep on nudging her gently.

Tuan Haji put many of the questions to Mahmood a variety of different ways in the hopes he might get a viable answer. The judge chastised Mahmood repeatedly for not answering. "Remember, if you keep quiet three times, it counts as an admission."

Tuan Haji pushed Mahmood gently, firmly, softly, loudly to respond to his questions about Mahmood's lies, perjury and deceit. An answer either way damned him and he stared malevolently at Tuan Haji.

Abruptly, in the middle of an especially damning line of questioning, the judge stopped the proceedings for the day. All nodded to reconvening at 10:00 A.M. tomorrow and we left.

Tomorrow it will all begin again. I am weary as I write this, but know I must persevere.

17 November

We assembled in the courtroom and Rahmat began his reexamination. "Tunku Mahmood, was your affidavit of 29 December, 1994 the truth, all of it?

"Yes."

"Did you divorce your wife ex-parte because you were afraid she would steal the children and you would never see them again?"

Tuan Haji jumped up at this and complained it was leading the witness and Mahmood had already refused to answer that question three times. Judge Lembut grimaced and Mahmood was released from the witness box.

The visitation dance began and Mahmood's hand was slapped for giving me only seventeen hours instead of thirteen days. I felt joyous when I learned I will have the children for forty-eight hours from the twentieth to the twenty-second of November and again from the twenty-fourth to the twenty-sixth and, further riches, from the second to the fourth of December. Thus ended another day in court.

Back in my room, the questions and answers go round and round in my mind. I feel as though this will go on forever, but Salwah told me decision time will soon be at hand. Dare I really have such optimism? Is redemption at hand? No and no. My life is in Allah's hands and I pray only for His permission to be with my children in two days.

20 November

The children are here. It is 11:00 P.M. and the last two hours have been hell. One problem followed another in rapid succession as I tried to put them to sleep. "It's too hot. It's too cold. Not this pillow. I want water. I want to go to the bathroom." Mariam went into angry hysterics over something innocuous and after a dozen shakes of the head, I hit on why. "When we were apart, did you sometimes think I didn't love you and had run away?" Nod. "Were you angry at me?" Shake. "Angry at Baba?" Nod. "Do you want to be with Baba?" Vigorous shake. "With me?" Vigorous nod.

"Do you know that Baba doesn't want us to be together?" She nodded and I started crying with her. Iskandar clung to me. Mariam clung to me.

"I am fighting very hard for us to be together and my lawyers are helping. We need to try and be patient when we're not together and trust Allah. Don't hate your Baba," I implored. "Be nice to him, because he is very unhappy and doesn't understand that mothers and their children need each other since he lost his mom when he was little. Soon," I promised with my heart in my throat, "we will be together always." I soothed them to sleep with a story about Michigan.

26 November

My second visitation period has ended. We had forty-seven and a half hours together. Iskandar was angry and contrary towards the end. "I don't want to go. I am going to stay with you," he chanted. I responded with the usual, "I want you to stay, I always want you with me. Soon we will be together. This is only for a few days. I love you, will miss you and think about you all the time, my wonderful little boy." He listened intently, curled up in my lap. He hugged me tightly, kissed me over and over and five minutes later, he was hating and hitting me.

Tears came to my eyes when that brave little boy had the courage to say to Mahmood when he came in, "I don't want to go with you!" Mahmood looked at me and laughed.

After they left, I caught a bus to Kuala Lumpur, slept at Alang and Lorraine's house then met up with Tuan Haji and Salwah at 6:00 the next morning for our drive to Melacca. As we rode to court, we talked about the affidavit on Mariam.

"I would rather lose them both," I said trembling, "than leave Iskandar alone with Mahmood."

"But," Tuan Haji said soothingly, "we see this as a device to get them both." He smiled at me, "Do not worry."

But he was unable to offer much in the way of concrete assurances. I have been obsessing over this affidavit and praying the court delays the hearing indefinitely.

Once in court, Rahmat's first witness, a henchman of Mahmood's friend, confirmed that yes, I did, in fact, read books and wear bikinis while the servant looked after the children.

The second witness was an exceedingly predictable Hajjah Maimunah. She testified that Noor Faridah wore improper attire, was never with the children and that Tunku Mahmood is a wonderful father. I can't imagine the lies Mahmood must have told her, a sweet woman of seventy, to get her to testify to lies for him.

At eleven-thirty Haji Ibrahim, to whom I'd written begging for help, was on the stand, looking old and unwell. Rahmat asked him a few stupid questions; he broke down a moment while relating a time when Mariam tried to follow his prayers. Then Tuan Haji stood up with a flourish. I think he's been looking forward to getting his hands on this guy.

Tuan Haji commented that maybe Haji Ibrahim was crying because it was sad to see Mariam without her mother. Then he went on. "For the marriage, Noor Faridah's address was listed as your home in Melacca, where she did not live, though the Melacca Code clearly states one party must reside in Melacca. Tunku Mahmood gave your address as his home for his divorce. Was he living with you?"

"No."

"No; Well, did you know your lie is also a crime?"

When there was no response, Tuan Haji then went over the letters exchanged between Ibrahim and me last fall. He questioned him on how he allowed Mahmood to divorce me when he knew where I was and why I'd gone back and that he'd promised to help me and stay neutral. Tuan Haji confronted him on every dastardly inconsistency and lie. Ibrahim's repertoire of excuses ran the gamut from "I forgot" to "I didn't know."

Ibrahim seemed genuinely shocked by the letters. Perhaps he felt sickened by the memories he'd been repressing suddenly hitting him one after another. I suspected neither Rahmat nor Mahmood had told him what to expect. I almost felt sorry for him.

"Now that you know the truth and have seen all the facts, do you think Noor Faridah has been treated fairly?" Tuan Haji asked.

"It's not my fault," Ibrahim replied.

After thinking it over for a few minutes during a recess, Tuan Haji decided to send me right into cross-examination with Rahmat, as any damage, he assured me, can be repaired in re-cross.

I looked over as Mahmood entered the courtroom. I knew by the bulge under his jacket he was wearing his gun. He probably had done this on purpose to destabilize me. Now that Mahmood was present, proceedings could continue which meant it was my turn in the hot seat.

I walked to the stand when summoned. For two hours I sat on a hard chair in a wooden box and answered loathsome questions. Were you ever in the hospital for anorexia? Were you into free sex on Tioman? Didn't you approach people to kidnap your children? Why don't you pray five times a day? You were a bartender? Why did you wear bikinis, knowing they are against Islam? Were you ever tested for syphilis? These questions went on even though Rahmat did not have a shred of evidence to back up any of the bad-character allegations. I started out frightened, relaxed toward the middle and began to get angry and frustrated near the end. The interpreter was a reassuring buffer.

Despite my fears of what he could do to me, when I returned to my room after the hearing, I decided to write a letter to Mahmood begging him to do the right thing and let the children be with their mother in these critical years.

Mahmood,

We both want the children to grow up healthy, happy and emotionally stable. We both want them to grow up within the light of Islam. We both want them to receive an excellent education and, I pray, we both want them to grow up together.

The affidavit regarding Mariam will be heard soon as it profoundly affects the continuation of this case. Tuan Haji has requested the judge to approve it at his earliest convenience and it is my hope that for the sake of our little boy we can resolve this today without the court's intervention.

Iskandar has become an unstable, deeply troubled child over these past fourteen months. Ninety percent of my tears are shed for him. I believe you have done your best for him under difficult circumstances. This is not about blame; it is about a little boy's desperate need for security, proper discipline and a normal life. He needs the unconditional and devoted love of his mother and he needs his sister more profoundly than you or I can imagine.

Mahmood, give me custody of Iskandar and I promise to commit my life to raising him up to be a man you will be proud of. I will raise him in a Muslim home and I will give you generous access to him and Mariam both. You are their father and should be an integral part of their lives. I promise I will raise them with love and respect for you, Malaysia and their heritage.

Mahmood, I don't hate you, nor do I have any intention of turning the children against you in retaliation for what we've been through. My only concern is getting on with the job of being the best mother I possibly can to Mariam and Iskandar. With Allah as my witness, I vow to fulfill the above promises because they are in the best interest of the children. Please. We have all suffered too much for too long.

Patty

15 December

I took the stand again and Rahmat tried to make me look evil and Mahmood saint-like. Because today is mosque day, when all the men go and get riled up by the Imam against Western decadence, we finished up a little afternoon. Salwah and Tuan Haji thought my letter was great and gave a copy to Rahmat. He read it, showed the letter to Mahmood, who read for a minute and then tore it in half.

I thought I did well on the stand and my "team" said yes, I was fantastic. Tuan Haji might ask me more questions on Tuesday.

As for visitation, Tuan Haji shared with the judge Mahmood's most recent violations and our chronic frustrations. Judge Lembut appeared outraged and lectured Rahmat and Mahmood for their misbehavior, then set another date for visitation.

17 December

Dear Mom,

The children are in a deep sleep. We went to the Merlin Hotel pool for nearly five hours today. Mariam is like a fish and I was in awe of her skill. She swam effortlessly in the deep water and even dove down to fetch things off the bottom. Iskandar was timid at first, but he soon found his sea legs and splashed around happily. I was wearing a conservative one-piece swimsuit and we were the only ones there, but I couldn't relax enough to stay in the pool for longer than a few minutes. After the interminable courtroom drama about my "immodest" behavior on Rawa, juxtaposed with the effort put into portraying me as a "good" Muslim woman, swimming with my children felt wrong and risky. So I sat on the sidelines, covered up.

These priceless, wonderful hours together pass so quickly and in ten more hours the children will be gone. My alarm is set for 7:00 A.M. so we can have a bit of time together before Mahmood comes to get them. I could easily stay up all night watching them sleep, but madness lies down that neurotic road. The bus to Kuala Lumpur, where I must see to some financial matters, must be caught at noon tomorrow. I shall try to fill the time with tedious tasks. Being busy like this has been my salvation. Every day these past few weeks has been blessedly full, giving me little time to obsess or self-destruct!

I love you! Do not worry about me. Patty

18 December

Mariam and Iskandar were dressed, fed and half shoed when Mahmood came in this morning and I hate myself for being so damn accommodating. I let him have them early even though it is my legal right to say no, they're staying until ten o'clock or for one more day or DAMMIT! In Mersing I am powerless and in his presence I am compliant. Otherwise, he gets angry and the kids suffer. I'm a wimp for them.

Mariam cried in her sleep these past two nights. She told me she had a dream last night about being tied up in a bag, unable to escape. Poor little girl.

I feel guilty about the problems Linus has had to contend with lately. He's struggled with malicious gossip for years and it's a big part of why he opened the new clinic twenty miles down the road. Now the petty, ignorant people here have a delicious new scandal to prattle over: Tunku Mahmood, his American ex-wife, their two children and the Indian doctor downtown. That they have made a big deal of this is a glaring example of how wretched a life here could be for me. As a Muslim woman, I should not be seen talking with men, going around with my head uncovered or wearing anything but long sleeves and pants. Any infraction, however small, could send Mahmood to the judge, harping, "See, she's not fit to care for those kids. People are gossiping and she's acting Western!"

With the case winding down, I'm able to look more clearly at the future and it's not a pretty sight. Unless, of course, it's only for a short time and there is a bright light at the end of the tunnel. I mean, of course, the bright lights of Glen Arbor.

19 December

Linus betrayed me. He wrote a letter to Mahmood saying my presence in his house embarrassed him and I haven't paid any telephone bills. He had the gall to write that I said, "Mahmood will pay them," and this was written after I'd left him a note asking how much I owed. Rahmat let Tuan Haji and Salwah read the letter, saying he was not going to submit it. Linus's guesthouse is no longer an option for me, our friendship is compromised and I want to sock him in the nose. When I confront him, he will say he is so sorry, Mahmood put him up to it, he was afraid of being arrested and the gossip was bad for his business. I just don't care. No, I do care and I have the right to be angry, not that it makes a whit of difference, so why bother?

Thankfully, my friend Khalid offered me lodging in his guesthouse. As I have little money to give him in return, we worked out an arrangement in which I will help by cooking and cleaning for other guests from time to time. At least, I am now relieved of one burden.

We arrived at the courthouse in Melacca at ten this morning and Rahmat showed up at noon, just in time for the lunch break, which lasts until two. The judge appeared in the court shortly after two-thirty and I went on the stand. Tuan Haji asked me why I should have custody and why Mahmood shouldn't. He instructed me not to hold anything back and I didn't. I gave an impassioned speech and, according to my lawyers, it was perfectly presented.

Rahmat's summing up then began. I don't practice Islam. I spoke with two men about kidnapping the children and Mahmood has serious fears I will run off with them. Mahmood's witnesses were good Muslims who testified about my dressing inappropriately and not caring for the children. I admitted on the stand I have had stress-related anorexia and have seen counselors and, as I am obviously unstable, there could be serious problems if I were given custody. Therefore I do not fulfill the criteria for custody. And, furthermore, Tunku Mariam and Tunku Iskandar have been with Mahmood these past fifteen months with no evidence of difficulty. In fact, Mahmood's three witnesses said that the children were fine with him. He went on that I have no family in Malaysia, no job, no citizenship and am dependent on my Christian family in the United States for support and can they be trusted? He finished up by reiterating that there are seven requirements for fitness to have custody and I fulfill none, while Tunku Mahmood fulfills all seven.

The courtroom is packed with curious onlookers and one wonders if the entire courthouse staff has abandoned their desks for this occasion. Then Tuan Haji Sulaiman, dressed in his big, black robe, began to defend me, "First of all, the reason we are all in this courtroom is to turn over an irregular and wrong divorce and custody order. Tunku Mahmood got his custody by lying blatantly and saying many other despicable things that were very, very bad." His voice had a steel edge as he went on. "The fundamental issue here is a mother's prior right to custody. Not by any stretch of the law or anything else has it been proven that Noor Faridah should not have been given her prior right to those children months ago. Why does she not have her children? Because of this law and that statute and all this other stuff—pure nonsense. Look at the overwhelming evidence of Tunku Mahmood's bad character. There is absolutely no evidence to back up any of the allegations against Noor Faridah."

Judge Ibrahim Lembut closed the case, saying thank yous all around. Now we have a month, perhaps less, to wait, but this is no ordinary case and, of course, he wants to get it right the second time. Visitation will be as usual—two days on, two days off—regardless of school. The twenty-second of January is booked for the judgement to be rendered.

26 December

The month has inched by. Except for my visits with the children, I have felt as if I were in purgatory. On Christmas Eve, Iskandar fell asleep right after stories, but Mariam stayed awake, determined to get some questions answered. She asked about whether Allah and Santa were real and why Santa doesn't come to Malaysia. Also, she inquired, why Baba is so mean and why he won't marry me again as she hopes and why we can't run away to America. I really struggle to answer her honestly and painlessly. The hardest question to answer was about Santa, in whose name I would give them a pile of presents if I could, but Mahmood would have taken my dangerous Western behavior right to the judge.

On Christmas morning, the children woke shortly after dawn and did not stop for a breath all day. A highlight was Hassan showing up for a visit. We hadn't spoken since July, but fell quickly into our easy rapport and had a good talk. He wanted to hear every detail of court and he wondered if the rumor was true that Mahmood and a servant were sleeping together.

Mariam was in the room, so we asked her. "You," she replied casually. In the same bed? "Of course," she said, amused by our dumb question. From her description, all four of them sleep in the same bed, though there is another bed in the room where Mahmood and the servant end up. They also kiss a lot and act loving, she told us. An interesting tidbit and, if I could get evidence, an extremely damaging one to Mahmood's case and a coup for mine.

27 December

My tourist visa runs out on 3 January. In the best case scenario, I take a bus to Melacca, collect my passport, take it to Melaccan Immigration, they renew it, I take it back to the courthouse and return to Mersing. There is no safe way to find out beforehand if this will happen in this bureaucratic nightmare of a system, so I'm anxiously formulating a plan that covers all snafus.

2 January 1996

Dear Mom,

I am in a constant state of anxiety, on the edge of tears, consumed with guilt, confusion, fear and a love for my children so frighteningly powerful I would endure one thousand times worse what I am going through.

Mahmood swooped in for the children at 8:30 this morning, I left for Melacca at 9:30, arrived at 2:45, got to the court at 3:00 and was out with the passport and a letter to immigration requesting an extension at 3:15. Ten minutes later I was at immigration and realized, after thirty minutes of the runaround, that they had no intention of extending my visa. I left in tears, made it to the bus station with twenty seconds to spare and cried quietly half the way back to Mersing. I'm now sitting on my bed wishing I were sitting on yours.

I cannot believe immigration would be so cold and bureaucratic as to deny the mother of two half-Malay children the right to stay. In Melacca today, they did. I may be luckier in Mersing tomorrow.

The registrar at the courthouse was expecting me to return my passport this afternoon. I'll phone Tuan Haji in the morning and he'll handle it, though the judge will surely hear and there's the rub. He might be hesitant to give me custody if my ability to stay in Malaysia is in jeopardy. Tuan Haji was too confident about my tenuous non-citizenship during the proceedings while Yusof Rahmat harped on it continuously. It is their one trump card.

The time may have come to take the bull by the horns and confront this country's unjust, illogical immigration laws. I would happily go up to Kuala Lumpur to plead my case (and that of hundreds of other foreign mothers) to the head of National Immigration Policy, the Prime Minister, whomever. There is not a single reason I should be denied the right to stay without hassle. This kind of stress is infuriating and terrifying.

Try not to worry about me.

Love, Patty

3 January

I'm on the road again. Mersing immigration said no. Now I must go to Singapore, so I caught the local bus to Johor Bahru as it was driving out of town, this time with ten seconds to spare. I will get a Singapore bus when this one lands and hopefully be in and out and back on a bus to Mersing without too much agony. Another day shot.

I'm a nervous wreck, because I could be denied entry back into Malaysia. I brought a scarf to put over my hair to soothe the Malay who stamps my passport. They have far more time and sympathy for a Muslim woman than another white female tourist with a suspiciously fat passport.

Two o'clock and Allah is great. The woman in the booth barely glanced up as she stamped my passport, granting me priceless security until the end of April.

The children have school and won't arrive tomorrow until one o'clock. I really want to visit their school, but I don't need the stress of asking Mahmood where it is and what classrooms the kids are in. Meeting the teachers and observing their classes would help rebuild the children's confidence in Mama as a part of their lives. Mariam says she hates school and usually has no idea what's going on since the teachers speak only Chinese. Things are easier in preschool for Iskandar, who only needs to know when to start and stop playing. Mariam, though, says she gets through the day by mimicking the other kids.

chapter sixteen

Toward Decision Day

6 January 1996

Mahmood returned promptly to pick up the children. Mariam and Iskandar were reluctant to leave until Mahmood opened the van door and there in a cage was a cat. The kids were so happy and I knew Mahmood was thinking, *Ha, you see! You think you won by getting visitation, so I got even by buying them a cat. You see how easy it is for me to win?*

We expect the judge's next ruling in sixteen days. I tell myself the worst is all but over and the children and I won't be separated again. Mahmood's not going to run off with them. He won't have me killed. I'm not going to have a breakdown. The children will not suffer more trauma and they are not irreparably damaged. I've seen the dark side of how Malaysian justice hurt two innocent children. In the past I've screwed up and suffered, but it was all my own pain. Mother-pain is an entirely different, deeper, more wrenching form of agony. No, it's not all my fault, but their healing and their future are my responsibility. I suspect I've finally grown up. I am committed, with unwavering certitude, to the children, to their stability, to the pursuit of them fulfilling each of their destinies.

18 January

I telephoned Salwah who said the hearing is the twentieth, not the twenty-second. I went into town, bought a bus ticket, left an updated message for Mahmood at the Rawa office and bruised my shoulder badly while jumping on the moving bus as it was turning a corner. Now I'm sitting on my bed in a daze. How could I have had the date wrong? In less than forty-eight hours, the immediate fate of the children will be decided and I can't lift my arm.

It's 9:00 P.M. and I just finished Isha, the final prayer of the day. Did all five today for the first time. Seems like I said goodbye to the children weeks ago rather than this morning. Why have I been on the edge of tears all day?

19 January

It suddenly hit me that the hearing date would be on the letter the court gave me for immigration. I find the letter, unfold it and the date is the twenty-second! Salwah, silly Salwah. She's made an error!

I'm giddy with relief, mostly for the twenty-four hours retrieved with the children. Also, to pray and to begin Puasa, the Malay word for fasting month.

I reach Salwah at the office and she brings me up to speed. The hearing is not the twenty-second, because the first weekday of Puasa is a public holiday in Melacca. The judge will try to reschedule ASAP, hopefully in the next week. This is wonderful, because I am still in Mersing and will have my babies for forty-eight hours and maybe another forty-eight hours after. If they are not suffering, all will be well in my world.

"As the hearing has been postponed, can I keep the children for my two scheduled days?" I asked Mahmood when he picked up the telephone. Silence. I prodded on. "Do they have school Monday?" He wouldn't volunteer anything...but Khalid might know. I hung up and called Khalid to ask him if the first day of Puasa is a school holiday. Yes it is, he told me, so I call Mahmood again. "Since Monday is a holiday, we'll see you late morning. Okay?" Mahmood just grunted.

21 January

The children and I went to town, went to the pool, went home, baked a rice and veggie custard, chocolate cake and pumpkin bread. They ate and bathed. Because it is Monsoon season and the nights can be cool, I've been carrying a pot of hot water over to the communal showers and giving them warm water bucket baths. They took forever to fall asleep, but they were so good and I got all my prayers in and was gung-ho to start fasting this morning. I have promised myself and Allah that I will learn to be a good Muslim.

23 January

Salwah phoned and told me the hearing, which had been postponed because of the holiday, is now on Monday, the twenty-ninth of January at 11:30 A.M. and the children will be here with me tomorrow at midday.

24 January

Whenever I feel as though all my ducks are in a row and take a moment for happiness, then another problem surfaces. Today the children did not arrive at noon, have not been in school the past two days and no one knows where they are. Salwah is out sick so I asked her secretary to call Rahmat and find out where my children are.

My mind shot immediately to the worst case scenario. Say, a private hearing with the judge, in which Mahmood has the children trained to say they hate their mother, she's insane and abusive and they don't even want to visit her. Allah, give me strength as I suddenly want to blow off my fast and have a cigarette. After thirty days of a beautiful, predictable routine, I am thrown by their absence and incensed by his ego and his right to take them wherever he likes without consulting me. I was naive to believe having them half the time meant something. No, he only complied because it was convenient and now, as the judge has surely made up his mind, violations won't matter.

Maybe he sent the children to Brunei, because he's heard or finally realizes I am going to get custody. Or, with the help of Azizah and Zahara, they could be in a third country. His ready compliance this past month may have been a diversionary tactic while he made preparations for hiding them. Well, if they don't turn up, I'll carry on here, go to the hearing on Monday, get my custody order and go from there. Wherever the children are right now, they are fine. I assure myself of this over and over.

26 January

Because of fasting, my body clock is upside down. I haven't slept longer than three hours in over a week, I'm more of an emotional wreck than normal and I've been constipated for five days. And the mosquitoes have discovered new holes in my net that I can't find to mend.

27 January

Yesterday Mariam and Iskandar arrived at 12:15! Mahmood was almost apologetic. "I have very important business in Johor Bahru and you can have them for four days." I was so grateful I did not chastise him for not calling or getting a message to me. I told him that, because of the hearing on Monday, he'd have to collect them early on Sunday. He didn't even know about the hearing.

Now it's midnight and I can't sleep. I suffered an agonizing anxiety attack while putting the children to sleep. Iskandar knows something is up, begged me not to go to Melacca and said he'll never see me again when he leaves tomorrow.

Is this our last night together with Mahmood holding custody? Will we be together every day, every night after Monday? Will Mahmood provide me with child support? Who can sleep?

28 January

My morning with the children was tense but wonderful. We got our Sunday papers and were contentedly reading the comics when Mahmood came for them. The moment they were gone, I went into final preparations to leave for Kuala Lumpur.

After all these months, the day of decision is almost here. I'm only drinking coffee; I'm too agitated to eat solid food. I feel strangely numb though I can easily break into a flood of tears within seconds.

By 9:00 P.M., I was settled into room 306 of the Grand Pacific Hotel in Kuala Lumpur. Took a hot shower and attempted to sleep. The wake-up call came at 4:45 A.M. I ran downstairs for the pre-fast, restaurant buffet extravaganza and stuffed my self. Afterwards, I returned to my room, prayed, dressed for court and packed. Hauling three unwieldy bags, I walked across the street to meet Salwah and Tuan Haji. Then we drove to Melacca to hear my fate.

Within moments of arriving in the courtroom, all my hopes were dashed. The judge ruled custody has to stay with the father, claiming "The children's immortal souls might be jeopardized as the mother was not born

Muslim and the father was. I must consider the hereafter" My shock turned to hysteria when the judge refused to rule on visitation during the appeal process.

A speechless Salwah and stunned Tuan Haji dropped me off at the Ramada Hotel on their way back to Kuala Lumpur. I telephoned my mother from the lobby after having the concierge send a taxi driver to take me to buy my bus ticket. Then I broke my fast with a cigarette and a tin of instant coffee while sitting on top of a toilet in the women's bathroom weeping.

Finally, I pulled myself together. I was still in deep shock, but after a year of coping with hell, I switched into functional autopilot. I had an hour to wait before the bus left and I spent it rationalizing.

Tuan Haji and Salwah will appeal. In the meantime, I must give three days notice to see the children and it will be at Mahmood's discretion.

I was on the bus by seven. It stopped for the few people breaking fast. An old man got off to pray. I held my breath to keep from crying out, leaking tears at a tremendous rate. I tried to shut down my mind, but there were too many triggers. My mind raced. *What will happen to me? Children...Oh, Allah, I can't say their names and thinking about them is too painful.* Again, yet again, I sank into a pit of overwhelming agony, wave upon wave.

When I got back, I telephoned my brother Matthew and Victoria. They cried with me, told me to do exactly what I felt to be right, said they would give Mother some money for me and that all the brothers would start chipping in. Another huge burden lifted. Next hurdle: getting maximum hours with the children.

30 January

I spoke with Salwah. The gist of the ruling, she reiterated, is I AM NOT MUSLIM and all other aspects of the case were irrelevant to the judge. Keep praying, be strong and patient, she counseled me.

I've been harboring an insane vision of the children arriving after school today. Realistically, Mahmood's going to buy their plane tickets to Brunei and send them off for a few weeks or months. He has the legal right now and I know he has the desire to assert his victory. Although there is little chance, Salwah put in a request for me to have the children in three days.

It is 12:15 and I've opened my door as this is the time they would come. In a half-hour, if they haven't come, I will close my door and cry, but now I'm perking up my ears and looking out the door whenever I hear a car.

No one comes. My heart is breaking. The children can count nights. They know they should be with me today. Are they asking, crying, begging to come? Is Iskandar angry, hitting, defiant? What is Mahmood telling them?

4 February

I lie in bed staring at the ceiling, my journal in my hand. How many hours will Mahmood give me? Will he be generous or stingy? Has his victory hardened or softened him? Is there a thread of compassion in him for me? Did my sobbing for the children in court touch his heart? Will he give me a few hours once a week, no more? Evil, of the magnitude Mahmood practices, is beyond my capacity. I am incapable and have been time after time, of believing or even conceiving he could do what he does.

I think I am in shock and have shut down emotionally. I am fed up with crying, gasping and banging my head against mattress or prayer rug as I implode with impotent fury. My stomach is a knot, my heart is a boulder and my mind is in a deep, deep chasm of denial that isn't quite deep enough. There is all this shattering pain agonizing over what to do and where to go and how all this will come out.

5 February

He's given me one hour.

Mariam said, "Baba says we're in his care now. Mother Azizah and Zahara came this morning. See what they brought us (A tiny doll house and a sword) and lots of other stuff. And Mother Azizah is going to buy me this and that and we're going to Brunei and I love you so much and what did you buy me and what can we play and Baba says we only have one hour and I want to draw a flower for Grammy; no, I want to give it to Baba and why are you crying Mama?"

Iskandar said, "See my sword. Read this to me! Read it again! Again! Again!"

I said, "I will always be here. We will be together soon."

Iskandar said, "No, we won't! Never! Never! Never!" And he threw things. Then he hugged me and said, "Sorry, Mommy."

The hour was over in five minutes. They left passively and didn't look back. I followed them to the van, begging Mahmood to say when I would see them again.

"You won't. You heard the judgement. Ha, ha, you lost!" He was walking so fast, ten paces ahead of me, rushing for the van. Tauntingly, he called back, "It's over."

6 February

Deeply discouraged, I have become obsessed with prayer, with seeking intervention from Allah. I'm sitting on my bed waiting for the sweet old man with a great voice to start the lilting call in Arabic from the mosque a few hundred yards away. Five times every day he climbs the stairs to a little room with a loudspeaker, flicks on the switch and invites the faithful to prepare for their prayers.

When I hear his voice I go into the bathroom and do my wudhu, or ablutions, with running water from the wall tap. I have to start out with niat, or intention, and for that I say to myself, "I am doing my wudhu with the intention to pray." Then I ritually wash each hand three times, rinse the mouth and nose three times, wash the face, forehead to chin, three times, wash each arm, right then left, three times, dampen the forehead then wash the ears three times and finally wash each foot and leg to the knee three times.

Without drying off, I go and lay out my prayer rug facing Mecca and put on my white, cotton, two-piece prayer dress. The skirt is a huge long tube with a drawstring waist and the top is a big circle that extends down to the knees and well beyond the hands. I push my face through a small lace-trimmed opening in the center of the circle so all that shows is a small oval from eyebrows to chin.

I begin my prayer by putting my hands up beside my head and saying, "I seek refuge in Allah from Satan the accursed. In the name of Allah, the most compassionate, the most merciful." This next sentence is my prayer niat and it is the only time until the end I use English, filling in the blanks by saying whichever prayer of the day I'm about to do and how many raka'ats, or repetitions. "Allah, I am doing my _____ prayer, __ raka'at for you." Then in Arabic, "Allah is the greatest."

I move my hands down and lay them across my stomach. I recite Al Fatahah, the Islamic equivalent to the Lords Prayer. "In the name of Allah, the most compassionate, most merciful. All praise be to Allah, nourisher of the world, the most compassionate, most merciful. Master of the day of judgement. To you do we worship and to you do we beg for assistance. Guide us along the right path. The path of those whom you have bestowed favors. Not of those who have earned your wrath, nor those who have gone astray. Hear our prayer, oh Allah. Allah is the greatest."

Next, I bend over, put my hands on my knees and say three times, "Glory be to Allah, our nourisher, the most esteemed, and all praise be to Him." Standing, I say, "Allah hears those who praise him, to you be all praises, oh, our nourisher. Allah is the greatest."

Prostration is next. I let my forehead and hands touch the mat and I say, "Glory be to Allah, the most high and all praise be to Him. Allah is the greatest."

Sitting, hands on knees, I say, "Oh, our nourisher, do pardon me my sins and be merciful to me and make me sufficient and give me provisions and guide me and give me good health and forgive me my sins. Allah is the greatest." Then one more prostration.

This is a raka'at, done once, twice or four times depending on which prayer one is doing. At the end of the series, I sit with hands on knees and say this final piece, "All respects which are blessed and all prayers which are good are due to Allah. Peace be upon you, oh Prophet, and the mercy and blessings of Allah. Peace be upon us and upon the righteous servants of Allah. I bear witness that there is no other God but Allah. And I bear witness that Mohamed is the Messenger of Allah. Allah, do shower your grace upon Mohamed and upon the family of Mohamed."

Looking to the left, I say, "Peace and blessings of Allah be upon you all." Looking to the right, I say, "Peace and blessings of Allah be upon you all." While stroking my face with my right hand, I say, "Allah, do shower your blessings upon Mohamed."

I have the prayer memorized, 90 percent of it in Arabic and, once it's mastered, I will learn additional prayers to supplement and expand my repertoire.

At the end of my Arabic recitation, I sit and go through it all in English once more. Though this unnecessary, I get a lot out of it.

Sometimes I cry and have to stop for a while. Sometimes, while doing an extemporaneous prayer at the end, I wail and bang my head on the rug. I always feel fulfilled afterwards and I feel especially virtuous at the end of the final prayer, having gotten through a sinless day of fasting and all five prayers.

Salwah told me that before she can begin preparing our affidavit for appeal, the court must send her official copies of the testimony and ruling transcripts. Melacca will stall and many weeks will pass before it's sent to Kuala Lumpur. Once she has our affidavit finished, certified and sent back to Melacca, they will deign to find a judge and a date to hear the appeal. Tuan Haji figures the process will take at least three months. In the meantime, we will vigorously pursue visitation, the financial settlement and getting that awful affidavit on Mariam's illegitimacy heard.

10 February

Dearest Mother,

On the telephone last night, you asked me if I had embraced Islam. The question startled me at the time and I've been mulling it over since. You are, I'm assuming, concerned about my practicing a religion fraught with controversy and stereotypes. In my vulnerable state, you fear I may become brainwashed and fanatical. Please believe me, I'm not going to begin wearing chador or support the anti-Western Islamic fundamentalism which, as we've discussed, is being seeded here. But that's not the real Islam.

Mother, I know there is talk in the family about whether I should give up, let the children go and come home. My family's rejection of my mission here is one of the greatest fears I harbor. It's beyond anything Mahmood could do. I'd snap. Madness lies behind that door. I won't believe it. You're all just feeling a bit burned out and I'm projecting my paranoia. I am simply in a place where thinking things could get much worse is an ever-present terror.

I still believe we're going to win this diplomatically or in appeal and I am as committed as I was the day I began this odyssey with Tuan Haji over a year ago. He will see justice served. He will not forsake us as he, too, is convinced I am the innocent, rightful custodian of Mariam and Iskandar. Mahmood is only one man and he will get his due. Another judge will hear the appeal and I have to believe he'll be honest.

All my love, Patty

18 February

Two weeks have passed in which I have been fighting frantically for access to the children, but I have just learned that Mahmood has taken them out of the country on holiday until April. I have gone through the usual emotions of anger, sadness and frustration at the news. Now I have decided I definitely am going home for a while.

Just telephoned the airline and the earliest I can fly using my mileage is 21 February. My passport is in Melacca and I can have Salwah request they courier it over and spare me a wretched day of travel.

Salwah says my presence isn't necessary for an ex-parte order on visitation, if one should manifest. The judge appears loath to give specifics and now has even less compunction to do so. "Use his violations in the appeal," he advised my lawyers. As for the affidavit on Mariam, taking her without Iskandar would be wrong unless there was a firm visitation order in effect. I can't conceive of separating the children. Mahmood then would have but one pawn to use and he would think nothing of forbidding me access to Iskandar as punishment for taking Mariam.

The children are in Brunei, I hear, but this time I have no legal right to see them. None. The closest I have come to justice since 15 September, 1994, were the four weeks of forty-eight hour visitations that occurred between the testimony phase of the hearing and the ruling. Those priceless days with my children were glorious and now they're gone...How long will it be until I see them next?

15 February

Today is Iskandar's fourth birthday. I continue to cry out for my babies. I've made my decision. I will fly home to Michigan. I need the comfort of my family right now. If I thought I could see the children, I would grovel. But I know Mahmood has no pity.

chapter seventeen

Mission Impossible

26 February 1996

I'm in Michigan, still fuzzy and emotional from jet lag and am suffering through strong bouts of sorrow, wishing I were back in Mersing. The children are too far away.

11 March

A week ago my brother Matt sat me down. "We are alarmed by your prayer shroud, rigid daily prayer schedule and your hostility toward our concerns. We feel you have been brainwashed and we need to help you if you are to have a clear mind which you must have to get the children back."

His words "get the children back" forced me to focus. "That is all I pray for," I said. Gradually and painfully, their attempts to deprogram me are beginning to bear fruit.

I've been working fifty-to-seventy-hour weeks since my second week back. Three of my brothers are paying me to clean their houses weekly and Bobby hired me to take over the kitchen at his bakery and shop, Cherry Republic. I told them all to give the checks directly to Mother.

13 March

There was a fax from Salwah waiting for me when I arrived at Cherry Republic to bake cookies this morning. "Please remit $2,000.00 for costs and deposit with Syariah Court, pre appeal." Enclosed was a translated copy of the judgement, finally. I cried, Mother showed up and we looked at one another. What to say? I read a bit of the judgement aloud and cried some more.

"Judge: 'I must keep in mind not only the welfare of the children in this world, but also in the Hereafter. Therefore, the father is more capable of looking after the children because he will assure that they live and die in Islam.'"

14 March

I had an ominous, awful dream last night. The children were apathetic when they saw me after I'd gone through hell to see them.

20 March

It seems the Fates, needing entertainment, threw me forty minutes on the telephone with Azizah last evening. She called Zoe, with whom I've been staying, pressed her not to tell my family or lawyers she'd called and breathlessly inquired, "Where Patty is?"

Zoe went into a frenzy and finally reached me an hour later at Matt's house. The usual crises ran through my mind: children sick or dead, Mahmood sick or dead, Azizah wanting to put me through another debacle. I fretted, being unable to reach her for two hours and then she called back.

Azizah began her monologue, "Zahara gone to shop. Coast is clear. How you are, Patty? I pity the children. They so happy in Brunei. They love the amusement park, Jerudong Park and all the clothes and toys I buy for them. The amah, that stupid woman Yati is so bad. She puts her clothes in the cupboard and the children's clothes on the floor! I don't like her."

At this point, I cut in to ask her if Mahmood and Yati were lovers.

"NO!" she exclaimed. "That's so bad. I can't talk to him. I stayed in Mersing ten days after I brought Mariam and Iskandar back from Brunei. I hate Mersing. The schools are no good. Too small. No friends for me, for the children. But Tunku wants them there, under his care. He says no to me when I ask for them and when I ask if they can see their mother. He is so crazy stubborn. When are you coming back to Malaysia? What do your lawyers say? Can you talk to Tunku, talk to your lawyers, try to get the children back to Brunei? I love them so much, I care for them so good. They cried when I left Mersing. Iskandar begged to follow me. I brought the photos and letters you left for them back to Brunei, because Tunku was angry and would throw them away. I will keep them here for the children to remember you."

Every third sentence, she expressed her pity for the children. She said Mariam confessed her secret that Azizah was not her mother and Azizah agreed with her. She said she slept with them every night, misses them, thinks about them all the time and wants to care for them for me. She's searching for ways to get the kids and wants me as an ally. I was friendly and encouraging. I stroked her ego and agreed I'd rather have the kids with her than Mahmood.

4 April

Today, my mother dropped a bombshell. "After careful consideration," she said, "I have decided I will not spend a dime on the appeal, which I believe will be fruitless, but I will, however, give you money for a rescue."

I immediately telephoned the man I'd contacted earlier in San Francisco. Yes, he will help us for $1,500.00 a day, plus expenses. He estimates the rescue will cost a quarter million dollars. No, we can't afford that. Mother said find someone else.

I called a couple to whom we'd been recommended in North Carolina and the wife will fly here on 19 April. They charge $250.00 a day each, plus airfare. Technically, they told me, they're not doing rescues anymore, but…she feel good about me and mine and will come so we can check each other out.

7 April

The couple from North Carolina backed out. I'm down to one apathetic prayer a day and back on the telephone constantly searching for help.

4 June

John Dohman, a longtime family friend whom Mother told about my ordeal, told her he might have a solution to my problem. He invited Mother and me to dinner at his restaurant last week. Once we were seated, he called out his chef, Ted, whose father, he told us, could get my children.

I left with a telephone number in Fort Lauderdale, which I began calling immediately. I had to wait, impatiently, for two days until Cal Fuller's full voice mailbox was cleared so I could leave a message. I baked, kept busy, cried, prayed, slept badly and then it was clear.

I babbled into the machine until there was no more time left. Again, I waited. Cal phoned a short eternity later and we talked for two hours. He hadn't slept in three days travel from Calcutta and was verbose, brilliant, empathetic and enthusiastic. We clicked, the conversation flowed effortlessly and we came up with five plans to peruse.

He called Marge, a friend of his, and asked her to do the rescue with him. She agreed. He'd already thought about cost and estimated the total bill at perhaps six thousand dollars.

Cal asked me to send him copies of the kid's passports, birth certificates, photos of Mahmood and the children and anything else I deemed important. I sent it all out the next day, in a huge Cherry Republic gift box.

14 June

For ten days I waited, fearing Cal's rejection, with diminishing hope and rising despair. For the twentieth time I tried to phone him and, Allah be praised, he answered. "Don't worry, kid," he assured me, "We'll get it done. We just have to find the easiest way with a high probability for success and then we go in and get your children. Relax."

His confidence thrills me.

25 June

I spoke with Cal for an hour and a half this morning while weeding my brother's garden. At the end of our energized exchange about the ins and outs of a hundred angles, he said to expect the children in the first part of next month. He and Frank, another of his sons, are doing it. I'm numb.

27 June

Yesterday, Zoe and I went shopping and I tried to buy clothes for the children. Impossible. I had a panic attack in the shoe department. I called Cal and he told me not to worry. He's done things far, far more difficult than this and succeeded. He will have backup plans. He may have the children here in less than fourteen days.

29 June

Tangible specifics. Cal says he's shooting for departure between the seventh and tenth of July and has looked into airfares out of Detroit. He mentioned he thinks his son Frank can handle the job alone. I quickly squelched that idea. "No," I asserted, "two people are a necessity and we are willing to pay for it." He acquiesced.

They'll fly into Bangkok and travel overland to Mersing, checking out the border and best route on the way.

On the other hand, he's ninety percent sure the United States Embassy in Kuala Lumpur is obligated to return the children to this country as innocent citizens, if he can get them there and demand asylum. I balked at this because Phillip French told me no way, that as long as Mahmood had custody in Malaysia, they'd have to give the kids back. At United States Embassies in most other countries, my rights as a citizen mother superseded his rights. But not in Malaysia. When I shared this with Cal, he admitted his mistake and said that's what he meant.

I got power of attorney for him using our local lawyer. I spent two hours at the courthouse entertaining the staff while getting true copies of all pertinent documents notarized with fancy gold stamps. I put together boxes for the children.

Cal and I are spending two to three hours on the telephone nearly every day. With each succeeding telephone marathon, I gain more confidence in him. He will bring Mariam and Iskandar home. He is thoroughly committed to not failing. Yet, at the same time, I cannot believe they will be home this month, in the flesh, in my arms.

The more Cal learns, the more seriously he is taking the job. At first he wondered why I hadn't just taken them out. Now he sees that would have been insane. The danger and complications only increase his interest. He wants fifteen hundred dollars for himself beyond expenses to buy shoes for forty orphans in Honduras (!!) and the same for his backup.

When we meet in Cheers Bar at Detroit Metro Airport on 11 July, we will sit and evaluate one another. If I want out, I keep the five thousand dollars in cash I'll be carrying in my purse and pay only for the telephone calls and his ticket from Ft. Lauderdale. Otherwise, we will rent a car, drive to Toledo where he has contacts, spend two nights there, drive back to the airport and he will fly off to Bangkok. Alone. When I questioned him on this, he said he didn't want to endanger his son and he'd be meeting up with someone to assist him in Kuala Lumpur.

When I asked him if this were his first child rescue, he answered by saying that every person, country, rescue is like a snowflake, anyway, and though he's not rescued kids, he's done enough operations to know the key to success is plenty of options.

10 July

I prepare a letter for the children so they won't be frightened of Cal.

Dear Mariam and Iskandar,

This is our friend Cal. He is very good and nice and he is smarter and stronger and tougher than Baba. He will take care of you and bring you to Michigan. Now it is time for us to be together with Grammy and Akasha and Uncle Bobby and Aunt Victoria and all the people in America who love and miss you. You are Americans and Michigan is your home, with me, your Mama. I am very excited and happy that Cal is helping us to be together. I will see you when you get off the airplane. I will have many presents and kisses for you and we will have a big party with a chocolate cake and balloons.

Baba can't get you. He is not the boss any more. The judge says for you to come to America with Cal on a wonderful adventure and live with me, your Mama. The judge knows you want to be with me in America and he says your Baba must let you go. So don't worry about Baba. He won't get you.

I told Cal all about my two beautiful, clever and wonderful children and he loves you. You can love him too, because he is funny and brave and our friend. He is very, very smart and he knows how to get you to America where I am waiting. Please do everything he asks you to do on your big and exciting adventure together and I bet you will like it very much.

Cal is going to buy you new clothes and some toys and books and everything you will need for your adventure. I gave him lots of money, because he is the cleverest man and knows quite a bit about children and everything about getting them to America. I am getting your room ready with so many toys and books and wonderful things for you. We are going to be a family soon—Mariam and Iskandar and Mama. I have a wonderful school for you where everyone is nice and all the teachers and other kids speak English. They are so excited to meet you.

When you get here we will go swimming every day and eat lots of delicious strawberries and cherries. We will go shopping and buy all your favorite foods and then we will have a picnic.

Please be nice to Cal and do what he says and so fast you won't believe it, we will be together and laughing and hugging. I love you to the moon.

Love, Mama

12 July

I have now met Cal and he is leagues from what I, in my fantasy, had imagined. When I first set eyes on him, I was speechless and quite taken back. Hands that shake, beer on the breath, a slur I hadn't noticed on the phone, a ravaged face, bad haircut, and ugly glasses.

I honestly do not know how I feel about him. He drinks far too much, but that's not abnormal in his line of work and I suspect he cuts way back when he's on assignment.

We walked through the airport making small talk, retrieved his luggage and went to the bar. I had coffee and a bran muffin from Starbucks next door and he had a corned beef sandwich and two drafts. Then we rented a car and drove to Toledo.

He knows less than I expected and he's not too concerned. "I'll get it done, but I just wish I knew a little more about that part of the world," he tells me. Words to inspire confidence? He is putting his neck on the line and he is the only person who knows what he can do. He's taking this mission, because he believes in himself and his talents with enough certitude to face enormous risk and possibly, death. Not for money, but for a beautiful woman (his words) and her two deserving children.

Our first stop in Toledo was to find rooms at a hotel. I freshened up and then we went out to a bar owned by a friend of his. I drank coffee and he drank Coca-Cola and coffee. The friend, a recovering alcoholic, joined us. He and Cal are close and his obvious good character gave me a boost of confidence. He knew nothing about me and his curiosity was immense.

At ten, we went to eat and, within minutes of returning to my room, I was asleep. During the night though, I kept waking as questions plagued me: *Will he be able to do this? Can he get the children out? Will the children like him? Will they go with him?*

13 July

At Cheers Bar, Metro Airport, I said good luck to Cal as he departed. He turned back to give me a serious lecture on reassuring my mother and family, "Do not let them worry. Tell them everything is perfectly organized and you are absolutely confident." Yes, sir.

I met his ex-wife this afternoon. I liked her immediately. While Cal was in the bathroom, I asked her if I had the right man or if his heavy drinking, shaky hands and obvious poor health meant I had made a mistake.

"No," she replied quickly, "Cal will get the job done. He gets his act together when he has something to do and he will succeed in bringing back your kids." I grabbed her hand and with tears in my eyes blessed her for the reassurance.

His friends truly love and idolize him. From the conversation, I learned that telephones were ringing all over Toledo when we rolled into town.

I have to believe he will succeed. The children will be here by the end of the month. I'm not going to tell my family about his drinking problem and other shortcomings. I don't want to alarm them.

19 July

He called at 9:16 P.M. "Hi, Patty, Cal here. Everything is going fine. I have the passports in my hands extended to the year 2000. Heading for Mersing now. Talk to you soon. You keep smiling, we will win."

I am numb and detached. Working twelve-to-fourteen-hour days and falling into my bed every night exhausted. Avoiding people. Obsessing. Jumping when the telephone rings. This is my life.

22 July

Azizah telephoned from the Royal Holiday Inn in Singapore. She spent the weekend on Rawa with the children. She saw Mahmood's relationship with Yati first hand and called me to rave and rant about it and Yati's neglect of the kids. "They're so thin. She doesn't feed them. She packed away the beautiful Cinderella dress I gave Mariam. I took back all the gold I gave the children to keep it safe. Tunku and that Yati lock themselves in the bedroom. The children must sleep alone outside. All the people on the island know they are together. That Yati has no respect. I'm not jealous, of course not. She will not listen or do what I say. She forgets she is the servant."

Mariam and Iskandar have a two-week school holiday beginning 14 August. They are flying to Brunei. Mahmood has given his permission for them to go and the tickets are confirmed. Azizah invited me to come and stay in her house with the children for ten days. She said I mustn't tell Mahmood or my lawyers and I must give her my passport to hold.

Cal must be in Mersing by now and he has surely met Khalid and seen my children.

25 July

The telephone rang once, then nothing. It rang again a minute later. I picked it up and said, "Hello, Patty here." There was a connection but no response. I listened for a bit to the void and hung up. My palms were sweating and my stomach was clenched. Mother looked at me wide-eyed.

Who else could it be but Mahmood, having just learned the kids are gone, wondering in his panic whether I am in Malaysia or Michigan? The call felt international. It would have been around 10:00 A.M. in Mersing. Could Sheldon have grabbed them from the schoolyard and Mahmood just found out? Will I get a call in ten or twelve hours from my free threesome over the border? Or at the embassy? Or tomorrow from Bangkok, giving their arrival time in Detroit?

I tell myself that if it had been Cal, he'd have tried again to reach me.

27 July

Cal, please call. No, 'please' is an insufficient word to express my inexpressible desire to hear his voice. Hell, the emotions I don't feel are not emotions at all but fleeting images of fleeing shadows of emotions I push away subconsciously. This mind in my head has warped into a creature I really don't have a handle on any longer. I can laugh and banter and sell and bake and clean and read and sleep and eat. I can verbalize the appropriate responses and theories as Cal's time out of contact with me lengthens. Damn him and damn this stupid mission.

31 July

It's finally Cal on the telephone. My heart pounds at the sound of his voice.

"Patty, I'm back in the States. I couldn't get close enough to the children to grab them. Sorry, not this time, but rest assured I'm determined to help you get them."

I am stunned, devastated. Cal was a six-thousand-dollar mistake. Reeling, I lock myself in my bedroom, too shocked and disappointed to weep.

2 August

I decided to call Azizah to see if I can still come in August and see the children.. Thank God she said yes.

10 October

It is two months since I arrived in Malaysia. I have seen the children a total of two hours. Azizah became frightened when I actually showed up in Brunei and tried to keep me from the children. I spent an hour with them in Brunei in August. They hadn't seen me in almost six months. They ran into my arms, but the traumatizing effects of our separation were obvious and agonizing. I saw them again in September for an hour, then nothing.

Since I arrived, I have been helping my friend Khalid run his resort in Muruing (on the sly; I might be deported if caught) and coping with the dynamics of living in a small Malaysian town. Everyone knows and watches me; the (now) single, white ex-wife of the prince and mother of the only two half-white kids in town. The stress is exhausting.

I resumed my ongoing battle to speed up the appeal process and get a visitation order. I began a marathon of telephone calls and meetings with Princess Zsa Zsa, Johor's Chief Judge, the Prime Minister's staff, women's organizations, a Singaporean private investigator and the United States Embassy. All useless...

The court, after months of promising an imminent date, scheduled a hearing for 20 May, 1997. At the behest of my family, I will be returning to Michigan next week for the fifth time in two and a half years.

12 October

I experienced my first tangible miracle at 1:15 this afternoon. While asking for guidance after last evening's prayer, I heard the words "BE PATIENT." When the call to prayer came today at 1:10 P.M., I nearly ignored it, so depressed and bitter was my state. But I prayed and let my anger out. When I was done I begged Allah to tell me what to do. Again, "BE PATIENT" came through. I was compelled to reach behind me into the drawer where I'd put my untouched angel cards. I held the bag for a minute, thinking to draw one (a waste of time) and sarcastically musing I might draw the patience card. I shuffled them for a minute then drew a card. The card I drew was...PATIENCE. I cried. I was humbled. I tried to accept its simple truth.

I leave tomorrow for Michigan where I must gather support and sustenance for my mission.

chapter eighteen

Crushing Blows

18 May 1997

I spent too many weeks in Michigan trying to finance a rescue. An anonymous article I wrote several months ago for the *New Straits Times* was finally published in February and is meeting with incredible response. I quickly wrote a follow-up article that came out in late April. My editor and I talked on the telephone and she encouraged me to go public. I agreed to let her send a reporter to the May 20 hearing. With my brother Matthew along for support, I flew to Malaysia a few days before the hearing. We are staying at Khalid's resort. To my great joy, I was given one hour with the children.

Iskandar was first as the children raced up the walk and threw themselves into my arms. He showered me with kisses and lovingly made room for Mariam when she clamored to join in our embrace. I introduced Uncle Matthew and they shyly looked him over, said hello and then turned their attention back to me. I noticed Mahmood coming up the path, motioned for Matthew to stay and carried the children to the chalet. We'd hoped that Mahmood might stick around, giving Matthew the opportunity to talk with him and probe a bit.

My darlings and I collapsed in a laughing heap on the bed, ate chocolate-covered dried cherries, looked at photos from Mama's many months in Michigan and talked about school, court and Brunei. Mariam was sad

233

and angry that Iskandar went to Brunei last month and she couldn't go because her passport was "wrecked."(?) She stayed home and said it was awful because Baba was in a bad mood.

I told them I would see the judge in two days and hoped he might tell their Baba to let us be together.

"What if he won't?" Mariam asked.

"Then the judge might be very angry at Baba."

"Baba might go to jail?" asked Mariam with big eyes.

Iskandar jumped in and said, "I wish Baba would go to jail 'cause he's so bad."

I quickly changed the subject, telling them Uncle Matthew was going to court with me and a reporter from the newspaper would be there, too, and wanted to do a story on us.

"Be patient just a little bit longer, my darlings, and know Mama is back in Malaysia working double, extra, super hard so we can be together."

They cheered and Mariam said, "I bet the judge will let me go home with you, because I want to be with you so much."

"No, I do," piped in Iskandar, "I want to be with you most, all the time. The judge will say, me too."

"Of course he will, sweetheart," I choked, praying it would be true.

Thanks to Matthew, who kept Mahmood engaged in a lively conversation about fishing after court, the children and I had an extra fifteen minutes to cuddle and exchange sweet nothings. Parting for them was not easy.

May 20

I'd asked Tuan Haji to start out by confronting the visitation fiasco and to keep today's proceedings from wandering off subject until there was a crystal-clear, impeccably worded, absolutely enforceable and generous visitation order clarified beyond the shadow of a doubt! Tuan Haji laughed, saw the serious desperation in my eyes, wiped the smile off his face and promised to do his best.

Judge Lembut entered the courtroom and the proceedings commenced. Tuan Haji jumped right to the crux and informed the court that his client had only seen her children a total of six hours in the previous fifteen months. The judge was outraged, demanded an explanation from Yusof Rahmat, scoffed at their lame excuses and, at Tuan Haji's prompting, ordered that visitation begin the following day and be for every alternate forty-eight hours.

Yusof had been whispering with Mahmood and, when he had the floor, expressed his clients fear that allowing Noor Faridah to be with the children was not safe, because Tunku Mahmood had been informed by reliable sources that she had engaged professional help to kidnap the children.

Judge Lembut did not seem impressed. He asked for evidence, and pointed out that there were always risks in cases of this nature, but in no way did Tunku Mahmood have the right to deny the children access to their mother.

Mahmood was apoplectic! He was huffing and puffing and I saw him fingering his gun. The thought that he might pull it out and begin firing passed through my nervous mind a few times. But he didn't and we all lived to prepare for the next hearing on the twenty-fourth, when the affidavit on Mariam will be heard. Court was adjourned.

Under Muslim law a child conceived out of wedlock is considered illegitimate and even if paternity is established, custody is automatically granted to the mother. I'd been waiting for this affidavit to be heard and the day would soon arrive. My lawyers, although I had at first objected to separating the children, were sure the aforementioned law would at least give me custody of Mariam.

Nervously, I asked Salwah what she thought about the illegitimacy affidavit's prospects for success. She sounded confident when she replied, "The law is absolute on this subject and there is no reason to suspect that the judge would dare go against the law and clear precedence. You can honestly expect to have legal custody and guardianship of Mariam within days of the hearing."

When I pressed her on whether the judge would have compassion for Iskandar and make an order giving me greater access to him so he could be with his sister, she said, "I don't know."

Tuan Haji, Salwah, the journalist from the *New Straits Times*, the newspaper's photographer, Matthew and I went to the Sheraton for their luncheon buffet. Then Matthew and I caught the four o'clock bus back to Mersing. Six hours later we were asleep in the chalet with visions of visitations dancing in our heads.

21 May

For three and a half hours now, Matthew and I have been sitting on the porch of our chalet, feet up on the railing, watching every car that goes by as we become increasingly more agitated by the children's failure to appear. The Judge clearly stated that visitation would begin today, 21 May, at 4:00 P.M.

The time is 7:30 P.M. and the odds of their showing up at this hour are nil. We have meticulously analyzed every angle, every horror and every nuance of Mahmood's warped psyche. We're both feeling a tad deranged and Matthew is going to force me to eat something now.

22 May

We both had horrible dreams. My most prominent involved two little corpses left on the porch sometime in the night and Matthew's slumber was filled with varying responses to men with guns crashing through our door.

Idiotic questions consume and sicken me...Are we being silly and they'll show up any minute? Has he run off with them? Where have they gone? Should I inform Salwah?

Life is a swirling, sucking eddy of despair with brief moments of false hope. Matthew is going to leave on the twenty-seventh and was really hoping he might get to spend some quality time with his niece and nephew.

Khalid and Matthew drove over to Mahmood's house and no one was there.

Hashim, the reporter, telephoned with a few follow-up questions, was shocked to hear that the children had not shown and said he'd definitely include it in his article, due to come out on the twenty-sixth.

24 May

Judge Lembut slapped Mahmood's hand with a hummingbird feather for denying me the children on the twenty-first, placidly pooh-poohed his excuses and ordered him to deliver them to me at 10:00 A.M. the 25th.

Then he said, "After considering the affidavit on the illegitimacy of Tunku Mariam Nabila, I have determined that everything will stand as is. I am disregarding the affidavit as I see no reason to change things since the custody and guardianship of both children was clearly determined and decided in my ruling of January 1996."

Tuan Haji jumped up. Both he and Salwah frantically pawed through piles of papers and reminded the judge that, in fact, the Mariam affidavit had been brought up during the custody proceeding and he was told to save it for a later hearing. Haji remembered clearly that he had attempted to convince the court that Mariam's illegitimacy was integral to the custody proceedings.

The judge denied that the affidavit had been brought up. "My decision is final," he said. Then he clarified that the next hearing would be 7 August on the financial settlement and adjourned. Tuan Haji took Salwah, Matthew and me out to lunch and then dropped us off at the bus station. We were silent on the bus that took us home. Matthew left for Michigan on the twenty-seventh as planned.

10 June

As I began seeing the children regularly and reestablishing my relationship with them, they gradually opened up and began recounting more and more tales of emotional and physical abuse by their father and his mistress/servant.

1 August

A bad couple of days. The children's behavior has deteriorated even further and I am having trouble handling them—especially Iskandar. I asked him what I should do the next time he misbehaves.

"Cut my penis off," he said nonchalantly.

"What?! Where did you hear that?" I asked, in shock.

"Baba says it all the time," he replied and Mariam piped in, "And so does Yati."

I said what I could to dissipate that whopper. Iskandar admitted he feels bad and angry when his father says this. He's probably terrified Mahmood *will* cut it off.

Half way through another especially stressful day, I watched Iskandar sitting on the porch coloring with a black crayon. I was also on the porch, reading, and Mariam was inside recovering from her brother's most recent outburst, curled up on the bed with dolly and sucking her thumb.

Out of the blue, Iskandar began to sway gently while chanting, "Shit! Fuck! Shit! Fuck! Shit! Fuck!" in a mature, deep voice I had never heard him use before. He was staring hard at nothing and he seemed unaware of his surroundings. I said his name a few times, but he was impenetrable and continued chanting, "Shit! Fuck! Shit! Fuck!" in exactly the same way each time, harsh and intense.

I was awestruck, trembling and confused. I'd never heard him use either word before and I sensed that this small being in front of me was not Iskandar. But who was it? Desperate to get him back, I went over, put my arms around him and carefully tried to get his attention without provoking him, as I feared he might attack me.

He stopped chanting, his eyes came back into focus and he looked at me strangely.

"Do you know what you were just doing?" I asked.

He glanced down, saw the crayon and paper and said, without a hint of guile, "Coloring?"

I can't call anyone over such a minor thing. Oh, but the symbolism is killing me. I want to go home. I want to give it up. I feel as though I am more of a burden to my children than a solace. I am destroying myself and doing nothing to improve their lives or their happiness.

Iskandar hits incredibly hard and Mariam and I have bruises from being slugged, pummeled and the target of his excellent aim. I'm pretty good at deflecting his fists and missiles or grabbing and holding his hands. But, alas and alack, these are temporary measures only.

Mariam and I try to do everything we can to keep him calm.

"I want to hurt people," he said when I suggested hitting trees or pillows instead of us.

"Do you want to hit your Baba?" I asked.

"No, I'm afraid of him," he admitted.

Mariam screams when Iskandar attacks her. The stuff of nightmares. He also makes her hysterical by wrecking or threatening to wreck her toys or her projects. Fighting back is not an option for her.

He is deteriorating at a rapid rate and I'm feeling more and more desperate.

I was in a near rage this afternoon while on the phone with Ivy Josiah, a counselor from Women's Aid. She'd cut me off when I telephoned earlier, because she was in a meeting, and promised to call back. How many times have I heard that...and then nothing. But she did call an hour later, though, and to every suggestion she made, I responded, "Done that, and that and that. Called them and them and them and yes, them too."

Once convinced I was in genuine dire straits, had exhausted every legal, political and media recourse and was no dummy, she asked, "Why don't you escape with them?"

I was shocked but coyly avoided the question for several moments. Then, then because I felt I could trust her, I told her, frankly, what the obstacles were and that I'd leave tomorrow if safe passage were assured.

"Let me talk with Salwah to get an overview of your case and do a bit of networking. Helping you and your children get out seems to be the answer, the only way to help you, your disturbed son and traumatized daughter end this hell and resolve a situation Malaysia's system has screwed up."

Ivy had terrible things to say about the Syariah Court and the uselessness of the government. "Organizations like Women's Aid are barely making a dent," she conceded.

She claimed to have personal access to the Prime Minister and asked if I'd tried his office. "Only a half dozen times," I replied, "all to no avail."

Ivy also said she personally had helped two women and their children get out. I tried to take comfort in her words.

15 August

It is two o'clock on my last Friday in Mersing. This is it. The children and I are leaving. Our Kuala Lumpur bus tickets have been purchased. We leave in forty-six hours. From the bus station, we'll grab a taxi to the airport and meet Ivy, who will stay with us until we're safely through immigration and on the last shuttle flight to Singapore. At 6:05 A.M. on 18 August, we fly to Tokyo, then to Detroit and again on a shuttle flight up to Traverse City.

The children left for school normally this morning and they suspect nothing. If they return on schedule Sunday morning for our visitation period, Khalid, my landlord whom I have come to trust, will drive us to the bus station on the ruse that we are going to Kuala Lumpur for a psychiatric evaluation of Iskandar on Monday. We'll return on the night bus, arriving at 4:00 A.M. Tuesday, and I'll send the children back to Mahmood as usual. Only Khalid knows the truth. And, now that I think about it, Mahmood probably doesn't even know we're going to Kuala Lumpur. How would he?

It's dusk and I said extra prayers for good measure. This attempt to get myself and the children to freedom is so I can get Iskandar some counseling above all else. He is becoming more and more out of control. Mariam and I could carry on a bit longer. Iskandar can not and with him as he is, Mariam and I are in danger.

16 August

I've been laying on my back staring at the ceiling. It is now 4:00 P.M. This is not how I imagined my last day would be. I am almost completely packed and the bag is only half full. I've been planning a bus and airport menu with remaining foodstuffs: prunes, crackers, peanuts, pistachios and cheese. I'll pick up some fruit and drinks at the bus station.

So little is left to do beyond the hardest part: enduring the next fifteen hours until I see their faces and then the four hours until we're on the bus, the six hours to Kuala Lumpur, the hour until we meet Ivy at the airport, the two hours until we go through immigration, the wait for takeoff and the long six hour night in Changi until the Northwest Airlines counter opens.

When will relief course through my veins? In spurts, I reckon, as each hurdle is cleared. The true tears of ecstasy may not flow until the jet out of Singapore rises into the air.

I relieved Khalid by telling him official government people would be meeting me in Kuala Lumpur and facilitating our departure. He's anxious and nervous about all this.

The children's passports are well hidden in my bag and are the only pieces of evidence that we're doing anything more than going to Kuala Lumpur for a couple days.

17 August

We were on the Kuala Lumpur bus getting settled. Mariam was drinking water and Iskandar was asking for a chewable vitamin C. I looked up and there was Mahmood looming over us.

Never had I been so afraid.

"Mariam, Iskandar, let's go. Come with me," Mahmood ordered.

Confused, they got up and followed.

Numb and impotent, I watched them go.

They looked back at me with vacant eyes. By the time I got off the bus they were sitting in the back seat of the car between Mahmood and Yati. His bodyguard, just climbing in, glowered at me.

Stunned, I stood and watched them pull out. Once the car was out of sight, I ran back onto the bus, grabbed our bags and walked into the bus station, saying over and over to myself, "What should I do? What should I do? What should I do?"

Get a taxi back to Khalid's? No, he was the only one I had told. Did he betray me? If so, I'd be helpless there...I rushed back onto the bus and sat down, breathless and determined to go to Kuala Lumpur and fight from there. There was not a reason on earth I should stay in Mersing. Mahmood won't let me see them now. I might be arrested.

The bus had a flat tire, giving me time to phone Ivy, tell her what had happened and change our rendezvous point. Finally, the bus pulled out and drove past Khalid's resort. Suddenly, I'm afraid the police may pull the bus over. I can't help but glance out the back window every few seconds. *Who told Mahmood?*

Halfway to Kuala Lumpur, we stopped for twenty minutes. I got off, drank a Nescafe and smoked two cigarettes.

Miraculously, I maintained my composure by silently chanting, "*I will not cry. I will cope. The children are fine. I will not think about them right now. I will succeed in Kuala Lumpur.*" All this and more I recited quietly as I stared out the window. I fought off the choking, screaming, unthinkable reality I could not allow to come to the surface until I was safe.

One thing I allowed myself to ponder was how Mahmood found out. *Was it Khalid or a tapped phone? If Khalid knew something, surely he'd have told me not to go. Maybe he told someone who told Mahmood. What does Mahmood know?*

I went over all the possibilities and consequences in my mind. *Khalid is the one who has the most to lose if things get hot in Mersing, but he'd have told me not to attempt our escape if he felt compromised, wouldn't he? Unless he wanted or needed me to be caught. Allah, I can't believe that!*

I left no evidence in the chalet of anything amiss. I can still deny everything, go back, demand my visitation, appear in court and carry on.

I wept softly and prayed desperately as the bus drove slowly along the winding, majestic pass through the mountains of old-growth rain forest. I felt close to Allah as I looked straight up at the tops of the trees and visualized him watching. *I beg of You, Allah, please strengthen my fragile thread, stay close and show me this is happening for a reason. There must be more You want me to do here before the children and I may leave.*

I continued on to Kuala Lumpur, met Ivy as prearranged and she took me to the domestic violence shelter where I spent the next three days strategizing with the Malaysian feminist elite.

Damage control was our first priority. We instigated a formal child abuse investigation and attempted to find out exactly how much Mahmood knew about my plans. My public excuse for going to Kuala Lumpur was to have the children evaluated by a social worker (at the shelter) regarding the child abuse. Pretending that I had done nothing wrong, I returned to Mersing for my next scheduled visitation, under advisement from my lawyers. When the children did not show up for the regularly scheduled visitation I filed a police report and my lawyers filed a contempt of court affidavit against Mahmood. A formal police investigation began because Mahmood and the children could not be located.

3 September

This article appeared in the *New Straits Times* today:

Child Abuse Allegations Against Businessman Under Probe

(Mersing) Police are investigating allegations that a prominent businessman, who is also a member of the Johor royal family, had physically and mentally abused his children.

Mersing District Police Chief Deputy Superintendent Hassan Jagar today confirmed that the businessman's former American-born wife, accompanied by a senior district welfare officer, had lodged a police report against him.

The report was lodged at the Mersing central police station on 29 August.

In the report, the businessman's ex-wife alleged that he had physically and mentally abused their six-year-old daughter and five-year-old son. She said she learned about the alleged abuse from the children during their visits.

The woman also claimed that the businessman had violated the terms of a Syariah Court order issued on 20 May, allowing her access to her children every forty-eight hours.

She claimed that her ex-husband had disappeared with the children seventeen days ago after learning that they (the children) were to undergo psychological evaluation by welfare officials in Kuala Lumpur to ascertain if they had indeed been abused. She said that the children had not been attending school since they were taken away by their father.

When she failed to locate her ex-husband and the children, she lodged a police report.

Deputy Superintendent Hassan said the police would work closely with the Welfare Department to investigate the allegations.

4 September

At ten last night, Inspector Gabriel arrived unannounced to begin his investigation. We discussed, in a mix of Malay and English, everything I could tell him about Mahmood and all the possible places he might be hiding the children. Gabriel's never met Mahmood, knew almost nothing about the case and hadn't even had a chance to read the thick file yet.

He asked about the abuse and I told him. "Those poor children," he said a couple times, with feeling.

It was strange. He had a big, ugly guy with him and often turned to him and related a fact or two in Malay. They were formulating strategy. He wanted to go over and over the same stuff and there was no bullshit. Three quarters of the way through, he told me, "They'll be arresting Mahmood and taking the children to the hospital when we find them."

So the article and my new reporter/advocate/friend, Thanum, who calls important people in high places and asks them difficult questions, are having an effect.

I can't believe Gabriel is so nice and honest and professes to really want to help me. He understands my deep distrust and cynicism with the Mersing police and even shares it!

I asked him what he would do if he found Mahmood and he refused to tell him where the children were.

"Hit him," he smiled, "And keep hitting him until he tells us. That's my job."

I told him my mother wanted the Mersing police to give me a twenty-four-hour bodyguard and he assured me that they would be keeping a diligent eye on the chalet and driving by a few times every night.

Mahmood has to be up to something diabolically clever to get himself out of this unscathed. He's been so invulnerable to any consequences, I continue to reject the idea that his gig may finally be up.

Bedtime, and I need to confess that every morning when I wake up, it is with a great sense of relief. I pray with emotion and thank God I am still alive. This only started when I returned to Mersing from Kuala Lumpur and the joy of surviving another night has increased with each passing day. Needless to say, I rarely sleep well.

9 September

I was summoned to the Welfare Office by a counselor named Karuna, a woman I had spoken to in the past about my situation and permitted to spend an hour with my children in her office. They were frightened, confused and hostile until the last few minutes, when they climbed into my lap, hugged me and began to open up...but then it was time to go. They left with their father, afraid even to look back at me.

Yes, Mahmood returned to Mersing two days ago and no, Karuna did not immediately remove the children from his house nor did Inspector Gabriel arrest him. Apparently, Karuna went over, had a nice chat and allowed Mahmood to take the children to the local hospital for a quick physical exam. No evidence of physical abuse, so no reason they can't stay with their father until their psychiatric exam.

"But what about your policies, your strict procedures and your promises to me, Karuna?" I strove to control my anger.

"The children seem okay and what can I do? Tunku Mahmood has custody and he says he has the right to deny you visitation because you...never mind. I don't want to get involved in court issues. Talk to your lawyers," she said, without looking me in the eye.

I've used all the despairing words that come to mind far too many times for them to have meaning any longer. I've felt these feelings that flood through my mind and endured this physical agony and written about days like today too many times to bother yet again. So I lay prostrate on my prayer rug, banging my head on its faded, tear-stained image of a mosque, while in hysterics I begged and bargained with Allah for relief, redemption or a simple reprieve.

As I write these words ALL emotion is drained from my body/mind. I am numb. I am hollow...I am okay and I'm still sane, determined and convinced success is inevitable.

1 November

Although I had all the right people in all the right places doing all the right things, I still only got to see my children for two hours in the past two months because "the judge and my lawyers were too busy to schedule a hearing." Our time together was an hour at the child welfare office and another in front of the psychiatrist doing the abuse evaluation. When the children saw me, they became hysterical and ran out of the room. It took twenty minutes to convince them touching me was alright; more brainwashing by their father and his minions. During these past two months I was praying frantically five times a day and doing the after-midnight "bonus" prayer in my desperation for justice, guilt over the latest rescue debacle and concern for the children.

I want someone to take charge and lead the children and me out of this nightmare. Maybe I can do it alone and in the end I'll probably have to, but I continue to search for professional, affordable help.

Ten weeks, ten angles, ten potential saviors, ten promises of help, ten seemingly sincere, sympathetic individuals outraged by the injustice... and then betrayals, lies and deceit. Nevertheless, if it weren't for those myriad options pursued, these weeks would have been unbearable. The untapped gave me reason to get up in the morning and incentive to endure another day. The not-fully-tapped were hopeful, helpful, productive fodder for my addled mind, my endless hours giving me a sense of control over my destiny and boosting self-esteem. And, despite the letdowns, my confidence in the righteousness of my case has never wavered. But I am weary.

2 November

Joe, Mahmood's driver, who has been friendlier since I loaned him some money a few weeks ago, peeked his head in my window an hour ago and asked what time I was leaving for Melacca tomorrow. Then he dropped a bombshell.

"Mahmood says he's sick and I will call you or come by as soon as I know what he's up to. Don't leave for Melacca until you hear from me. I'll probably be taking him to the clinic in the morning," he said, glowing with the thrill of being devious and the joy of doing good. Then he added that he's quite sure Mahmood will have no trouble getting a letter from a doctor (a necessity) because he intends to get even with me and have the hearing postponed. Shortly after Joe left, I cried pitifully and banged my head my prayer rug at the proscribed prayer time shortly after Joe left.

So be it. I try to remember what Allah taketh away with one hand He gives with the other. Good things may result from this delay. The psychiatric evaluation may be done. My advocates will be angry and more motivated to help. Few, if any, will believe Mahmood is really sick and opinions of him will drop further, I told myself.

I'm resigned to the continual delays but I had my heart and mind focused on seeing the children before this week was out and reconciling my emotions with THAT disappointment is the hardest thing to bear.

3 November

Joe came by last night and told Khalid that Mahmood sent him to every clinic in town after he left here yesterday afternoon to get a medical note, but all the doctors were suspicious and refused to write a note without seeing the patient. Of course most would. But I knew how much power Mahmood had and that he wasn't about to be thwarted.

Noon. Joe called twenty minutes ago to say Mahmood got his medical letter and I immediately telephoned Salwah. She was dismayed, but latched quickly upon the idea of going to court anyway and confronting the judge with the seriousness of the situation.

She went to find Tuan Haji and called me right back to confirm that he definitely thinks we ought to go...so I'm off on the four o'clock bus to Melacca.

Salwah and Tuan Haji were planning on driving down with Ivy and Laura, an intern from Minnesota, and they still want to come. However, Ivy will call the press and others who were planning to be in the courtroom and tell them not to bother this time.

5 November

The bus to Melacca had two other passengers and no shock absorbers. It delivered me slightly bruised, but unscathed. I found a reasonably palatable Chinese hotel, tried to sleep, got dressed in a Malay dress Ivy had given me and a fancy velvet scarf Khalid's sister had lent me and caught a taxi to the courthouse.

When I arrived there, Tuan Haji and Salwah were sitting on a bench in the lobby. Ivy and Laura showed up and we talked about nothing and everything for twenty minutes, then went upstairs to the courtroom.

Tuan Haji put on his big black robe while Salwah bustled around, laying out notebooks and such, and soon all was ready for a normal day in court. Salwah had informed Mahmood's lawyer we were coming. He should have been there, but he wasn't.

At 10:15 the judge's assistant called Tuan Haji into Chambers. Salwah stood up to go with him but was told the judge wanted only Tuan Haji. When they were gone she said, "Discrimination starts here!" It was said as a joke but she was really disappointed. She should have been in the judge's chambers because she did 95 percent of the work on the case.

The four of us discussed gender issues and Syariah law. Both Ivy and Salwah related cases of suffering and injustice that were unthinkable. Ivy was livid about the situation here, but she calmly talked about ways to rectify the system and inform the public. After twenty minutes, the assistant came for Salwah and, ten minutes later, she and Tuan both returned.

"The judge," Tuan Haji told us, "was shocked and furious (as usual) by Mahmood's continued contempt for the court, by Yusof Rahmat's absence and by the suspicious nature of the doctor's letter." (They did not tell him what Joe had revealed to me, but apparently the letter looked like a forgery.) He continued, "A summons for both Mahmood and Yusof Rahmat to appear in court at 2:30 P.M. on 18 November will be issued. The summons will clearly state that, unless Tunku Mahmood has a damn good reason why Noor Faridah is being denied visitation, he will be thrown in jail." Tuan Haji permitted himself a smile as he lingered over the word "jail."

When Salwah received the copy of Mahmood's medical reprieve from his attorney, she also received a note from him saying he was completely booked until next March! This did not please the judge, who noted that Yusof was scheduled to appear in his courtroom on another case the morning of the eighteenth. He joked that he would grab and force him to stick around for the afternoon session.

Tuan Haji and Salwah were pleased with what had transpired. The judge saw no reason to give a visitation order in the meantime, because he assumed Mahmood would ignore it! Reality may have finally sunk in.

The eighteenth, we all agreed, would be a climax in the case. Ivy began to strategize about filling the courtroom with spectators, doing a fax appeal and contacting VIPs and the media to be there.

As I read the paper that evening I saw an article reporting that someone telephoned the United States Embassy threatening to kill four Americans in the country. Anti-American sentiment among the extremists, some of whom Mahmood knows, is continuing to build. For a few moments I felt especially vulnerable being well-known. If the sentiment for revenge is being promoted among the radical minority, they could strike. Ah, well, just one more thing to worry about.

17 November

Mahmood told Joe, and Joe told me, that after Mahmood wins tomorrow, he's going to sue me for slander for two million dollars. When he wins that, too, and I can't pay, he'll have me deported! He may have stepped over the edge and become truly insane now.

I'm leaving in four hours for Melacca and I can't sit still or think straight or find anything to focus on except the clock.

18 November

I telephoned Salwah at 8:00 A.M. from my hotel in Melacca but she won't be in the office for another two hours. Dr. Kasmini's finished psychiatric evaluations of the children was going to be delivered to her yesterday evening and I can't wait until I see her this afternoon to hear what it says.

She returned my call at eleven. I wailed and gasped for air. I feel so very, very alone...

The report states no evidence of abuse. According to the psychiatrist, Mahmood is an excellent father. Mariam and Iskandar are normal and well-adjusted. They repeatedly said to Dr. Kasmini that they wanted to stay with their father and were afraid their mother would take them to America. The only thing she wrote that was true is that they should spend time with me.

I walked the streets for twenty minutes, fighting hysterics. Everywhere I turned, I saw mothers and their children living normal lives. Choked up, I rushed back to my hotel room to let my frustration out.

I know I must set the evaluation aside. So be it. I need to look forward. There are going to be a dozen or more supporters and reporters and television cameras in the courtroom and I need to be calm and composed. At the very least, the judge will rule visitation must resume. I will not expect more, lest I be disappointed and make a scene.

How much of the children's and my future will be decided today? How much good can be accomplished for them? Visitation is but a panacea, albeit a necessary one. The only true, indisputable and ever present good I can achieve for them is to get us home to the United States. This simple truth is always, always with me and lives in every breath I take and in every word I write, speak, pray and silently scream in despair.

When I arrived at the courthouse at two, I saw Tuan Haji and his wife standing on the verandah and went straight to them. Things became hectic when Salwah showed up to ask me questions and some women came over to say hello. We all went into the courtroom, Mahmood and Yusof Rahmat came in and before Tuan Haji even had a chance to zip up his funky robe, we were asked to rise. The judge entered and the proceedings began.

Tuan Haji started with a speech about Mahmood's contempt of court in strong language and stressed, stressed and stressed again that, "Tunku Mahmood must be punished for his litany of sins and blatant disregard for the esteemed Court and Your Honor." My grasp of courtroom Malay has become excellent so I rarely had to ask Salwah for a translation.

Yusof Rahmat stood up in his ill-fitting black sports coat and brown trousers and spouted tired justifications: "Noor Faridah didn't have the right to take the children to Kuala Lumpur. Tunku Mahmood feared she was trying to run away with them."

Tuan Haji brought out that, in fact, Mahmood was the one to run away with the children and Noor Faridah did have the right to take them on a short trips and, "Don't forget, Your Honor, he's in contempt of court and his excuses are lame and he needs to have the book thrown at him and didn't you say you would throw him in jail?"

The judge ignored Tuan Haji, cut in regularly, asked questions, criticized Mahmood's naughtiness and said visitation must be restarted, bad boy Tunku, welfare of the children, compromise, blah, blah, blah.

Tuan Haji continued to harp on Mahmood's criminal disregard for the law and the exemplary behavior of his client, the long-suffering Noor Faridah, to no avail.

The Judge didn't want to hear it. He was anxious to make a ruling and be done with us. I was feeling panicky and whispered to Salwah that two days with me/two days with Mahmood was not good for the children and please tell Tuan Haji not to put the children and me through that again...

But before she could get his attention, Tuan Haji brought up the forty-eight days of visitation I lost over the last three months and the judge latched onto that as the way to punish Mahmood and ruled Noor Faridah would get four days to Tunku Mahmood's two until the forty-eight days were used up.

Then they got into passports and the debate went around and around. Tuan Haji was determined that his client should not have to give up hers because she had a clear record and Tunku Mahmood was the one whose passport should be held. But the Judge said both. I whispered to Salwah that the children's passports were really the only ones they needed to hold, so she whispered this to Tuan Haji. He told the judge and the judge said "All four passports," the end. And it was over.

I was stunned. We had to move out of the courtroom quickly. Other lawyers were filing in and the next case was starting. Clenching my jaw, I took shallow breaths to control hysteria. I half-stumbled out of the court-room physically supported by others. The doors pushed open. I walked through blinding flashbulbs, video cameras in my face and Mahmood's bulk, two feet in front of me, sucking all the air out of the hallway. I rushed to a corner, followed by a half dozen women.

"How do you feel? What do you think of the ruling? Isn't it wonderful you get all that time with your children?" they asked, smiling and concerned.

My words came out jumbled. I said something about being disgusted, about the same old scenario and Mahmood getting away with his crimes and, and, and.... Then the cooing started and there were arms around me

and words meant to console, "But at least you got to be with your children..." and I was off again on the insanity of my being happy because I
get to see my kids again! Oh, I was in a state for five, maybe ten minutes
and then I looked around me at all these sympathetic female faces.

I calmed down, went through the niceties, said the right things, got
through the next ten minutes, then gracefully escaped to find Salwah and
Tuan Haji to ask a couple of pressing questions.

"I have only had three weeks left on my visa. I need to make a Singapore
run before surrendering my passport." Tuan Haji assured me I could do it
and get back without causing any problems.

Then I asked the question consuming me. "And when exactly is visitation going to resume?" I inquired.

"We aren't sure," Tuan Haji admitted. And I began to cry.

21 November

We went to the court again. Somehow my courage returned. This time
I had with me about twenty influential feminist supporters and the press.
The judge gave Mahmood a strong rebuke and ordered that he "make up"
the visitation I had lost by giving me four days with the children to his two,
starting immediately. He neglected to address the affidavit on child support
(legally I am not allowed to work for money in Malaysia and I am fast
approaching serious penury), putting it and the affidavit on marital assets
off until January. He did, however, hold to his original order of confiscating
everybody's passports in order to placate Mahmood's ranting about my
abducting the children.

25 November

I was waiting anxiously for the 5 January court hearing to address
child support and the distribution of marital assets when I learned that for
the first time in the history of Syariah Court in Malaysia the registrar "forgot" to send the affidavits to Mahmood's lawyer, whose office was just a
block away and who was in the Registrar's Office nearly every day. Yet
another court date was scheduled for 19 March. When Tuan Haji learned
of this, he cornered the judge in his chambers and, miraculously, the hearing was reset and confirmed once again for 5 January. Though slightly

buoyed by Tuan Haji's small success, I was still disheartened that the change in dates occurred in the first place. I felt certain Mahmood was behind it. Because legally I couldn't work in Malaysia except surreptitiously, I had little money left. Since threats weren't working, I guess he hoped to starve me out so I would have to go back to the United States.

I continued to pray daily, kneeling enshrouded on my prayer mat, seeking a savior to manifest and liberate us. I fought tears of fury, my sense of hopelessness—no justice, little money, no knight on a white horse and little strength left. Yet I knew for the children's sake I had to go on. I somehow had to make it to the next hearing in January.

chapter nineteen

One Step Forward, Two Steps Back

1 December 1997

I waited for the children three days beyond confirmation of my passport's arrival at the courthouse. Salwah sent a few demanding faxes to Yusof Rahmat and the judge. Between 8:00 A.M. and 5:00 P.M. on the twenty-fourth, twenty-fifth and twenty-sixth of November, I hated myself for giving Mahmood what he wanted—my suffering. A simple trip to the bathroom was fraught with trepidation that the children might show up at that moment, not see me and leave.

Then, out of the blue, at 2:00 P.M. on 27 November, after 102 days apart, Iskandar was running pell-mell into my arms!

"Mama. It's you! Do we get to stay? I miss you so much," he chattered, as we held each other tightly, drunk in the joy of mother and child.

Mariam, on the other hand, had a strong compulsion to show me how angry she was about our separation. She clung to Yati and refused to get out of the van or look at me. I spent twenty minutes politely and unsuccessfully trying to extricate Mariam, kicking and screaming, from Yati's neck. Yati was no help. I tried to be gentle, but quickly came to the realization Mariam (and Yati) needed a bit of firmness. My daughter was testing me and I rose to the occasion, pulled Mariam off Yati, ignored my daughter's attempts to bruise and draw blood from me and marched to the chalet with a small she-devil in my arms.

By the time we reached the porch, Mariam was quiet, though still seething. When I put her on the bed inside, she moved to the far corner, stuck her thumb in her mouth and refused to look at or communicate with me. I was in a near panic that, for the next four days, she would be silent and withdrawn. Feeling helpless, I let her sit there and began showing Iskandar all the new things in the chalet. Five minutes later she was in my lap and ALL was forgotten.

Day two was quiet time. After the first day, Mariam stopped calling Yati Ibu (mother). I chastised her firmly and left no doubt in her mind that I was their one and only mother. Mariam, Iskandar and I spent day three in town. We lunched at Kentucky Fried Chicken, a special treat because they were behaving so well, and Iskandar noted that his Baba had brought them to KFC after he took them off the bus. He also noted that he was very scared at the time thinking that Mahmood had done something to me and was about to do something to them. Mariam concurred and added that Yati told her crazy and mean stuff about me that really confused and frightened her.

We lingered in the library while waiting for the highlight of our day, watching *George of the Jungle* in Mersing's beat-up old cinema with a cement wall for a screen, terrible acoustics and two ten-minute snafus. Nevertheless, we loved every fabulous, funny minute.

Mariam was in a bad mood on day four and decided she was going to take all her stuff from Baba's house back to Baba's house. She went around the chalet meticulously gathering her possessions into her little suitcase.

"Yati hates you and I hate you too and this is my bouncy ball," she said.

"Why do you hate me?" I asked.

"Because you're, you're...because you're skinny!" she finally said. "And this stupid house doesn't have a television or a video and it's only one room and we have to go outside for the bathroom and the toys are stupid and boring and you don't have a car and I'm taking my Bikini Barbie." She glared.

Iskandar sat in my lap listening. Only sometimes he defended me, but never did he agree with her. He stated firmly, "I'm leaving all my stuff in Mama's house."

I got her back in a good mood by filling Khalid's washtub with water and letting her splash around while Iskandar read with me and patiently waited for his turn in the tub.

The next morning, our last morning, Iskandar had his first tantrum. He
hit me a several times, threw things and yelled, "I hate you. I want to kill
you." Finally I calmed him down.

We walked the entire one-mile length of the street market and had a
blast. We bought second hand clothes, a big washtub of our own and gorged
on fresh warm tofu in syrup, sugar cane juice and other Malay junk foods.
The children were determined to christen the tub with long, happy baths
when we got home.

When Yati and Joe came at two o'clock on the first of December to pick
them up, the kids ran into her arms and excitedly told her about their time
with Mama—a good sign. I realized four days was a long time to be away
from their surrogate and felt no resentment.

4 December

My babies are back with me. A plague of mosquitoes have arrived with
the monsoon rains. They seem worse this year... Iskandar is a magnet and
endures five bites for every one Mariam or I get. They also seem to irritate
him more poor boy, and his legs are already scarred from past infections.
He's a compulsive scratcher and scab-picker and it's worse now that he's
stopped biting his nails. And Mariam, though she still sucks her thumb, has
given up her dolly. I wonder and worry about what Mahmood did to break
them of the habits.

8 December

Dear Mom,

We arrived home at noon today and the children left two hours later.
Our three nights away was a happy interlude and I'm glad I took the risk.

Mariam and Iskandar were emotional wrecks until the bus pulled out
of Mersing. They anxiously watched every car, checked every face and
turned to me for constant reassuring. They became panicky when I
wanted to go inside and buy a bottle of water for the trip.

"NO, don't go, Mama," they implored frantically and held me down.

"We can go together," I suggested. That was also quickly rejected. They
promised me they wouldn't be thirsty, so I dropped it and stayed with them
on the bus. I admit I was no better, but hid my nervousness from them. I'd

hardly slept the night before. Logically, I was sure Mahmood wouldn't disturb us, but my subconscious had a mind of it's own.

Once the bus was in motion and on the road out of town, I cried a few tears of relief and we all loosened up. We talked openly about our feelings and it was a therapeutic milestone.

Iskandar took the opportunity to complain about his father. "I hate my Baba so much. I never want to go to his house again. We can hide or lock the door when Joe and Yati come. Why is Baba so bad? When he yells at me, I run and hide under the table where he can't get me and I won't come out for the whole day. One time he hit me one hundred times and I wanted to poke him in the eye with a sharp stick and kill him."

Later, while I was making dinner, I heard crying. Mariam was wailing and Iskandar was chanting, "Crybaby, crybaby. Mariam is a stupid crybaby." He refused to stop until she stopped and she refused to stop until he stopped. I managed to make light of it and got them laughing. Now I must seal this and go to sleep.

Love, Patty

11 December

Dear Grammy,

How are you? I miss you and I know you miss me so much. I love you. I am seven years old now and Iskandar is almost six.

Today we made the little Christmas tree that you sent Mama last year so pretty. We used shells and ribbons for decorations and we found many starfish for the top.

The rain was really hard this morning and made rivers everywhere. We sat in the restaurant and played until it stopped. We helped Mama make breakfast for two people from England and I helped cook the eggs. Then we made four puppets—two girls with cats and a snowman and a teddy bear with a rabbit.

Last night a family of jungle pigs came to the rubbish bin at the back door of the kitchen while we were eating. There were seven babies and they were so ugly and cute. Khalid yelled at her and chased them away. They eat his plants and make big holes in the yard and he really hates them. Iskandar and I were excited and scared because they were so close and the mother had little tusks.

Yesterday we went to the library and got six books—two Dr. Seuss, two Christmas books, one of scary poems and a learning book. We went to the cinema and saw *Starship Troopers*. It was really bloody and had lots of giant mosquitoes and the people wanted to find the giant brain. Mama wanted us to leave, but Iskandar said no way!

We are so happy with Mama and Khalid and the best would be for Yati to live here, too. Merry Christmas and I want Barbie dolls and a magic wand from Santa. Kisses and hearts, Mariam

P.S. Iskandar wants Spiderman toys, a sword, a slingshot and remote control cars from Santa. But he is naughty so he better watch out!

20 December

Mother dear,

I worry that something horrible just might happen and my list of fears could fill a few pages. History is on Mahmood's side and I can't shake this angst.

For example, I'm suffering Christmas guilt, indecision, remorse and a desire for self-flagellation. Guilt because I dare not give the children a proper, manic, over-stimulating fulfillment of all their Christmas fantasies, lest it backfire and put me in jail for celebrating the birthday of a minor prophet. Mahmood has threatened to try and get Mersing's medieval religious police to arrest me.

Indecision because I don't know how much of a holiday to attempt. Remorse because I didn't shop weeks ago when I had the time, but didn't know if I'd have the kids. Finally, self-flagellation because I can't think of anything creative, wonderful and cheap with which to surprise them. They know every toy in Mersing and I feel like a fool for obsessing over this. Your box of goodies did arrive intact and is hidden away, so at the very least we'll have Santa Grammy!

Love, Patty

22 December

Since we won't be together on Christmas, I've decided to have Santa come tomorrow. I was able to put them down to sleep earlier than usual tonight, a bonus.

As soon as the children were asleep, I set to work. I put up strings of lights, arranged their thirty small plastic animals around the tree, drank the water and ate the candy cane cookies (we'd made earlier) that they'd set out for Santa.

I had flutes, fruits, sticker books, puzzles, Christmas crackers, rubber balls, more dominoes, a doctor set, chocolates, books, other odds and ends and Grammy's gifts. I spent a long time fiddling with the arrangement, went to bed and couldn't sleep. I felt so sure they'd be disappointed.

23 December

At seven, I got up, plugged in the lights, lit candles and lay back down pretending to be asleep. A short time later, Iskandar sat up, looked over at THE spot and quickly woke his sister. They rushed over, sat down by the animals, were speechless for a few moments, then said, "Mama, wake up! Santa came and oh, wow, look at this and this and this. He has been watching us and he knew just what we wanted, but he didn't get us any of the junky, expensive stuff and that's okay. Oh, Mama, this is wonderful. Oh, Santa went to Michigan and got us T-shirts from Uncle Bobby's shop and he gave us fruit just like you got when you were little."

Tears of joy and relief streamed down my cheeks.

1 January 1998

Mother dear,

I opened my *New Straits Times* this morning and there I was looking back at me, on the front page, in full color. The photo accompanied a small headline, Woman Advance Against the Odds…on page six, section two.

To quote, "One case of injustice highlighted this past year was that of Patricia Noor Faridah, who sought and lost custody of her two children to her husband, a member of royalty."

"Patricia's husband was in contempt of court when he did not allow her to visit her children for over a year. Despite her many attempts at seeking redress from the court, it only gave repeated warnings to her husband. After undergoing so much hardship, the court finally decided to give her more access to her children in November. But one wonders if this mother should have suffered at all?"

"This is but one of hundreds of cases where mothers are subject to unfair treatment when they present their cases to the Syariah Courts…"

My few paragraphs are surrounded by a long article about the Malaysian system and other areas where women have and have not advanced. Accompanying the article is another big picture of me.

Today is the first day of Ramadhan and I'm fasting. This is my fourth year fasting in this purgatory of a life.

Iskandar's behavior has become exasperating at times and he has come very close to crossing the line more than once...but he doesn't do it! He's discovered and is respecting the boundaries. Mariam and I still get hit, things are thrown, ugly words are spat, but recovery is quicker and there are promising signs.

Khalid took us to a swimming beach one afternoon, we went to the library twice, did a bit of baking, caring for those staying at Khalid's guesthouse and visiting in our neighborhood.

I need to get to Melacca on the fourth for court the next day. The fifth is the first day of the children's new school year and they should attend, though I am sorely tempted to take them to Melacca with me. Court falls during my visitation time but because of school, Mahmood can leave them with Yati and Joe while he and I are in court. I still turn to anxious jelly when I have to deal even indirectly with Mahmood. The children also get really worked up. I suspect they intuitively and helplessly seek to protect me from him.

4 January

I said goodbye to two unhappy children at two o'clock and left Mersing two hours later. The bus was freezing and the Malay music was deafening, but I did get my newspapers read. At 7:18, I broke my fast with a hundred other travelers at a rest stop for buses.

I arrived in Melacca and I'm staying at the Straits Heritage Lodge, a small, tasteful establishment with ten rooms opening up to a beautiful stone tiled lobby. My room has a large, proper bed, a telephone, television, small refrigerator, coffee and tea set up, air conditioning, hot water in my own loo and even toilet paper! The last place I stayed had none of these amenities and I am grateful for the small luxuries.

I'm sitting on my bed now eating Nasi Lemak, rice cooked in coconut milk with a dried anchovy chili sauce, half a boiled egg and two slices of cucumber washed down with a carton of milk. Not what I wanted, but what I found after a ten minute walk once I checked in. This neighborhood is full of bars, snooker halls, Karaoke clubs and upscale restaurants out of my league and interest.

There is no arrow pointing toward Mecca in this room and I can't ask, because the front desk is closed. This provides a fair excuse to skip final prayers and go to sleep. I have asked for a wake-up call for prayers and food at 5:00 A.M. My appointment with courtroom destiny is at 10:00.

5 January

At 8:30 Salwah phoned to say the hearing's been rescheduled for tomorrow. We talked about strategy, fasting and the kids for a while and said goodbye.

6 January

I came at nine because Salwah and Tuan Haji are always early, but they are not here yet. This room is so cold, the sweat on my palms is steaming. I am functional but pale, weak and anxious. I am alone now in the court-room. It is nine-thirty. Mahmood is downstairs gesticulating to his lawyer.

At 10:30, they still haven't shown. No one's bothered to tell me what's going on and I'm too anxious to ask. I'm sitting on a bench outside the courtroom, because Mahmood, Haji Ibrahim and Yusof Rahmat are inside and without my buffers (Salwah and Tuan Haji) I can't breathe and am in danger of hypothermia. Every two minutes I jump up to peek over the promenade, hoping to see them pull in.

Finally, at 10:45, Tuan Haji and Salwah arrived. They got caught in a bad traffic jam leaving Kuala Lumpur. I ran down to the car and helped them carry three huge cases full of files, two briefcases and other paraphernalia. When I commented on the materials amassed, Salwah said they were but a small percentage of what my case has generated.

We went inside, Tuan Haji put on his robe and the judge was informed he could start.

Tuan Haji began the proceedings by noting that because there was no interpreter and two relevant cases in Kuala Lumpur were awaiting deci-sions, he wanted to postpone the Distribution of Marital Assets affidavit. Agreed. ("For the best," Salwah whispered. "We must delay until we can get more evidence of his assets.")

Yusof Rahmat happily told the court, "I've never received a formal copy of the affidavit from the court registrar." So, it definitely has to be postponed.

Tuan Haji said, "Fine, but we must get an interim order for maintenance, as my client has received nothing and is broke!"

The judge nodded, "Okay, but only for food, since she has to have shelter anyway."

Things deteriorated from there. Yusof Rahmat, who was being pushed by a furious Mahmood, began a short speech about my wealth.

"If she is so broke, then how is it she can afford the best lawyers? And if she is so broke, maybe she should just go home, give up the case and visit the children a few weeks every year," he said.

At this juncture, Tuan Haji became very irate and eloquent. He made a long, impassioned plea, quoting Syariah Law, the Prophet Mohamed's teachings and the deeper meaning of fasting month to express his disgust with their premise that I should give up my case over money. "All of it, all of it, is the father's responsibility," he stated again and again.

The judge told the two sides to work something out and he left the room for a half-hour.

Mahmood and Yusof Rahmat went to a side room and then Mahmood came out and Tuan Haji went in and five minutes later he came out and told me their bottom line was that Mahmood would send food for the kids, but they refused to discuss school transport.

The judge returned and a long, petty argument commenced about how much taxis would cost Noor Faridah and in May Noor Faridah said she'd cover transport and if it was a burden she should just give up visitation! The judge cut in and chastised both sides for being unable to compromise and come to an agreement. "Therefore," he ruled, "no interim order can be made and everything will be put off until the next hearing on 19 March. Court is dismissed."

Stunned, we all sat there for a couple minutes. Finally I broke the silence. "Salwah, tell Tuan Haji to tell Yusof Rahmat to tell Mahmood I'll take the kids back at two o'clock on the eighth." Down the line went the message and back to me in the same way came his reply—"Okay." The lawyers began shuffling papers and Mahmood went back to Haji Ibrahim. They sat a minute, stood up as if on cue and left. I looked at my watch. It was 12:30. There was supposed to be three days of court. Things were going to be decided once and for all this time. This ninety-minute debacle was hardly what I'd waited so long for. I'd been teary-eyed through most of the proceedings and was still trying to maintain my composure as I quietly discussed my anger and cynicism with Salwah. Tuan Haji returned from the judge's chambers where he'd been chatting and sat down, in no hurry to leave. Getting a grip on my emotions, I asked them some hard questions, trying to get something, anything concrete from them about the appeal, Mariam's affidavit, prospects for a decent, enforceable financial settlement and other matters. All their answers were non-answers, evasive rhetoric and bullshit. Never had I been more disillusioned.

We left and they dropped me off so I could buy some groceries for the kids. I wandered around in a daze before going back to the hotel.

Changing out of Malay dress, I freed my sweat-soaked hair from the scarf. As the day turned into night I tried to make some plans, but my head ached and my brain was like jelly. Finally, exhausted, I fell asleep still wearing my clothes. I slept fitfully, images of unfair court proceedings and escaping the country with my children flitting through my mind.

chapter twenty

Countdown

9 January 1998

Early in the morning I telephoned my mother to tell her what had transpired in court. "We will never get justice here. Somehow, I have to get the children away," I said soberly, "and somehow, I will find a way." My mother said she'd never heard me so determined.

As soon as I hung up I looked up the name of the Malaysian reporter for *Asiaweek Magazine* who had expressed interest in my story. I intended to convince him we were worthy of a story. I telephoned Kuala Lumpur information for Rajen Davidison's number.

I tried again and again but I got no answer. While in Melacca, I tried again and a man picked up the telephone.

"Is this Rajen Davidison?" I asked.

"Who are you? How did you get this number? What do you want?" he asked in a perturbed voice. "I know no one by the name Rajen Davidison. The number you've called is unlisted."

Why he didn't just say, *Sorry, wrong number*, and hang up was the first miracle.

"What do you want?" he asked again. He sounded angry.

I took a deep breath and poured out my story. "I'm the American mother of two children whose father is Johor royalty. He's tried to have me banished from here and threatened to have me executed. Though I have fought hard and have the best lawyers, the courts have supported him." I told him of my long struggle to be with my children, my disappointments with the local media coverage and my theory that international exposure could put pressure on the Malaysian powers that be to expedite justice. I was rambling and couldn't seem to stop. There was something about this man's strong, self-confident voice and on-the-spot comments that drove me to keep talking until I'd convinced him to offer help...I feared if I stopped speaking before he was sold on my merits, he'd say "Sorry, can't help you," and hang up.

"I know no one by the name of Rajen Davidison and the number you called is unlisted," he repeated a little more calmly then before. "My name is Arvin Shivaya. I am a freelance writer of investigative crime and court articles. I also do social work. Perhaps," he said slowly, "I can help you. But tell me, what do you *really* want?"

Slowly, nervously, I moved from the innocuous to the profound, "Ah, well, truthfully, my dream is to get the children to the United States. They have suffered so much and so have I and I don't know if we'll ever get justice in Malaysia. Their father would probably have me killed if I ever did get custody and I have a wonderful family in America, and, and..." I was off again on a desperate monologue of the 10,000 reasons he should help us get out. He encouraged me to keep talking and I did, until suddenly I shut up because he'd said something that stopped me in my tracks.

"I have a close friend," he said again, sure he had my full attention, "who lives in Padang Besar, on the Thai border, and he's a smuggler. I went back and forth with him a few times without my passport while working on a story last summer. The border is very loose and he travels to and fro freely. He has a big heart and I think it would be a small matter and not so expensive for him to take a white woman and two children across."

He went on, "I believe your making contact with me was a manifestation of the Divine. I am a devout Hindu and have devoted my life to helping others. God has brought people to me in the past, and now you are here. I know it is my destiny to help you."

We were both uncomfortable talking about my problem on an open phone line and had just decided we needed to get together when someone knocked on his door. "I can't talk any longer," he said. "Call me at eight tomorrow morning."

I made the call at 8:00, but he had someone with him and couldn't talk. I waited all day to hear back from him but no avail. Before I went to bed, I prayed that Arvin Shivaya would really be the savior I so desperately needed.

11 January

I sat by the telephone staring at my watch at 7:45 A.M. I had decided in the middle of my sleepless night that if Arvin answered, still committed, I'd go to Kuala Lumpur during my next break from the kids. I dialed his telephone number.

"Good morning, Patricia," he answered cheerfully, "I pray you slept well and are not worried too much. I promised I would help you and here I am, at your service. What do you say?"

"We need to meet in person as soon as possible. I've been deceived too many times and must see you in the flesh before I can think straight about this thing. This may be the miracle I so desperately need, but I have to be sure. Can you meet me at the bus terminal in Kuala Lumpur at five-thirty in the morning on the thirteenth?" I was talking much too fast.

"Sure, no problem. But, better to meet in the Indian restaurant across from the terminal. Then you can sit comfortably while you wait and there will be much less people. Okay, then, see you at five-thirty."

He must have noted my anxiety because he added, "Telephone me from a call box a couple of times in the interim just to say hi and relieve your worries! Remember, God is with us, my dear."

When I prayed later, I asked Allah to grant all necessary help and guidance to get me through tomorrow and beyond.

I told Khalid I was doing an interview while in Kuala Lumpur so he wouldn't get suspicious. He's going to drive me to the bus station tomorrow and on the way I'll tell him I'm meeting an undercover investigative reporter who I want to look into the biased rulings Mahmood and his lawyer obtained from the Melacca. That should satisfy and entertain Khalid's big mouth and if it gets to Mahmood, he'll think, *Ha ha, let her try!*

12 January

I am on the bus. It's 9:50 P.M. So far, there is only one other passenger. I keep my eyes down and try not to show how nervous I am. Two other passengers come on board. I cast a quick glance at them—a man and a woman

immersed in conversation. They pay no attention to me and I relax a little.
Soon we're off.

13 January

It's a few minutes before 5:00 A.M. and I'm sitting in the only open
restaurant across the street from the Kuala Lumpur bus terminal. It's
Muslim and Arvin said Indian, but I feel confident he'll find me. I'm drinking a large mug of strong coffee and eating a Malay-style pancake with sugar.
I am the only woman in this restaurant, half full of men hanging around,
drinking tea and smoking cigarettes while they wait to begin their fast.

There are two transvestites in here looking very pretty. They're getting
more stares than I am, especially just now, when they saunter out with
bulging Adam's apples, wearing tight jeans, stuffed bras, sexy tops and
heavy makeup.

I breathe a sigh of relief. I don't look too much out of place here, I tell
myself. They get a lot of single, white women backpackers who are
expected to be independent, oblivious and above local customs.
Notwithstanding my lack of a backpack, I try to feel anonymous and comfortable.

I have the children's American passports, birth certificates and a nega-
tive of myself to use if we decide I should get another passport. If IT'S going
to happen, I'll need a new passport at some point.

Later. It is now 5:20 P.M. I've been wandering around Kuala Lumpur
since I left the American Embassy at 11:30 A.M. I have four more hours to
waste before the bus takes me home. Unfortunately, there wasn't an earlier
direct bus and, if I had gone the roundabout way, I'd have arrived in
Mersing well after dark with no transport home. This bus will drop me off
at the end of the lane leading to Khalid's resort, a two-minute walk.

I'm half-dead with exhaustion, but now I'm just five minutes from the
main bus terminal enjoying solitude and a cup of thick joe in a Lebanese
restaurant. I finally have time to go over the day's events in my mind.

Arvin, a dark-haired man, had arrived at the restaurant at 5:40 A.M. I
was pleasantly surprised to see that he was handsome with big soft eyes,
thick curly hair and strong hands. He seemed older on the telephone. We
moved to a corner table and talked about generalities for half an hour to get
comfortable with one another.

After a while, our conversation turned toward the serious. Since there seems no rhyme or reason why we connected, we are both convinced that our contact is a miracle orchestrated by God. His full name is nothing like Rajen Davidson and he's never written for *Asiaweek*. He does however have that friend who smuggles people and things across the Thai border. After recently accompanying his friend on such a journey without his passport, Arvin knew for sure it was possible. Mind blowing, I thought.

Nevertheless, I was exceedingly cautious while we talked and listened with rapt attention, but not once did he say anything that I found even remotely suspicious.

I was staying fairly well-detached, though my mind, when I allowed it to wander, pondered… Pondered if IT could be done as soon as the last week of this month when the children have no school (Chinese New Year/Hari Raya holidays) and I could easily say I was taking them to visit friends in Melacca.

I tried hard to keep my wits about me. Memories of past knights/scoundrels wanting to rescue/rape/swindle the damsel in distress have not dimmed. I was really, really rabid to get to know Arvin and discover whether he's more than just another mistake, Allah forbid.

He ordered black coffee and I ordered another cup with cream. I paid when the coffee came and he nodded his thanks. He wanted details about my living situation at Khalid's, my relationship with Mahmood's family and any potential threats he might be exposed to in helping me.

"Patricia, forgive me, but I did some research to check you out. My feeling for you was good from the beginning and I know you are sincere. Still, I wanted to see what others had to say to you. I got a copy of Hisham's article from the *New Straits Times* and I spoke with Aishah Ali about you. I was very surprised with what she said."

He hesitated here and my heart went to my throat. Could she have discouraged him from wanting to help me?

He smiled broadly, "Aishah says you are an extraordinary woman. She thinks you are brave and heroic to not give up against so much injustice and to always fight, fight, fight for your children. And she wished you could get your children out of Malaysia because she believes that maybe you will never get justice here. The article and her words convinced me one million percent to help you and your children escape."

I was speechless. I remember thinking, *Is this the moment, here in this crummy little restaurant with a cup of awful coffee and a man I've just met, that my prayers are being answered?* Allah, I realized, works in strange ways.

So, with all the certitude I could muster, I said, "Arvin, I believe in you and trust you and I will do as you say. Please get us out."

We drove around in his car for another hour. On his car phone he contacted his friend on the border. Arvin had the speaker on and asked his friend to speak English, so I could know the facts and not worry that they were actually conspiring against me. I thought it a sweet and effective gesture. "Is it doable? Will you help?" Arvin asked.

I heard a pause, then a deep voice pause reply, "Yes, it's doable and I will do it."

They sketched out a plan while questions flew back and forth.

"That's it," Arvin said, after ending the call, "If you're sure about this, we can go ahead and get you and the children out the last week of this month."

I choked out, "Yes, Yes, Yes!!" and we moved on to the next step: getting my passport. After that we concentrated on the details. "The kids and you will take the 4:00 P.M. bus to Melacca on the twenty-sixth; I'll meet you there at 10:00 P.M. and we'll drive the twelve to fourteen hours to the border town and my friend's house. He'll cross with us and I'll stick with you as long as you think you need me."

I am embarrassed but ask, "How much?" Arvin tells me he feels it would be wrong for him to take any compensation beyond gas for his car and meals while we're together. As for bribes and payment to his friend, he reckons another five hundred dollars should more than cover it. Excluding airfare and what happens in Bangkok, this can be done for less than one thousand American dollars!

"Arvin, I want you to know I'm scared, insecure and traumatized, but also brave, determined and able."

He smiled. A little before 9:00 A.M., he dropped me off at a shopping center five minutes from the United States embassy. Nothing was open, so I phoned the embassy, spoke with an administrator and she advised me to have photos made, come in and meet with Hugh, a First Secretary to whom I had spoken in the past. Then I read the newspaper until the photo shop opened, got the prints and was at the Embassy at 10:15. We went directly

to Hugh's office and discussed politics and my adventures of the last few
months. Then we got down to business.

"The court in Melacca has my passport, Hugh, and I want another one,"
I said politely.

"Why?" he asked, smiling.

"Do you need to know?" I asked warily.

Yes, Hugh the diplomat did, and he read me the guidelines. Then he said,
"We don't want to cause an awkward situation for the United States
Government," and spoke about needing to sit down with the Ambassador and
the necessity of informing the State Department to get their opinion. He went
on about the importance of consensus and the seriousness of what could happen...

Hugh did not patronize or minimize. He treated me like an equal and
our little conference brought out a side of him with which I was unfamiliar. He was tense and took notes with great earnestness. Hugh knew it
would be his ass if this exploded and he wanted it covered. "What about the
courts?" he said.

I endeavored to convince him the odds of my getting justice in Malaysia
were nil and that the Malaysian Government would, in fact, be relieved if I
left with the children. "Mahmood will never relent an inch; he is determined to drive me to suicide, penury and/or deportation." Further, I
reminded Hugh that his predecessor, Philip French, assured me they could
issue another passport the last time the court took my passport and under
similar circumstances, passports for the children were issued.

While we were going through all this, I asked how the embassy in
Bangkok would react if I showed up there without a passport.

"Oh, they'd issue you one immediately," he replied without hesitation.

"Considering everything?" I sputtered, dumbstruck he hadn't told me
this at the outset.

"Sure. It wouldn't be a problem at all," he said confidently.

"Okay," I asserted confidently, "if you and yours deny me a passport,
then the kids and I will still go across the border and make our way to
Bangkok. I've discussed this scenario with my contact and it's feasible."

At this, he spent a long time writing, but had no comment.

From the beginning of our lengthy conversation, I'd sensed the
United States Embassy in Kuala Lumpur would not approve my request

for a passport and confronted Hugh on this suspicion. He was evasive and changed the subject. We got on to the subject of the kids' passports and I pulled the diminutive green documents out of my back pocket to show him. While we were talking about them, he said, "You know, I suddenly have a completely different perception of this whole thing."

We'd also been discussing the court holding the children's Malay passports, the gray area of the judge's right to hold my American passport and the embassy's right to intercede, because passports are United States Government property. I'm not sure exactly what changed the direction of his thinking, but changed it was. Another miracle? He expressed a willingness to speak with the Ambassador and State Department on my behalf!

I spent quite a bit of time telling him how my leaving would be a good thing for Malaysia. I stressed that Malaysia is living with an explosive situation in ME, a strong, assertive, vocal mother who's been royally f——d over by the system and Malaysia knows it's culpable.

"I'll be going over the border with or without a passport and wouldn't it behoove you guys to help me now and get this resolved. I'm a very small bone in your throat today, but the potential is there for me and mine to make a whole heap of trouble. I'm not going to give up until I have Mariam and Iskandar home in Michigan," I told him. "If necessary, I might just create a huge international stink one of these days."

Hugh seemed impressed with my character and conviction. We parted on a good note and I walked back to the shopping center.

Arvin and I had agreed to refer to the passport as a book I was buying in all our telephone conversations... So, when I called I told him, "The bookstore clerk needed to talk to the boss and head office before he can sell me the book, but he said buying the book in Bangkok would be a simple task."

He understood perfectly but stressed, "Buying the book in Malaysia would be best, so telephone me as soon as you hear from the clerk." He went on to tell me not to worry and to trust him and to remember we can always go later and he's with me 100 percent. I ran to the nearest toilet stall and bawled with gratitude, relief and fear.

14 January
Perhaps because I felt comfortable with Arvin and my decision, I slept like a rock on the bus and for another five hours in my chalet. I've had

twelve hours rest and I'm bright-eyed, bushy-tailed and gnawing at the bit for the children to show today. If they do, Mahmood probably has no suspicions and, even if Khalid thinks I'm acting strange and up to something, he wouldn't know what or when...

I am tremendously paranoid, yet I must live every minute as normally as possible. In these next twelve days, I shall strive to convince Khalid, the kids and Mahmood I intend to be around for a long time.

It is now 1:30 P.M. In half an hour I will know if all is well. When I see Mariam and Iskandar's smiling faces a tear of joy will fall, because if Mahmood sends them now he will send them next time and the next (AND FINAL) time.

Not twenty minutes after the children arrived, Karuna from Child Welfare showed up! She sat on my porch and asked one hundred questions about the case, the court and the kids. She observed them and, luckily, they were in great and affectionate form. She'd only seen them with me once, for that unmentionable hour in her office.

I shared my disappointment with the psychological evaluation, but said, "It appears Mahmood was frightened by the investigation, because he no longer hits the kids." I don't think she had an agenda beyond doing a follow-up for her report and, if she did, I passed with flying colors. The children ignored her and were constantly interrupting to ask me things. They were surprisingly well-mannered about it and I complied with long-winded answers to their questions. She got the hint and left.

Having failed twice, I know the success of this hinges upon risk management and, with that in mind, I'm going to keep my mouth shut about my plans this time.

18 January

Dear Zoe,

On the brink again and whilst in this state, my thoughts naturally turn towards home and loved ones. By the beneficent grace of Allah, Mariam, Iskandar and I hope to reach Michigan before this missive reaches you. I am praying for our success.

In thirty-six hours, Hugh, First Secretary at the Embassy, is going to telephone and tell me whether the government has approved issuing me a second passport for the purpose of leaving the country. If he says yes, I'll request it be done at midnight on the twenty-sixth. If he says yes to that, the children and I will take the afternoon bus to Melacca, get picked up by our savior when we arrive and he'll drive us to Kuala Lumpur and the embassy. Then I'll pop inside and take care of my passport while the children sleep in the car. When it's done, we'll head north to the border, meet savior number two, go across and then home. Once we're in Thailand, we'll be safe.

If Hugh says no passport in Malaysia, we'll go across without it and I'll get one in Bangkok. Savior's number one and number two have already said they'll take us across with or without.

Getting caught and arrested at the border doesn't faze me. My saviors are risking their necks, too, and won't let it happen. If it does, look for me on CNN. No, if it does, you'll see me catatonic in the corner of a padded room, lamenting all I've put my poor children through, in the hopes I could give them a better life...

I will breathe the (first in a series) breath of freedom once our bus has pulled out of Mersing and away from Mahmood.

To keep Mahmood ignorant I know I must keep Khalid ignorant. I just can't trust him anymore. I told Khalid we're going to stay with my women friends in Melacca for three nights and will probably spend the fourth with his landlady on the way back. We've done this before and I think he'll buy it. I'm also going to tell him I intend to meet with the headmaster at the kid's school about teaching English the week after the holidays.

I have the children four days between now and then. I can't tell them either, so the status quo will reign. It will, in fact, reign and reign as long as possible, preferably until we're over the border.

It's 9:00 P.M. on a Sunday. The children left for their forty-eight hours with their father at two this afternoon.

I've been dreadfully restless since the kids left and have jumped from reading the papers to making idiotic lists to organizing clothes and stuff into piles and then disassembling them as I tell myself, *Stop, you bloody stupid woman! Status quo, get it?*

In truth, I have abundant time during next weekend's forty-eight child-free hours to pack THE BAG. Above all else, this chalet must look the same or even more settled. Maybe I should start a remodeling project like adding a bathroom, a kitchen, a living room, an extra bedroom, a closet or a little shelf on the wall as a diversionary tactic.

Oh, my friend, are the Fates going to let us go home this time? Have I finally found the right person to help us and formulated the plan that will work? Have I paid my karmic debt? Suffered enough? Is the miracle of my contact with savior number one really the "miracle" we've all been praying for these many months? Or is this a devilish ploy? Is it destined to fail? Am I destined to be arrested, to raise political, international hell and become the unwilling, precedent-setting poster child for suffering, custody-challenged women and kids everywhere? Can I really trust saviors number one and number two? Can I trust the embassy not to rat on me? Is *I'm going to escape* written all over my face? Is it seeping out of my pores? Does Mahmood already know and is he chuckling over how this time he may make good on his threats to kill me?

These are but a few of the demons that plague my warped and fragile psyche. Some others are: Will the police bang on my door tonight and confiscate this letter, the only tangible evidence in this chalet of my intentions? I do have the kid's United States passports (hidden under bras and panties in a basket on the wall). I can say, "Look, guys, I've had these passports for over three years and they're useless without entry visas. I keep them in case of emergency and my lawyers know about them and approve, so there." But would they believe me? Ah, there's the rub…

So, will all be well when I drop this in the postbox, or are they (WHO?) going to grab it out of the box, read it and what? Tell Mahmood? Lock me up? Steal the stamps?

Now, on the other hand, there is the possibility Hugh or the Ambassador spoke with someone, say the Malaysian Prime Minister or his deputy or whomever, about my plan, got approval and the way will be quietly smoothed for our departure. It behooves the United States Government to inform the Malaysian Government that the best interests of all parties are served by letting us go. That Patty Noor Faridah will never give up, shut up or go away…she's a ticking bomb who could go off at any time and embarrass both governments, especially the Malaysian.

I put a lot of energy into convincing Hugh of my unwavering quest to liberate Mariam and Iskandar one way or another, of my justifications for doing so and of my willingness to face arrest, prosecution and international news cameras for trying to free two innocent children from a cruel father and an unjust system. I was eloquent and there was fire in my eyes.

I'm not going to tempt fate by writing about our reunion plans. If I'm still in Malaysia when you get this, don't worry about me. God knows I've been knocked down before and have always managed to get back up to fight on and persevere.

I know we'll get home one of these days. Success is and ever will be inevitable…If only I didn't have this day-to-day, sanity-sapping agony of fears, ubiquitous mosquitoes, hand washing piles of children's clothes, living in a fishbowl, being white and feeling guilty because most of the women in this neighborhood have it so much worse than me. I hate this life and I love my children with all my heart. The three of us belong together and together we shall be. All else is meaningless. I miss you and oh how I pray I'm leaning over your shoulder when you read this during a break in our Scrabble game after Mariam and Iskandar have gone to their beds.

To be continued…

Love, Patty.

24 January

Two more days. I am fasting today and trying to overcome the block of fear that has iced my neurotic mind for too many days.

What do I fear? Most importantly, Mahmood taking the children off the four o'clock express bus to Melacca tomorrow. I've already bought the tickets, but I've had it in my head, until just a few minutes ago, that I must use them, must not take another way and add more expense. Like a few insignificant dollars lost is worth a risk so easily eliminated.

My mind conjures up alternative plans. Shortly after the children arrive tomorrow, say at 2:30, I telephone the taxi stand for a taxi to Kluang (halfway to Melacca) and in fifteen minutes or less one arrives here and takes the kids and me straight to Kluang. There we hop on a bus if it's convenient or into another taxi to Kuala Lumpur where we'll meet up with our man. We will be in and out of Kluang before Mahmood expects us to leave Mersing and NO ONE will be the wiser, because I'll tell Khalid, if he's around, that we're going into Mersing early to hang out. And if he's in the restaurant and there's no way to order a long-distance taxi without him knowing, we'll take a local taxi into town and hire a Kluang taxi from the taxi stand. As long as we are well out of town at four o'clock in any direction, we'll have a huge head start.

I'm so excited by this cognitive leap of beauteous simplicity and embarrassed by my stupidity, by the mental wall that prevented it from manifesting earlier.

Yes, the children and I can be in Kuala Lumpur by 8:00 P.M. and Arvin can get us anywhere and we can be off on our adventure hours earlier. There isn't a reason on earth why we need to go to Melacca. None, none, none!

The more I dwell upon altering tomorrow's plan, the better I feel. Where, though, should Arvin meet us? The safest would be Kluang. If Mahmood sends out an alarm at four o'clock and there is a lookout for taxis and buses and questions are asked of drivers, we'll fare infinitely better in a private car.

Maybe we should meet at the A&W hamburger joint in Kluang—no, better would be a hotel lobby restaurant. Oh, yes, Allah, yes and there's one a short walk from the taxi stand. What is the name of that hotel? Argh, I'll look in one of the tourist guides Khalid has for guests.

It's 7:15 P.M. and moments away from the siren ending the fast and my ice cold sugarcane juice. My head is ready to burst, but I am proud to have endured this day and gained inspiration from it. I pray, eat a doughnut and pack the things I've laid out: three dresses and a couple of silk shirts that weigh nothing, two T-shirts the kids and I can share and so on…95 percent of my possessions stay behind. I may decide to keep the children in the clothes they arrive in to speed up departure and keep them out of the chalet. I'll telephone Khalid in a week and ask him to distribute the contents of the chalet to the poorest people in the neighborhood.

Never have I felt so alone. I want, need, ache for someone to talk with and share this day of waiting. I won't call anyone though. It's too risky. I have my prayers and the angels who surround me.

I'll call Arvin early in the morning about meeting in Kluang. I got a tourist guide unobserved and have the name of the hotel I hadn't been able to remember earlier. We'll meet there around 4:00 o'clock.

I'll try Hugh one more time in the morning, though I have little faith in his involvement. I wrack my brain for any other hitches that may arise. One I'm contemplating is the children's behavior as the day progresses.

I've just completed my fifth prayer of the day at 10:00 P.M. and intend to perform the "power" prayer at midnight. Also, Allah willing, I'll fast tomorrow and break it north of Kuala Lumpur at 7:25 P.M. Fasting, I tell myself, will be added incentive for angelic protection, divine approval, blessed success. Also, on a practical level, fasting keeps me occupied and mellow. But I will not beat myself up if I break early and Allah will forgive me. Tonight I need to sleep well so I can think well tomorrow.

It is almost midnight and in a few minutes, I'm going to wudhu, brush my teeth, pray fervently and go to bed.

chapter twenty-one

The Perilous Journey

26 January 1998

I called Arvin at 9:30 and we set the time and place for our rendezvous. He was worried about money and so am I. Without a passport, I'll be unable to make cash withdrawals anywhere but Mersing and don't want to raise suspicions by going back to the bank today. I can use my credit card and have enough cash to get us to Bangkok, but…Arvin's going to bring as much money as he can get his hands on, just in case. Bless him.

As I went over our plan, stomach knotted, mind zooming, I compulsively rummaged around the room and through the bag for things to take, leave and agonize over. I kept telling myself, *I can handle this—Allah knows I've been at this juncture before*. I sighed, remembering that every other time has ended in failure…

When (I will not say if) the children arrive, our journey home is really, really going to be put into motion. How will the minutes flow? How will I breathe, talk, move normally? Why does this attempt feel more intense than any previous attempt? I know the script and I know how to improvise. I must carry it off. I am trying to convince myself I can do this damn thing blindfolded and with one arm tied behind my back. It's no big deal, biggest deal of my life, no big deal, biggest deal of my life…

In approximately six hours, not so long, we will be with Arvin, our Knight, Hero, and Savior and our journey will begin. That is what I long for.

The time is inching by. How can I occupy myself these last hours? I've run out of insignificant things to do and my eyes are riveted on the clock which hardly seems to be moving. I need to turn this time over to a Higher Power.

At 1:15, I prayed, packed the prayer stuff, showered, dressed and prayed in my own words, once more.

Noon. I'm glad I ate well early, because I know I will not be able to swallow a morsel until later, maybe much later...

Looking out the window I see the wind is really high now, the sky is dark and it is beginning to rain. Once more, I look at the clock. Despite my fears that it is standing still, time is passing.

1:50. I sit in the gazebo, eyes darting furtively from entrance to wrist-watch, my fear growing exponentially with each slowly passing minute. They aren't going to show—yes they are—no they're not—yes they are—no they're not.

Finally, at 2:15, Mariam and Iskandar arrive. I went to the van to greet Yati and their driver, wish them a Happy Hari Raya and, with my voice cracking, remind them, "Remember, we are going to Melacca until Thursday." I took the bags of food and clothes from Yati, waved at Joe and turned to the children.

We went to the kitchen first. I took out a loaf of white bread, a jar of strawberry jelly, a box of macaroni and cheese and two oranges. I kept the fruit to add to the bag I'd prepared and left the rest on the counter so it would look like we were going to return soon. With heart pounding I tried my best to answer the kids steady stream of questions about our impending trip. "What toys did you pack, Mama?" "Where are we going to stay?" "What time is the bus?" "Can I take this toy?"

A light rain fell as I did a final check of the room, rifled through the bag Yati sent for the children, grabbed a couple unstained T-shirts, checked off the essentials in my head and kept the kids out of the bags, as they clamored to add the dozen things they didn't want to leave behind.

"It's time to go, kids," I struggled to keep my voice normal.

Taking a deep breath, I locked the chalet door, dropped the key in my shoulder bag and we walked through the drizzle to the restaurant. There I telephoned the taxi stand for a car to Kluang. No taxis. I waited five minutes and tried again. No taxis. I tried to keep my voice from shaking as I told them to send a town taxi for us and we went over to the porch of Khalid's house, where he was sitting.

Casually, I mentioned that we were going to visit with friends and wait for our four o'clock bus.

"Let me drive you," he offered.

I shook my head, "I've already phoned a taxi."

My lips were dry and my palms were sweating. Was Khalid suspicious? Did he speak with too much friendly enthusiasm? I could not help wondering if his behavior was part of a conspiracy, so great was my paranoia.

Iskandar insistently demanded the right to open his toy box and both children complained about the rain and taxi's delay. After ten minutes, I re-phoned the taxi stand again. On the way, they said.

I withstood five more interminable minutes of Khalid's idle (sinister?) chatter. Then our taxi pulled up to the entry and honked.

"Salamat Hari Raya-Qong Qi Fau Choy. Happy Hari Raya and Happy Chinese New Year," I enthused as we said our good-byes. My arms around them, I walked the children quickly through the rain to our chariot. We climbed into the oldest and most beat up of Mersing's taxis and rattled off. The driver was an elderly Malay man who had driven the children and I many times before.

To the taxi stand, I told him in Malay, where we planned to get a taxi to Kluang. He asked why we were going there. For a moment my heart quickened. Then I said as smoothly as I could, "We're meeting a friend there who will take us to Melacca."

I turned to the children who were demanding access to their toys and begged them to be patient. Meanwhile, my own heart pounded so loudly I was afraid it could be heard.

The taxi stand was packed with people waiting for out-station taxis. We put our things on the edge of a bench. The drivers all wanted to say hello to Tunku's ex-wife and ask inane questions. Johor Bharu taxis pulled in and out. Kota Tinggi and Rompin taxis pulled in and out. I was trembling and each breath was an effort.

Suddenly, without permission, the children ran off through the rain and puddles to a shop. I ran after them to bring them back. Iskandar refused to budge until I bought him a toy. I ignored his angry tears and dragged them back. Both were noisy and irritable, which probably helped in the end, because the local drivers convinced one of the Johor Bahru drivers to go out of his way and take us to Kluang. He asked for $15.00, one third more than standard.

After one lame attempt to bargain the fare down failed, I said, "Yes, thank you. Let's go." We pulled out of Mersing at 3:15.

The driver was young and Chinese, a godsend, but wanted to practice his English, a curse. We discussed how long the trip would take. I'd told Arvin we'd be there between 4:00 and 4:30, but the driver said making Kluang before 4:30 was impossible. I agonized over whether to have him stop so I could call Arvin and decided it didn't matter, he'd be there.

When we passed the turnoff to Mahmood's house and his van wasn't waiting there ready to intercept us, I nearly cried out. And even when we'd gone another mile I constantly glanced behind us for his van or a police car. Luckily, the children settled in and were quiet. Finally I began to relax a little. The driver and I chatted about the holidays, America and the economy.

I vacillated over whether to ask him to drop us off at the hotel or the taxi stand. In my mind, I went over the pros and cons of each option and decided upon the hotel. Although it would only take a few minutes to walk, I was terrified by the prospect of interception at the taxi stand if Mahmood thought to question the drivers in Mersing. I hoped the driver would just turn around and return to Johor Bahru from the hotel rather than go to the taxi stand and face the possibility of unknowingly betraying us. I considered confiding in him...for about ten seconds.

I suspected I was making a monumental blunder and should have him stop the taxi so I could phone Arvin to change the rendezvous location to somewhere else in Kluang. But I didn't know Kluang well enough to come up with the name of another hotel or shopping center.

I endured a massive panic attack, my worst yet, while the children sat chatting on either side of me, oblivious. I told myself to stop the paranoia that could put me over the edge (into what? I didn't want to know). I lay my head back, closed my eyes and silently chanted, *Arvin will be there waiting. We are surrounded by Angels. Mahmood does not know.*

But *what ifs* soon filled my mind. What if Mahmood was waiting to grab the kids off the four o'clock bus as he had before and we didn't show? What if he began to search and he went to the taxi stand? What if they told him we were going to Kluang and he got his local police to alert the police in Kluang and they were waiting for us? Looking at my watch, I saw it was already after 4:00 and I could visualize this disastrous chain of events with growing panic.

We pulled into Kluang at 4:30. The taxi stopped in the street outside the hotel. I paid the driver, watched him drive off in the direction of the taxi stand and hustled the children into the lobby.

My heart ricocheted and then stabilized. It was empty. I set down the bags and searched for the coffee shop—no Arvin. "Where is the closest pay telephone?" I asked a maid. When told it was a couple of minutes walk away from the hotel, I faltered, ready to cry. The maid I'd asked kindly took us through the employee's door and pointed to a row of phones across the street. She stood and watched while the kids and I rushed across and I called Arvin's cell phone. He answered, "I'm nearby; wait at the entrance." We went back through the hotel. I grabbed the bags and went out the door.

I was delirious with anticipation to see Arvin's face and frantically hoped I could relax and begin to feel a semblance of optimism once we were in his company.

"Patricia," he called. I turned around. He looked smaller, different, somehow less heroic than I remembered. Oh, but when I touched his arm and saw his calm, confident face closeup, my trembling decreased and I managed a smile.

Arvin took one of the bags and we set off for his car, parked on the other side of the taxi stand in a back parking lot. I held my breath as we walked within sight of the taxis and drivers. I angled my body away and urged the kids and Arvin to "Hurry."

We arrived at his Mercedes sedan, loaded the stuff in the trunk, the kids into the back seat and ourselves in front. The motor ignited, Arvin reversed out of his parking spot then moved forward into the traffic inching its way out of town. I slouched down in the seat and barely heard him, so great was my fear that somehow we had been followed. But Arvin reassured me, "Everything will go just as we planned. Please believe that."

We'd discussed earlier what to tell the children Arvin's name was and had settled upon George, but ten minutes into the drive, we decided to find another name because George was one of my nicknames for Iskandar and things became amusingly complicated. Iskandar came up with a new name for him, Davey Crockett, and we used that.

The children's questions soon began, "When do we get to Melacca?
"We're not going to Melacca."
"Why not? I want to go. You said we were. You promised."
"We're going somewhere better."
"Where?"
"It's a surprise."
"How long will it take?"
"A long time but you'll both be happy once we're there."
Iskandar and Mariam tried to get concrete answers, but I wasn't telling. Eventually they gave up, unpacked their toys and began to play.

I stayed low in my seat until we were on the expressway. Even then, I was unable to feel anything but a frenzied trepidation, fearing there was still danger even though we now were on our way to the border. Arvin's reassuring conversation and genuinely calm demeanor had no effect upon my rising anxiety level.

When I next looked at my watch, an hour and a half had passed. I had drink boxes, fruit, granola bars and candy for the kids and it sufficed nicely for snacks. Arvin, though, was hungry and the children needed a hot meal, to use the toilets and run around. The prospect of stopping unhinged me and I pressed Arvin to put it off time and again. But the kids became more and more demanding…

At dusk, we pulled into a rest stop packed with people waiting to break their fasts. The kids and I left Arvin and went to the bathroom. Afterwards, they begged to spend a few minutes in the small playground and I acquiesced, as it was close to the kiosks where I could get them hotdogs, fries and juice. But I kept my eyes on them all the time.

We headed back to the car and intercepted Arvin. I needed to return to the bathroom and left the kids with him. When I got back to the car, Iskandar wasn't there and Arvin said he'd followed me. In a panic, I rushed up the stairs. I looked up and all around but didn't see him. But this time my heart was pounding and I expected to see Mahmood with Iskandar in his arms. Luckily, just at that moment, my son saw me and ran towards me yelling, "Mama, Mama. I lost you."

In tears, I scooped him up and carried him to the car.

With the last rays of the sun fading in the distance, we got organized and set off again. The kids squabbled on and off, mostly over space and toys.

Iskandar hit Mariam regularly and she cried each time. I was duly embarrassed, upset, angry and unsuccessful in trying to mediate. In fact, Iskandar had fallen into the habit of slugging me on the arm whenever I threatened consequences and he had a strong arm.

Arvin was pathetically hilarious in his attempts to control them, saying, "I won't friend you if you're naughty," and other similar nonsense the kids ignored. Dealing with them was actually a welcome respite from my mental hell. I knew they'd only go so far, that we were in an enclosed space with plenty of distractions and this, oh so normal acting out, would tire them.

Meanwhile, I began to go over in my mind how to tell them. I needed to prepare Mariam and Iskandar for our journey, yet didn't dare tell them yet that we were going home to Michigan. If this rescue failed, I wanted them innocent of any knowledge, guilt or disappointment.

Story-time was fast approaching and I outlined a Curious George adventure in my head. "Settle down, children," I said. And this is the story I told them:

Curious George was living in America with Uncle Bobby and Aunt Amy. He often heard the family talking about Uncle Bobby's sister Patty and her two children, who were living in a country far, far away. They were not happy in this country and wanted very badly to come home to Michigan. All the aunts, uncles, cousins (except for Uncle Paul, Aunt Kimberley, Akasha and Keeston who lived in Maui every winter), Grammy and Curious George would get together and think of ways they could help them.

They loved and missed Patty and her children very much and worried about them all the time. They talked about the children's father who had a very bad habit of trying to keep the children and their mother apart and the judge, who wasn't trying hard enough to help them be together.

One day when everyone was talking about the judge, Curious George had a brilliant idea.

He jumped up and down excitedly and Uncle Michael said, "I think George wants to tell us something. What is it, George? Do you have an idea?"

George nodded.

"Is it a way to help our family far away?" asked Uncle Matthew and George nodded again.

"Let's see," said Aunt Becky, "Does it have something to do with the judge?"

George nodded vigorously.

"But Patty has tried everything to convince the judge she and the children should be together," said Uncle Timmy, "Is it something we could do?"

Again George nodded, getting more and more excited. Everyone thought hard but no one could figure out how they could help.

Frustrated because he couldn't talk, George looked around the room for a way to show them his idea. Suddenly he had it. He ran to the desk, grabbed paper and pencils and passed them out.

"What do you want us to do," asked Aunt Victoria, "write someone a letter?"

While George nodded, Cousin Vanessa jumped up and said, "I know. George thinks we should all write letters to the judge asking him to let our cousins and Patty come home."

George was so happy they'd figured it out, he fainted with joy. When he woke up, everyone was writing his or her letter. He wanted to do something, too, so he drew a picture of the family having a picnic on the river. Then he drew another picture of the cousins playing in the snow. For his last picture, he drew an airplane with Patty and her children peeking out the windows, smiling and waving. He wanted to be sure the judge understood his three pictures; so, being very clever, he drew an American flag on each one.

Grammy checked one of Patty's old faxes from the court to get the judge's address. They put all the letters and George's drawings in a big envelope and mailed it that very day. Then they all held hands and prayed that the judge would get their letters quickly, read them with a loving heart and change his mind about letting their cousins and Patty leave.

Every day after that, George begged to go to the post office with Uncle Bobby. He waited anxiously in the car until Bobby brought that day's mail out and was dejected when Bobby said, "No, nothing from the judge, George. Maybe tomorrow."

The family explained to George that the letter would take two weeks to get to the judge and then he'd have to find someone to translate the letters from English to his language so he could read them. They further consoled George by saying the judge might not even respond to the letters, but would call Patty instead. So from then on, George jumped every time the phone rang, hoping it was Patty calling to say they were on their way because the judge said yes.

One night, three or four weeks later, the family and Curious George were together at Grammy's house when the phone rang. It was Patty. She'd gotten a letter from the judge that day giving her permission to leave, but their departure had to be very, very *secret. No one could know, especially the children's father. In the letter, the judge gave* her the name and phone number of a man who could help them sneak out.

Patty was crying with joy on the phone and said she would not call again until they were safely out of the country. She wanted everyone to be patient and pray for them.

Curious George was so happy, he fainted. When he came to, the family was talking about the phone call and George suddenly didn't feel very happy. He felt scared and nervous for Patty and the children. He quietly crept into a corner and shut his eyes, hoping the bad feeling would go away.

Like a flash of lightening, a wonderful, magical picture appeared in his head. He saw Patty and the children holding hands in a field of wildflowers on a perfect summer day. The sky was blue and the sun was shining and the three of them were surrounded by Angels, hundreds of them. George opened his eyes and looked at the family. They were still chatting happily. With a big grin on his face, he went over and climbed in cousin Sam's lap.

A few days later the call came. They were over the border and would soon be on their way home. When the glorious day arrived, Curious George and the family went to the airport. When the plane rolled up to the terminal, George wondered if he was the only one who saw the Angels. . .

"Is the story about us? Is it true? Is it real?" Mariam and Iskandar asked a dozen times while I was relating the tale of Curious George.

"Maybe," I said and smiled demurely, "Maybe one day soon Angels will surround us and help us find our way home to Michigan."

Afterward, I tried to get them settled and to sleep. It was an arduous affair.

"Why do we have to sleep in the car? When will we get to our surprise? Mariam's leg is on my side. Iskandar's kicking me. I can't get comfortable. We want another story."

I answered each question and dealt with each argument through gritted teeth. If I could stay calm, they might be convinced everything was okay and go to sleep. All the clothes from our bag were being used as padding on the floor of the backseat or for pillows. My two sarongs were blankets.

I sat cross-legged as my floor space was packed with toys, books, toiletries and food. Arvin, in the driver's seat, was unruffled.

It was 9:00 P.M. We were on the North-South expressway somewhere between Kuala Lumpur and Penang and at least eight hours from the border. I kept checking the rear window for the flashing lights of a police car, but not as often.

"We want another story, please, Mama. Then we promise to go to sleep," begged Mariam.

"How about Curious George and the cowboys?" suggested Iskandar.

"Settle down, be quiet and think about sleeping with happy dreams. No more questions. No more arguing. No more talking and I'll tell you a story about Curious George and the cowboys," I pleaded. It worked! They bustled for a few minutes and were soon ready...

I babbled a long convoluted story, throwing in enough drama to stave off complaints. Success. There was silence when I finished, hoarse, having thoroughly exhausted the subject. Arvin and I sat on tenterhooks, hardly daring to breathe. We wanted to be sure, sure, sure the children were really sleeping.

However, as soon as I was convinced they were asleep, my nemesis, paranoid obsessing, reasserted itself. I'd been so thoroughly consumed with the children, so stressed and obsessed with mothering and so comforted by a role I was used to, that with them sound asleep and no longer taxing me, my mind returned to Mahmood, interception and failure.

A routine roadblock was coming up and questions would be asked for which I didn't have answers. In my mind a new scenario began. Arvin and I will be arrested and the children put in a car (screaming for me) and taken back to their father. To calm down I told myself roadblocks were a common occurrence and we'd already been waved through two. The police were looking for bandits and drug dealers, not white women kidnapping their kids. Not yet, anyway...

I looked over at Arvin and considered how best to get him talking.

He broke the silence. "Get some sleep."

"An impossibility," I replied, "until after we cross the border." Understanding my suffering, he accepted the excuse and, with some encouragement, began to tell me more about his life.

27 January

At 4:45 A.M. on Tuesday we arrived at Padang Besar, the border town. Arvin parked under a streetlight near a hospital. He didn't want to disturb his friend before six in the morning and we both needed some air and to stretch our legs. We stood outside the car. Soon the streets would fill with people on their way to the mosques to perform the first prayer of the day. We would stick out—a white woman and an Indian man. We had discussed what we'd say if the police questioned us and having a good alibi gave me no solace. I was sure they would know we were lying.

As I looked around I saw everything as potentially threatening, from a car that didn't pass to a look that lingered beyond a half second. Twenty-four hours without sleep and little food were taking their toll.

Looking at me, Arvin suggested we both take a thirty-minute nap. I suggested we wake his friend and get it over with. He reminded me for the third time that we couldn't cross the border until after the shift change at eight o'clock, when his friend, Ugo Ganesh, felt more confident the border guards would be those he knew.

We got back in the car, Arvin put his seat back and within a minute was snoring softly. I stared at him and at my children sleeping in the back and cried softly with a sort of mellow hysteria that could have escalated in a heartbeat. I forced myself to breathe deeply and bit my lip to still the trembling.

I lay back and soothed myself with positive affirmations. Thankfully, there was very little traffic and the predawn stillness helped me to calm down to a functional level.

After twenty minutes I felt guilty, but I could stand it no longer and gently nudged Arvin.

"Let's go meet Ugo Ganesh and his family," Arvin said, as he looked at his watch. It was 5.55 A.M.

Less than ten minutes later we were there. I woke the children, grabbed our bag and we followed Arvin to the door.

Ugo, heavy-set and a few years younger than Arvin, met us at the door with his wife, Lakshmi. She hugged the children and me, ushered us into the house and asked whether we wanted to eat before or after our baths. After, I smiled and said, yes, toast, fruit and hot chocolate would be wonderful. The children followed me into the bathroom and I was relieved to see a shower with hot water. The morning was chilly and I knew they'd have balked at cold water. As it was, both argued halfheartedly as I helped them undress and wash. I was amazed by their mellowness. Beyond a couple innocent questions about our location and itinerary, they were mute.

They wanted to wait for me, so I showered quickly and, wrapped in towels and sarongs, we went to the bedroom Lakshmi showed us to get dressed.

The table was set when we came out. Ganesh and Lakshmi's two teenage daughters were up and eager to meet the company. After we sat down the questions began. I told them of the past three and a half years in a quick synopsis, emphasizing the children's suffering.

The conversation moved on to working out the details of our imminent journey. By this time, the children were fed and restless and the younger daughter took them off to listen to her read a story.

Lakshmi and Devi, the daughter who stayed at the table, offered to go with us across the border to enhance our everyday look. "We will say the American wife of Ugo's friend, Arvin, accidentally left her passports in Kuala Lumpur and wants a few hours shopping in Thailand with my mother and me." It would be victimless crime with a small price tag, a few hundred dollars spread among the half dozen guards on duty at the Malay and Thai checkpoints. Lakshmi held my hand through this discussion and her touch was comforting.

Ugo Ganesh went off at exactly eight on his motorcycle to prepare the border for us and we emptied all my stuff out of Arvin's car and into the trunk of Ugo's.

There was a large Hindu altar in the house at which they prayed, for the family was devout and, like Arvin, believed helping us was their religious duty. With Iskandar and Mariam watching, Mother and daughters prayed and put ash on their third eyes. Moments after they walked away, Iskandar went up to the altar, mimicked their motions, put his finger in the ash and made a large mark on his forehead.

The women, who had been watching, were transfixed. "This is a miracle and a sign from God," said Lakshmi. "We have nothing to worry about!"

They fawned over Iskandar and he wore the ash proudly until it faded away, two days later.

Ugo Ganesh returned and said, "Let's go."

We went out to the car, a nondescript gray sedan. The men sat in front. I was in the middle of the backseat and the children sat on the laps of Lakshmi and Devi on either side of me. Lakshmi found my hand and I caressed Mariam's arm with the other. "Children, please keep quiet for our little drive. We are on our way to do some shopping," I said. They sensed something was happening and were silent.

Unadulterated, 200-proof, paralyzing terror engulfed me as we pulled out of the drive and set off through the busy streets of Padang Besar. Less than five minutes later, we were at the border, a series of drab cement buildings, fences with barbed wire at the top and directly in front of us, a customs booth with two men standing beside it. The Malay checkpoint.

"Keep your eyes down and try to look relaxed," said Arvin.

Ugo Ganesh slowed down the car to a crawl and inched past the two men. They looked us over as I tried to breathe normally. Time stood still. They asked a few questions which I somehow answered. Then, giving me one last lingering look, they waved us on.

Arvin turned to me and smiled, "That was the big one."

I nodded, unable to speak.

We drove on. As we approached the Thai side of the border, Ugo slowed down the car. Two men and a woman stood by the booth. They stood looking at us for what felt like an eternity. Then they whispered to each other and finally nodded to Ugo Ganesh. Suddenly, we were in Thailand.

I cried softly, as not to alarm the children, and struggled to still my trembling hands.

"Please," I begged, "can we go to a hotel right now? I don't feel well and need to explain what just happened to the children."

Ugo found a Chinese hotel. I gave him money for the room. "I don't care what it looks like—just get the key." He did.

The room was a dump, yet it was beautiful. There was a beat-up television in one corner and the children found Sesame Street. The reception was fuzzy, but to their delight, Kermit and Miss Piggy were speaking English.

The bribes were to be paid at 11:30, during the guard's lunch breaks. Ugo needed to take the women back and would return on his motorcycle.

Overcome with gratitude, I embraced Lakshmi, unable to speak. I kissed her cheeks, hugged her daughter and pushed Mariam and Iskandar forward to say good-bye. We'd been with them for a few minutes shy of three hours. In this case, a lifetime.

Arvin hadn't had the opportunity to bathe earlier and, after making sure that I was okay, he took over the bathroom. Ten seconds later he came out. "Keep the door locked," he lectured, "and don't open it for anyone. I'll hurry." I laughed and chided him to relax.

Finally he went back into the bathroom and I had Mariam and Iskandar to myself. I turned the television down, called the children over to the bed where I was sitting and pulled them onto my lap.

"Something very, very wonderful just happened, my darlings. That family helped us to go across the line between Malaysia and Thailand. We are not in Malaysia any longer and now we are free to go to America." My voice shook with emotion. I feared I was making too great a promise. We could still get caught and sent back...

"But what about Baba? Won't he get us?" asked Mariam nervously as Iskandar looked on.

"No, Baba won't get you. He doesn't know where we are. You don't ever have to go back to him again. We are going to America and he can't stop us."

With this, Iskandar let out a cheer and started bouncing on the bed.

Mariam wasn't so sure, "What about Yati? She's going to miss me."

"Don't worry about Yati. She'll miss you for a little while, but she'll be okay. She and your Baba will take care of each other."

With that, she joined her brother in a laughing, bed-jumping jamboree.

"Yea, yea, Baba can't get us. We're going to America. We're going on an airplane. We're going to see Grammy and Akasha and Uncle Bobby and everybody." They sang, danced, embraced and were, quite literally, bouncing off the walls with joy.

"We got through every barrier," I said, smiling at the children, "because angels have surrounded us and they're still very much with us. There are a few more checkpoints before we fly to Michigan. We have to get to Bangkok and go to the American Embassy to get me a passport and then we have to get permission from Thailand to leave. We sneaked into their country and they need to ask us some questions before they can give us permission to go. But don't worry, the embassy and the President and everyone will help us because they are all so happy we got out of Malaysia safely."

Arvin came out of the bathroom, looking quite dapper and smelling of Old Spice, my father's favorite cologne. I shared the children's reaction with him and we thanked our liberator, with loving gusto.

Ugo Ganesh returned. We had an hour until the payoff rendezvous and needed to purchase three bus tickets to Bangkok. Ugo knew where to go and we set off walking.

The next bus was at 4:30 and it was full— no, there was one seat available—no, two seats were available and yes, the two children could share one seat. We bought the tickets and on the way out Arvin confided in me, "I think we just witnessed another miracle. The bus was full. For sure, no seats. The sign said full. The sheet was marked full, but when the man looked the second time, there was a seat, then one more. God made two seats for you."

Spontaneously, I hugged him.

It was then I realized I was attracted to Arvin, but knew a relationship with him was impossible. Still, my overwhelming gratitude for his selfless act would last forever.

A short while later we walked to the restaurant rendezvous. I ordered noodles with prawns and vegetables for the children and coffee for me. The two thousand Malay dollars (in hundreds) was still in my pocket. Arvin had told me earlier that half would go to Ugo Ganesh and the other half would be distributed among the border guards.

When Ugo walked in and sat with us, Arvin asked for the cash. Then he and Ugo left us, though they were never out of sight at a table in the corner. Nervously I watched the guards come and go from their table at short intervals.

We went shopping for the children. Iskandar bought a hand-carved cobra walking stick that, serendipitously, was broken in half. It was still very cool, an incredible bargain and would fit in our luggage. Mariam found a coloring book of dancers from around the world and we got a box of colored pencils.

With the bribes paid, I felt paranoid and exposed. Arvin confessed he also wanted to get out of sight. With money in their pockets and a few drinks under their belts, we feared Ugo or one of the guards might talk too much and pique the interest of a cop or immigration official.

Meanwhile two determined children endeavored to convince me that buying more toys to celebrate our escape was sensible and necessary. "Yes, you may each buy something," I promised with a chuckle, "and then we'll go back to the hotel and rest until we leave."

I was punchy with exhaustion and imagined Arvin was also. He intended to stay with us until the bus pulled out of town. He had to be back in Kuala Lumpur the next morning for an appointment he couldn't break. When the men returned, we said good bye to Ugo until four o'clock.

We went back to the room. It was two o'clock. The children assured me they were not tired and would play quietly with their toys on the floor close to the television. Japanese cartoons were on and they quickly became fixated on them.

"I am falling in love with you," Arvin whispered, pulling me towards him and pressing his body against mine.

"Oh Arvin, no." I pulled away. "I need to go home and recover my sanity, Arvin, before I can consider a relationship with anyone. You think you're in love with me, but you've just saved a damsel in distress. It's not possible for us to be together and I'm sorry."

At 3:55, Ugo banged on the door. We let him in and scurried around, packing the detritus of two children. I reminded the kids to go to the bathroom and brush their teeth. I also did a quick toiletry.

At 4:10, we were out the door and at 4:20, we were staring at a huge bus. There were dozens of people milling around, but I was the only white person as far as the eye could see.

Arvin and the children followed me onto the bus. The floor was uncarpeted and the seats were narrow, but the arm rests came up and there was plenty of floor space to make a bed. "We'll be fine," I said softly. I left the nonessential bags on the seats and we went out, with fifty pairs of eyes watching. I felt panicky. The odds of encountering one or more roadblocks was high and I didn't have a passport. Neither did the children, for all practical purposes, because theirs had no entry visas for Thailand.

I pulled Arvin aside and asked him how I should handle it if we were questioned.

"Relax, my dear. Just tell them your passports got lost and you are on your way to Bangkok to get new ones at the embassy. Don't say they were stolen, because then they will want you to file a police report. And remember, don't talk much and act very shy. You are so smart and brave, my love. Trust God and soon you will be home in Michigan, U.S.A. Don't forget me and maybe someday I can come to see you."

I embraced him and the children came over and put their arms around us for a moment, then grabbed my hands.

"Let's go, Mama. Everybody is getting on the bus. Hurry, Mama. Goodbye, Davey Crockett. Goodbye, Mr. Ugo."

I kissed Arvin on the cheek, shook Ugo's hand and let the children pull me onto the bus. While they puttered around, taking out their toys and building a universe in a few square feet, I stood in the aisle and looked out the window, my eyes meeting Arvin's. He blew me a kiss and I blew one back. Turning, I looked over at my children and smiled as the bus began to roll.

"Sit down, Mama." "Look, we made a spot for you." "Isn't this a wonderful bus?" "How many miles to Bangkok?" "What's for dinner?" "What day is it in Malaysia?" "When will we get to Grammy's house?"

chapter twenty-two

Destination Freedom

28 January

The first stop the bus made on its way to Bangkok, the children got off with me. We needed food, bathrooms and time to walk around. No one spoke English and in Thai I could only say, "How are you?" and "I am fine." Thankfully, our agenda was straightforward—don't miss the signal to get back on the bus and secure a taxi to take us to the embassy when we arrive in Bangkok. At the rest stop the bathrooms were clearly marked, food was displayed for easy pointing and I'd gotten more than enough Thai currency in Bang Besar. I should have felt confident but I was consumed with fears and massive foreboding, visualizing Mahmood waiting behind every corner, in every shadow. *I have to manage such thoughts*, I told myself, *for what choice did I have?*

The second time the bus stopped, at two this morning, I felt slightly more relaxed. I disentangled myself from the sleeping children and crept off the bus, went to the bathroom, smoked half a cigarette and then had a panic attack. Now I imagined a new enemy. The vision that compelled me to run pell-mell through the rest stop was that of pimps who would steal my children to sell into prostitution. I felt so vulnerable to this new threat, a fragile-looking single woman who couldn't speak Thai and left her kids alone on the bus. *What am I thinking? I could have been knocked out in the bathroom or, or...*

I literally ran back onto the bus, so great was my terror the children would be gone/stolen/disappeared. Weak-kneed and trembling, I stood in the aisle gazing at my priceless cargo.

I lifted Iskandar's head and slid under it, pulling my feet up under me so as not to disturb Mariam on the floor. I stroked his forehead and rhythmically banged my head softly on the seat back, cursing my foolish self.

We pulled into Bangkok at 6:45 A.M. and a taxi driver with a grasp of English appeared in front of me as we disembarked.

"Where you go?" he asked.

"American Embassy, please hurry," I replied.

"Okay, 400 Baht. Where your bag?"

I didn't know or care enough to haggle with him. Eight dollars U. S. seemed a bargain at that moment. In fact, any price was a bargain.

"Where you come from? How you like Thailand? Where you stay Bangkok? What you name?" His questions came rapid fire and I answered, only half-conscious of what I was saying. The children were wide awake, demanding breakfast and our itinerary.

I gave them each a granola bar, a juice box and the promise we'd have a big meal once our embassy business was completed and we'd found a hotel.

The embassy was open when we arrived at seven-thirty. Oddly, I hadn't even thought about what we might do if it didn't open until nine or ten. I showed the Thai guard at the gate the children's empty passports. "I am here to get mine replaced." He let us in and I went to the counter, gave the clerk a quick summary and was ushered through a door. We were put in a small interrogation chamber with a glass divider over a table dissecting the room. Second's later, a tall blonde man appeared on the other side of the glass.

"Hi, welcome to Bangkok. I'm Joshua Edmonds, First Counsel for American Citizen Services and I hear you have a story to tell." He introduced himself with a questioning grin.

"Is there a spot where the children could play?" I asked timidly. He suggested the waiting room. Iskandar and Mariam refused to leave me, however, and promised to color quietly on the floor. I began. He took notes, said "Wow" a few times and asked many questions. After an intensive twenty minutes, we both came up for air.

"Congratulations! What an incredible story. I think you've accomplished something phenomenal by getting this far and I do believe we can help the three of you get the rest of the way home to Michigan. There is a major hurdle to jump, though: Thai Immigration. You crossed their border without passports and they're going to demand some answers about where, when and how you entered Thailand."

"I hadn't even thought about that," I said shakily, gathering my thoughts. "They're going to want the name of the guy who took us across and I can't get him in trouble. I don't want to get anyone in trouble. This is awful. I wonder if I could act stupid, say I don't know the name of the town, I don't know what time it was and I had my head down, so I don't know how many. And I gave the money to a middle man and I never looked at the guy who took us across."

I was feeling panicky and rushed on. "Oh no, but they're going to interrogate me and they'll know I'm lying and they will force me to tell them the exact time and how many guys were bribed and what they looked like and then those people will get fired or beat up and even if I don't tell, they'll give the name of the family who helped me and, and..."

"Patricia, Patricia, slow down," cut in Joshua. "I doubt very much that your friends will be approached. The entire border is extremely porous and I'd hazard a guess that there is a lot of corruption on both sides, considering the huge volume of contraband that crosses day and night."

He went on, "Let's approach calmly and look at the facts. You're an American woman with two kids and you were unable to use passports to leave Malaysia. You have a friend of a friend, who's a small time smuggler and knows the border situation. You give your friend a couple thousand dollars, he gives it to his friend, you cross, and a bribe is paid, no big deal. No drugs, no guns, no important friends or relatives of the Malaysian Prime Minister. Just two little half-Malay kids whose mother can show good cause why she came across illegally. Thailand has little affection for Islam and loves children." He paused and looked at me for a long moment and then went on, "I think you did a heroic thing by escaping."

He did have a caveat, however. "Nevertheless, you will have to endure their bureaucracy and it can get pretty hairy at times. They could make you go through a formal court appearance and pay a large fine. But, hopefully, with your cooperation and the American Embassy's help, they'll waive the consequences. This is definitely a humanitarian case and you have two cute kids with you to remind them you had excellent reasons for entering Thailand as you did."

He paused for a moment, then added, "I'm getting ahead of myself. First things first. You need a passport and we can't issue one until I've corroborated your story with the State Department. Considering the time difference, that should take me about twenty-four hours. The embassy in Kuala Lumpur is closed until Friday, but I think we'll be fine without their input and can issue you a passport tomorrow morning."

"Thank you, thank you, thank you," I said.

He smiled. "Wait until it's done before thanking me. There's a hotel close by that we recommend. It's clean, comfortable and relatively inexpensive. Shall I have someone call and see if they have a room?"

"Yes, please." I was suddenly feeling very, very tired.

He left and Mariam immediately asked, "Mama, why was he like that, with the glass window between? Was he afraid of us? Are we in trouble? What about going to see Grammy? Do we have to stay in Thailand?"

Iskandar jumped in. "Is Baba going to find us 'cause you have to tell how we sneaked out? Will they put us in jail? Is Mr. Ugo going to get an arrest?"

"Come here, my darlings," I said and they scrambled into my lap, "I think he was behind the glass because that's the rule when they talk to someone they don't know, just to be safe. We are definitely not in trouble and in a few minutes we're going to a nice hotel. Mr. Edmonds says the embassy is going to give me a new passport tomorrow and help us with the officers at immigration. He said they really like children, so you two have to be extra polite and charming. They might ask you some questions about Malaysia to be sure we did a good thing in leaving."

"I'll tell them all about Baba being so bad and the judge not letting us be together and that we want to go to America and stay with you always," said my little prince.

"Me, too," said Mariam, "And I can tell them about the school and how the teachers always hit me and Baba didn't care, but you did and would cry 'cause you were sad for me."

"Yes," I said with tears in my eyes. "Tell them exactly that kind of stuff and the nice people at immigration will want to help us fly to Michigan and then we will. Baba won't find us and Mr. Ugo won't get arrested. Mama is so proud of you for being brave and smart and wonderful."

I was drying my tears when the door to our side of the chamber opened and there was Josh, the nice man, not Mr. Edmonds, the diplomat. He shook our hands, asked to see the children's artwork and gave me a map of the neighborhood with the hotel clearly marked.

"Come back at nine tomorrow morning and we'll go from there. In the meantime, get some rest and don't worry. We'll get you home, maybe by the weekend."

Our walk to the hotel was pleasant. There was an abundance of trees and flowers, the air was breathable and the traffic light. I felt like we were on a garden path, rather than in the center of one of the most polluted and snarled cities on earth. The children ran and played and picked me a bouquet of bougainvillea.

At the hotel, check-in went quickly and I made tentative airline reservations for Saturday with the in-house travel agent.

Then we went up to our room, which is the height of luxury, larger than my chalet in Mersing, with a king-sized bed, a small fridge, a roomy bathroom with all the amenities, clean carpet and round-the-clock Cartoon Network.

Once we finished admiring the room, my thoughts turned to Michigan. I hadn't spoken with my mother in nearly a week and she only knew that I was planning to make another attempt to rescue the children in the near future. I doubted any of my letters had arrived and realized our escape thus far would be—what? All words/idioms/metaphors seemed cheap and inadequate for describing the impact of my news on familial ears.

I picked up the telephone and endeavored to stay relaxed through the time-consuming headache of the hotel operator transferring me to the international operators who struggle with English, until finally, "Hi, Mom, Patty here. Mariam, Iskandar and I are in Bangkok watching Bugs Bunny on Cartoon Network."

"Oh, oh, oh. I can't believe it. In Bangkok! What does that mean? Are you okay? Did you cross the border? What happened? Does Mahmood know? Oh, God, I can't believe it. Are you safe? Did you..." She was gasping, stuttering and slightly hysterical.

"Mom, take a breath!" I laughed, "We're fine. I've been to the embassy and they're going to help us. The kids are great and we're safe. We're trying to work out everything so we can leave, so relax, please!"

Mariam wanted to talk, "Hi, Grammy. We have the best room and we even have a little 'fridgerator. I missed you so much and now we are going to see you and everybody. I am so happy and I don't even miss Baba one bit and…"

Iskandar pulled the telephone from her. She tried to get it back, I intervened, informed a determined Iskandar he was wrong to grab the phone, hugged a crying Mariam and allowed her to talk another minute, while I held Iskandar down. Then it was his turn and she gave him the receiver.

"Hi, Grammy…This is Iskandar…I…I miss you…"

He was tongue-tied and I could hear Mother chattering away while he listened intently and nodded or shook his head in response. I trembled with love, pulled him onto my lap and gently took the telephone away.

I answered Mother's many concerns while the children jumped on the bed and chanted, "We want fried eggs. We want bagels. We want pineapple juice." We'd gone through the room service menu before I called Mom and stupidly, I hadn't ordered their breakfast first.

"Mom, I've got to go. The kids are starving and I have to order food before they attack me. It's morning here and we're going to hang around the room most of the day, so feel free to give out this number. I love you, bye."

I hung up and immediately ordered a huge room-service brunch. While the kids ate, I washed two days of dirty clothes in the sink.

A short while later, my best friend Zoe called. Then my brother Matthew and his wife Victoria called. After that, Mother called again and it began to really sink in—we're going home.

We showered and, feeling restless to get out of the room and away from the phone, went for a walk to a nearby shopping center for groceries and to take a local toy inventory. By then it was lunchtime and the golden arches seduced us; the kids got one-dollar takeout Happy Meals and we decided to go to our hotel's rooftop oasis and eat.

It's now six-thirty and the sun set a half-hour ago, but the heat is still stifling on the rooftop of our hotel. The children are ecstatically playing with floating ice cream containers, handkerchiefs and small rubber animals in a bubble-less, cool water Jacuzzi. They're wearing underpants for bathing suits and oh, how I envy them, as I have nothing remotely appropriate to wear. I am reclining in a deck chair smoking a decent (fifty cents a pack) cigarette and drinking milk coffee from a tin.

Reality is sinking in slowly, leaving me numb and with a myriad of questions. Are we really going home? Really free of Malaysia? Really safe? My psyche is neurotically cautious. When will it release my emotions and allow joy, untainted? When I have my new Passport in hand? When we have exit stamps from Thai Immigration? When I hold the plane tickets? On the way to the airport? At check-in? At our gate? In the plane? On lift-off? In Tokyo? Detroit? When I see the Traverse City skyline? My mother's face?

I suspect that, as each of these happen, the happiness will come and build in degrees to a crescendo. Oh, dear Allah, I hope so. This flat feeling unnerves me and is tinged with fear, a fear I desperately want to be rid of, because I'm concerned it may actually take a very long time to dissolve, may last until Mahmood dies...regardless of the precautions we take.

In my mind, I just did the math and realize I haven't slept in sixty-one hours. I sense a crash is imminent and suddenly feel as though I should get the children back to our room and into their pajama's.

"Mariam, Iskandar, time to go. Mama needs to sleep right now."

29 January

Our next step, however, was not as promising as I'd hoped.

We arrived at the embassy, got my new passport and Josh called ahead to alert Thai Immigration that we were coming. We took a taxi and got out in front of a huge, ugly and intimidating building—Thai Immigration Offices. I'd been briefed on what floor, what room and who to ask for, so with a child's hand in each of mine, we set to conquer. With me were my new passport, the children's old passports, a few affidavits, copies of newspaper articles from Malaysia I'd brought and an official letter from Josh on embassy stationery. It said:

Dear Commissioner of Immigration,

The purpose of this letter is to seek your assistance in facilitating the departure from Thailand of United States citizen Patricia Sutherland and her two United States citizen children, Tunku Mariam Nabila Binte Tunku Mahmood Shah and Tunku Iskandar Shah Bin Tunku Mahmood Shah. Ms. Sutherland and her children entered Thailand from Malaysia on 27 January, 1998. However, due to circumstances beyond her control, she did not have her passport when she entered Thailand and neither she nor the children completed formal immigration processing at the border. The U.S. Embassy has issued a passport for Ms. Sutherland and she would like to return to the United States with the children as soon as possible.

As always, your assistance is very much appreciated.

Almost immediately upon arrive at Thai Immigratioin, we were confronted by a very rude official, who all but threw the passports at me, saying, "Why you come here? Go back to Malaysia and solve your problems. You can't come here and make us solve your problems."

The children stood beside me and the three of us stared at him, horrorstruck. The kids were trembling as I marched back to the man who'd sent us to the officer and related what he'd said. He called the guy over, chewed him out in Thai and then told me, "You'll have to appear in court and pay a fine."

Well, after hearing they might send us back and/or send us to court, I returned to an official named Proon, our first contact at immigration, who'd been briefed by the embassy. I had him phone Josh and, after a long conversation, it was determined that the kids and I should return to the embassy, write an official statement with official U.S. Government stamps and a cover letter and then return to Thai Immigration to start over.

I got the starving children takeaway Dunkin' Donut sandwiches to eat on the floor of the embassy while I wrote the statement.

We later returned to Thai Immigration and the sea of desks and staring men in uniforms. The tide turned when Proon and Suksopan, another official, sat down with me in an empty conference room and began to ask questions. The children played on the floor, on the table and in my lap.

Slowly Suksopan, with Proon acting as occasional interpreter, came to an understanding of what we'd endured in Malaysia and why we left without using passports. Suksopan understood the dynamics of Malaysian royalty and the grip Islam has on the courts. He agreed that if the people at the border had seen the names on the children's passports, they wouldn't have touched us with a ten-foot pole.

Suksopan promised to smooth our path, but there was no way around the formality of his boss's approval. Suksopan assured me he'd have it by three the next afternoon and we left him late Thursday afternoon with the children and me thinking we'd be able to fly home Saturday morning.

30 January

The deadline for the children being declared AWOL passed at 2:00 P.M. My unending fear of Mahmood increased, as did the bureaucratic nightmare unfolding.

We called and then went over to Thai Immigration at three-thirty, expecting our approval to be done, but no, a decision will not be made until after three on Monday.

Suksopan, the Lt. Commander, is very sympathetic and helpful. He's going to waive the court appearance and 5,000 Baht fine, but not the approval from his boss, which is slow in coming.

Iskandar was listening intently while Suksopan spoke to me yesterday afternoon, in confusing broken English, "Sorry, sorry. I try help you get visa today, try make no problems. I wish you and babies to go home. I working hard for you, try talk to boss yesterday, today. But, big problem, no boss. Monday he come, for sure, then you get visas, get plane tickets, go home."

Iskandar spoke up: "You promised Mama we would get the stamps in our Passports today. You said! Every day we have to come here. You promised! Call the boss right now! You said!"

Suksopan was taken aback, then he smiled, tousled Iskandar's hair and said, "Hey, little boy. You smart, you a good boy, take care your mother. Don't worry. You go to hotel, look at television, relax. We get you home quick, I promise. Monday, not so long."

When we got back to the hotel, Arvin called. He had telephoned my mother in Michigan and asked for me. Once she got over her shock, thinking he was Mahmood at first and then realizing out who he actually was, she told him I was still in Bangkok and would be there for at least another three days.

"She shouldn't be alone there. If you can pay for my flight, so sorry, but I can't afford it and I won't take any other money, then I will go and look after her."

Arvin called me a half-hour later. "Hello, Patricia dear. I got your number from your mother. I have to tell you something upsetting. Your ex filed a police report in Mersing and there is a manhunt on for you and the kids. I'm going to see what I can do to put them off your trail. Your mother is going to wire me the money so I can fly there to be with you. Okay?"

My fears exploded. I teetered on the edge of hysteria. "What will the Malaysian police do? Call Thai Immigration? Demand an extradition? Could Mahmood send people here to look for us? I am scared, Arvin. Come tonight."

"No, no, you'll be fine. No one knows where you are and they won't suspect Thailand for days, if ever. Stay put, don't worry and I'll call you tomorrow when I arrive. Goodbye."

1 February

I've been up an hour. Iskandar is sleeping under the bedspread on the floor and Mariam, thumb in mouth, is half-awake and tangled in sheets on the bed. The children have lost track of the days. I'm carefully avoiding the subject and reassuring them. Yesterday they asked whether Baba knows that they're gone and I said I didn't know.

A minor reprieve from relentless anxiety: it's a weekend and Thai Immigration is closed—even to Mahmood. But even if the offices were open, the Malaysian police would have no reason to suspect we were in Thailand, especially after Arvin had a friend drop hints about an Indonesian destination. Also, there are two more days of the Hari Raya holiday slow-down in Malaysia and the Mersing Police questioning all the likely suspects could take days. I had told no one what we were doing and I hoped no one was being hassled too much.

I felt antsy. I tried to think of more reasons to relax: I have the support of the United States Government, for the time being, anyway. The Thai Immigration officials seem to like the kids and me. I don't think they are going to send us back for what is sure to be a horror. They'll be tight-mouthed if Malaysia calls and, as far as I know, we aren't in the Thai computers yet.

And finally, Arvin knows the system and knows how Malaysian crime investigations are carried out and he'll do everything he can. Nevertheless, my anxiety is building.

It's 5:00 P.M. We're spending the day in the room, because I'm too afraid to go out in the street. The embassy is closed.

Lastly, I tell myself Allah is good, because the children are surpassing my expectations, behavior-wise. There are only brief, fleeting moments of rage, hitting, screaming and throwing of heavy objects. Moments that send my heartbeat into orbit; nonetheless, I fear escalation, but consistently they go to the edge and rein themselves in.

2 February

It was a rough, rough bedtime last night. Both children were crying for an extended period over the "spot," a small tent I'd made on the floor that neither was going to give in on and allow the other to sleep in. Midnight was fast approaching when I finally pulled an angry Iskandar away and held him down while Mariam fell asleep in the tent.

He refused to close his eyes and threatened to take over the tent if I let go of him. He sat, a prisoner of my lap and chanted, "There's nowhere to sleep. Only the tent will work. There's nowhere to sleep, nowhere to sleep, only the tent, only the tent..."

Soooo, feeling more than slightly deranged and biting back tears, I picked up Mariam's sleeping body and carried her to the bed. Iskandar went down in the tent, the television went off and he was asleep within seven seconds. 12:30 a.m.

Exhausted, famished and extremely relieved there had been no bloodshed, I wolfed down a yogurt with a hunk of bread and cried myself to sleep.

Arvin said if he hasn't telephoned by noon today, he's on his way...

The kids woke at eight-thirty. I fed them cereal and haven't stopped moving from demand to crisis. Mariam caught her bowl of milk and cereal in a towel and it flew onto the carpeting and her clothes.

The bureaucratic nightmare has continued. Joshua Edmonds just telephoned from the embassy. Proon told him that Suksopan gave assurances Thailand won't contact Malaysian Immigration for three to five days after we get our approval. Proon also told Josh that the delay is simply the ubiquitous paper shuffling, avoid responsibility at all costs workings of a Third World bureaucracy. I pray that is true.

Josh also spoke with Hugh at the Embassy in Kuala Lumpur and said Hugh is thrilled and relieved to hear we're in Thailand, sends his kudos and regards.

"EVERYONE," Josh asserted, "wants you and the kids on a plane soon, Patty. You've done everything right and I commend your patience." I was glad he could not see within me—the anxiety, the fear.

Noon came and the children were being wonderful, though I was on pins and needles waiting for news from immigration. We were straightening the room and packing things into bags for check-through or carryon. The room was nearly empty. *Oh,* I prayed, *let the approval come today.*

Arvin arrived mid-afternoon and I savored a flush, a blush and a rush of pleasure at the sight of his gentle face.

My call to Suksopan (who promised he'd have the approval) at three was put off until three-thirty, because he couldn't find his boss and then at three-thirty he took my number and said he'd call me back! The children were restless, Arvin was tense and I was tremulous with general frustration.

Suksopan finally phoned at 4:45 and sheepishly admitted his boss hadn't come in all day, but he was sure the man would be in early in the morning and promised to call me by noon with the approval.

He made a point of mentioning Iskandar and wanted me to tell my son that we would have the stamps very, very soon and how sorry he felt and crazy that his boss didn't show. He called me Patty, spoke with genuine compassion and exhibited all the signs of being on the level. Still…

At five we set off for Central Shopping Center. I felt better having Arvin beside me. Still nervous, but no longer terrified, we went up to the toy department's play area where Iskandar had a longish fit over a too-expensive Batman toy. He relented in the end, though I did have to carry him. While the children played, Arvin and I sat and held hands, talking about miracles and Mahmood.

Then we walked to McDonald's for Happy Meals and to the supermarket for fruits and nuts. At eight we returned to the hotel and missed Mother's daily call by one minute. The children ate, watched television, talked with Grammy when she called back and listened to stories.

Arvin went to his room at ten and I tried to sleep next to my darlings while visions of the next day danced in my head. Earlier, I'd shown the children where Arvin's room was and told them if they woke up and didn't see me, I'd be there, talking with Davey Crockett.

3 February

Arvin came to our room at seven-thirty. We shared a pot of coffee and watched the children sleep.

Suksopan had said he would call in the morning. I was on edge from eight o'clock on waiting for him to call.

The children got up; we ordered breakfast, ate, packed, showered, dressed to go to immigration and waited. And waited. Again and again I tried to reach Suksopan without success. My anxiety grew.

At noon, I phoned the embassy and Josh promised that when people got back from lunch he'd have someone who could speak Thai call immigration and find out what was going on.

At 1:10, Josh called and said, "Suksopan had to leave the office and Kirip, our liaison, has the files. She's trying to reach him and she'll stay on it until we get an answer. Patty, remember I said there might be problems, but we're solving it. Hold tight."

Less than five minutes later, THE CALL came, "Hello, Miss Patty. You confirm your flight! You come get passports!"

"Where do I come? What is your name?" I asked but he only repeated those two sentences, so I said, "Okay, we come now," and hung up.

I called Arvin's room, but the line was busy, busy, busy. Finally I got him and said, "THIS IS IT. Let's go!"

He knocked on the door just as I was opening it, we ran down the stairs to the lobby and I grabbed 6,000 baht from my safe deposit box in case there was a fine to pay (the embassy suggested it might be necessary). I told my none-too-affectionate travel agent to confirm our flights for the following morning and we walked out the door into a serendipitously waiting taxi.

I held my breath...until we arrived at Thai Immigration, took the stairs two at a time and left Arvin in the hall as the children and I went into the main office. The scar-faced, underweight, undercover, bad-guy-looking dude who made me nervous every time I saw him, jumped up and without a smile said, "Come."

We walked past Arvin in the hallway as we followed our escort to an interrogation room full of official-looking men.

Proon was there and pointed to three chairs, but the kids wanted to stand and look at different currencies displayed under the glass of a nearby desktop. The owner of the desk, though, was in the process of questioning a guy and shooed them away, so they stood by my chair.

Nervously, I watched as our passports moved around the table and listened to an animated and incomprehensible conversation in Thai. Just as I was beginning to think we were in trouble, a pretty woman with a stamp used it in our passports and did some writing. I was called up to the head of the table to sign a document in Thai.

"You confirm flights?" asked a man who looked like the boss.

"Yes," I replied.

"Show me tickets," he demanded.

"I don't have them. They're with the travel agent. Northwest Airlines, 6:00 A.M. tomorrow," I hoped facts would suffice.

He repeated "6:00 A.M." a couple times and seemed satisfied.

When the passports and a three-page document were put in front of me, he barked, "Now you go tomorrow!"

"Yes, sir!"

And so our fate seemed to be sealed.

Dazed, I walked out with two unusually quiet children lagging behind. I smiled and flourished the passports as we met Arvin at the elevator door.

"A man confronted me while you were inside. He was very serious and asked me who I was, what was I doing here, where was I from," he said, visibly rattled. "I told him I was waiting for a friend and I was from India and then he went off."

Ironically, Arvin was the one feeling paranoid as we left and walked across the street to a shop for some snacks. He suggested we be very careful. "Careful" was the operative word in my mind, too.

I was manic to get back to the hotel, put the passports and money in the security deposit box, call the embassy and my mother and regroup. A lighthearted giddiness consumed me as I looked at the kids. I felt like

screaming, crying, laughing and dancing. They felt it, too, and were delightfully goofy and affectionate.

Josh was relieved and happy for us. I couldn't reach Mom. I left the kids
with Arvin in the room and went down to the lobby and had them run the
bill. It was much lower than I'd anticipated. I confirmed our flights and
ordered a taxi for 3:30 A.M.

After an hour at the hotel, we set off for a late, celebratory lunch at
TGIF. I knew the children would love an American-style restaurant and
they did! Arvin and I shared pasta primavera, his first Italian food.

In our exultation, we wandered the streets, enjoying sidewalk vendors
and wide-eyed tourists. I bought Arvin a tie, a female deity for Mother, a
porcelain doll for Mariam and an ugly plastic monster for Iskandar. Just
walking was nice and the kids knew to stay close. Arvin was often way
ahead or inside a shop somewhere but popped up regularly at my side. He
was an easy person to be with, patient, steady and amiable. I shuddered to
visualize the last two days without him.

It was after dark when we headed back to the hotel. I grabbed two
Happy Meals, which the kids had wanted, on the way. Mom phoned two
minutes after we walked into the room and I told her my good news!

Television, food, organizing, packing, long showers, Mariam having a
tearful meltdown, Iskandar being too sweet and finally, both settled on the
floor at eleven. But they were too excited, couldn't sleep and wanted to
talk until nearly midnight.

I sat by my babies, stroked their heads, puttered quietly, checked the
bags for the nth time and finally lay down beside the children when Arvin
left.

At 3:00, I called Arvin's room and at 3:10, I woke the children. At 3:25
we all were in the lobby. I paid the bill, emptied the safe deposit box and
we walked out the door to the last leg of our journey homeward.

4 February

Just when I thought my problems were over, leaving Bangkok was more
troublesome than I'd anticipated. The Northwest desk handed me three
entry forms to fill out because the passports didn't have any. I hadn't
thought about this and wished immigration or the embassy had given me a
clue.

I had to destroy my first two attempts because I fumbled with awkward questions like, "How did you enter Thailand?" and "What is your purpose here?" Arvin helped me get them right and we felt it prudent to say good-bye sooner than we wanted because I might encounter trouble with the exit stamp process.

Hugs, promises, thanks and goodbye.

It took the immigration guys about twenty seconds to close our passports and call in the supervisor who led us to a table. I felt confident (though the FEAR was there) as he perused the letter I'd been given, made some notes and gave us the stamps.

I knew Arvin was anxiously waiting outside the restricted area. I asked the man if I could run out for a moment to tell my friend all was well. At first he said no, but I pleaded until he acquiesced and agreed, but only if I left the passports with him.

We jumped up and ran out, leaving our bags behind. Telling him what happened, I gave Arvin a final hug, then the children and I ran back inside.

The long walk to our gate was a happy one and the plane was loading when we arrived. We slept most of the way to Tokyo and were there three hours longer than scheduled due to mechanical problems. The only real annoyance was a video game obsession Iskandar refused to shake as we walked up and down the stairs to the transit lounge half a dozen times, ate free sandwiches and phoned Mom about the delay.

From Tokyo to Detroit the plane was packed, but we were luxuriating in the first row of economy with our own movie screen. Mariam got the window without an argument. We slept, ate, did well.

We landed in Detroit at 2:30 P.M. and I knew we'd miss the 3:10 to Traverse City. Our luggage took sooooo long to come and the immigration ladies were friendly as they examined our passports, then looked up startled and said, "What is this!?"

I told them in a few sentences and after their chorus of "Wows!" we were sent through. I checked the toy and clothes bags up to Traverse City and, unencumbered, we caught the bus to the domestic terminal.

My teeth chattering, I telephoned my mother to say "We missed the 3:10, we'll be on the 5:00 and please have coats for us." We went to our gate shivering with cold. I put my T-shirt on Mariam and my denim shirt on

Iskandar, but I was freezing in a light rayon dress. I convinced Iskandar to give me back the denim shirt and I'd carry him. Mariam was okay in three big T-shirts over a long dress.

Then we took a bus out to the twenty-seven passenger turbojet on which luckily both children had window seats. Nevertheless we were anxious to land and when we did I saw familiar shapes through the window as the plane pulled up to the terminal. Over twenty-four hours and twelve thousand miles later, we arrived in Traverse City, Michigan. Exhausted but wired, we raced two thousand yards through the icy cold to Grammy, who held up jackets and a sweatshirt.

The children ran into her arms, laughing and yelling, "Yahoo! Hi, Grammy! Here we are!"

I followed in a daze. My aunts, brother, sister and Zoe were upstairs. Seeing everyone for the first time in so long made our liberation REAL to me. REAL, REAL, REAL! Their faces, touches, joy and smiles of love penetrated my numbness. I pulled Mariam and Iskandar to me and we basked in the glow of our long awaited reunion.

An hour and a half later the children were in front of their Grammy's house, playing in the snow.

Epilogue

Dawn is breaking over the snow banks outside the window. My world is surreal. Where am I? How did I get here? Why did the Fates set us free?

Four years ago, on our first morning in America, the children were waiting in their snowsuits for the sun to rise. I can't remember much about that day beyond confusion. There were so many people around and we had a new world to discover and navigate.

My mother had been busy while we were in Bangkok. She shopped, borrowed and was given the makings of a new instant life for the children and me. Our half of her house was full of furniture, clothes, toys, books and all the other accoutrements of middle-class America. Seeing these wonders, the children were almost speechless with amazement. "Wow, Mama. It's a miracle," was what they managed to say.

My son was behaving so well that I hardly recognized him and both children took to my family effortlessly. My three and a half years of frequently talking about our friends and relatives back in Michigan was bearing fruit.

I spoke with Arvin our second day back. Mahmood had gone public. He believed we were at large in Malaysia and appealed to the public to call him with information. Arvin said he was faxing me the newspaper article.

When it came through, the headline read, "American Ex-wife and Two Children Disappear." Mahmood was quoted as saying, "I am sure the three of them could not have left the country as our passports are with the

Syariah Court in Melacca." A court he well knew was prejudiced in his favor.

Arvin telephoned again to report that Mahmood had been interviewed on a forty-five-minute segment of a popular television show, *Malaysia Today*. Mahmood said he knew we were not in the United States, but if he learned we were, he'd send someone over to check things out... A statement which sent shivers running through me.

Salwah sent my mother a fax on 7 February asking for any information on my whereabouts. Arvin's advice was not to contact anyone in Malaysia and I didn't.

During those first weeks, the children and I slept together in the bedroom, either all on the bed or me on a couch by the door. I couldn't have slept any other way. Even so, I woke up in a panic at least once a night, sure they were gone or that someone was in the house or the yard, ready to shoot me and take them.

When I registered the children for school, I met with the county sheriff and the principal at the school. Everyone, it seemed, knew our story and we were treated like fine china on the one hand and extraordinary heroes on the other. Did we seem so fragile? So special? I did know that a blessed sense of vindication sustained me. Mariam and Iskandar deserved this life and I had earned it for them.

Mariam had early problems with reading and writing after four years in Chinese School, but Iskandar loved kindergarten. Within a year, Mariam was reading well above grade level. In fact, both children are voracious readers, mainly because we don't have a television set, computer or battery-powered games. Iskandar devoured the Harry Potter series three times and Mariam has read all the young adult fantasy and sci-fi novels in our village library.

In March, 1998, I went to help out in Mariam's class and ended up subbing there all day. It was structured chaos and somehow I succeeded. I'm glad I had no warning and was spared pre-teaching jitters. By April of that year, I was subbing regularly. Overall, the children were doing well, but Iskandar still was fearful. He and I talked about "Fear of Baba" before he fell asleep one night. "I'm still scared of Baba. Give me more reasons not to be scared, Mama," he said a half dozen times and I told him another reassuring fact. Poor baby, it was harder for him with his limited grasp of geography and politics to really understand how far away Malaysia was and how safe we were here. Though I asked myself many times in those early days, *How safe are we?*

As spring turned into summer, I discovered that I was eligible for a free attorney to help me get legal custody of the children. The three lawyers I'd telephoned earlier all wanted thousands of dollars up front and went on and on about how difficult getting custody would be because of the international angle. I told them that the case was simple and straightforward, but they did not see it that way. Legal Services, on the other hand, agreed with me, took the case and assured me nothing would be sent to Mahmood.

However, in June, when my lawyer went on maternity leave and a different lawyer took over, Friend of the Court informed Mahmood of our whereabouts. They apologized profusely…

Several weeks later, on July 26, 1998 Arvin faxed me an article with the headline, "Man Claims Ex-wife Kidnapped Children." It read:

"A member of the Johor royal family has claimed that his former American wife abducted their two children and wrongfully obtained custody over them in a Michigan court in the United States this month.

"Tunku Mahmood Shah alleges that Noor Faridah Abdullah, 38, deceived a family court Judge in Leelanau County, Michigan to obtain custody of Tunku Mariam Nabila, seven, and Tunku Iskandar Shah, six, on July 1.

"'I was shocked to receive the order on July 22, granting legal and physical custody of the two children to my ex-wife without my knowledge,' he told reporters at a press conference yesterday.

"Tunku Mahmood added that the court also ordered that the whereabouts of Noor Faridah and the children be kept confidential.

"He added that he was perplexed how Noor Faridah and the children left Malaysia when the U.S. Embassy had denied providing travel documents to the children.

"'It is puzzling how a Caucasian woman manages to take two Asian children out of the country without passports and without arousing any suspicion among the immigration officers,' said Tunku Mahmood.

"'I have instructed my lawyer Yusof Rahmat to file an official protest to the U.S. court and the U.S. Embassy over the court's decision.'

"'I have been greatly wronged and my children should be sent back to Malaysia as the Melacca Syariah Court had awarded custody of the children to me first,' he said.

"Tunku Mahmood related that he was still searching for the children inside Malaysia and was surprised when he got a questionnaire relating to

Noor Faridah's custody application from the Friend of the Court in the U.S. on July 14, two weeks after the court granted custody to his ex-wife.

"'I believe Noor Faridah had not informed the court in the U.S. about the decision of the Melacca Syariah Court nor about their kidnapping,' he said.

"Tunku Mahmood said the religious education of the two children will be affected as Noor Faridah was not a staunch Muslim and did not have relatives who practiced the faith."

I knew Mahmood wouldn't come here to get the kids. No, if he wanted them, he'd hire men who would be only too happy to retrieve his children from the Western infidels. Sometimes I saw them behind every tree in the yard.

As time passed, my night panics fell to less than twice a month. For a long time Iskandar wouldn't sleep in a room alone and both children found comfort in talking about what they would do to escape if bad people tried to steal them. I endeavored to empower them and, with the help of good advice, we planned for different scenarios, going so far as to play them out. Our martial arts teacher, Sensei Karen, was invaluable in bolstering my self-esteem and that of the children.

Towards the end of the 1998-99 school year, I was working full-time as an academic tutor for Native American students struggling in the public schools. The children and I moved twenty-five miles north, where they attended the school at which I worked. During this period, we were rarely more than a hundred yards away from one another all day, every day. I did this full-time for the next two academic years.

As for my social life, I went out with a few men the first couple years, but nothing was serious, because I was…and still am…what? Odd? Detached? Uptight? Happier mothering? By choice, I haven't had a date for over a year.

Janice, my traveling buddy, and I have renewed our friendship. She has married and has two young children of her own and two stepsons.

I ran my first marathon in the spring of 2000, a few weeks after turning forty. I loved everything about it, especially being in the best shape of my life and, Allah willing, I intend to run at least one marathon a year until I'm ninety. I also meditate, study yoga and am a student of Thich Nhat Hahn, a Buddhist monk and peace activist. Mariam ran a three-mile race two weeks ago and thinks she wants to be a runner, too.

Until this spring, both children were in counseling. For Mariam, it was as much for coping with Iskandar as it was for her Post Traumatic Stress issues. At this time, she is popular, well-adjusted, wise and very brave. She enjoys speaking in front of an audience, carried a placard in one of my activist walks and likes being the center of attention for her flexibility in yoga class.

Iskandar has had more problems. On the one hand, he is athletically gifted, witty, affectionate and overly compassionate towards all forms of suffering. But until recently, he was also sometimes violent, cruel and unpredictable. He was tortured by the side effects of Oppositional Defiance Disorder and Post Traumatic Stress Disorder. Not surprisingly, Mariam and I bore the brunt of his acting out and there were times I had to bring in help. Things got worse before they got better, but this spring, my sister-in-law Amy, who is studying Naturopathic Medicine in Oregon, called me. In one of her textbooks on homeopathy, she discovered a remedy that matched Iskandar's symptoms and suggested we try it. We'd been through a few non-traditional treatments and though their success was limited, I was praying for a cure. From the very first day of Iskandar's homeopathic treatment, his dissociate chanting, defiance and violent outbursts ceased and have not returned.

Legally, both children still have their Arabic names and I have no intention of changing them. They are still Muslim and, although we don't practice all the tenets, we are a Muslim family. The nearest mosque is two hundred miles away and there are very few Muslims in Northern Michigan. As far as I know, we are the only ones in our county. I had two Saudi boys from a local prep school tutoring us in Arabic and Islam our first two years and this past year they had a Sufi martial arts instructor who prayed with us. And just recently, I met a devout Palestinian man who is giving religious instruction to both children.

In the spring of our second year in Michigan, contact was reestablished with Mahmood, Azizah and Zahara. Once Mahmood knew we were in Michigan, it seemed foolish to pretend otherwise. And I knew if he were planning to make an attempt to get the children, their contacting him would be irrelevant and could even be preventative. Also, despite all he had done to keep the children from me, I knew the children needed their father and he needed them. For the sake of both the children and their father, I had Mariam and Iskandar write letters to Mahmood.

He responded, sending a long letter and a box of clothes and toys. Soon he was calling on their birthdays, letters were flowing back and forth and he sent the children beautiful, traditional clothes they enjoyed wearing. I carefully monitor what the children write and censor his letters' cruel comments about me.

I send him copies of report cards, schoolwork, awards and other paraphernalia related to the children's lives, although he and I have no direct contact. If I answer the phone when he calls, he says, "Is Tunku Mariam there?" in a gruff tone. When he first started calling, I was unable to sleep those nights, but gradually my fears have quieted.

Mahmood and Yati married and have a son and daughter. Rawa has been transformed into a high-class resort.

I have told Mahmood he has an open invitation to come to Michigan or meet the children anywhere (supervised) on United States soil, but because of all that transpired, I will not send the children to Malaysia. He has a long list of excuses about visiting here, the most recent being that, after 9/11, America isn't safe for Muslims. There is, of course, a wry irony about that excuse.

Lorraine and Alang divorced. Azizah telephones regularly to complain about Mahmood and chat with the children and me. Zahara married the Sultan of Brunei's Chief of Protocol (and shook President Clinton's hand as he disembarked from Air Force One when he went to Brunei for an economic conference in 2000). She has a daughter, thrilling Aunt Mariam and Uncle Iskandar. She and I have become friends. I cherish both hers and Azizah's places in our lives. They send us wonderful packages of Malay foods, clothes and religious items such as prayer rugs and books. They also have an open invitation and I hope they will visit one day.

Beyond being a record for my children, it is my hope that this book will raise consciousness about the many thousands of women and their children presently in circumstances similar to those my children and I endured. Like us, they are victims of unfair international custody laws and suffer because of societies that treat women and children as second-class citizens. I feel these women's pain and am trying to bring their plight to the public attention.

I also hope this book will bring to light the plight of Muslim women in culturally repressive countries and the sacrifices and risks mothers of all faiths and in all lands are willing to undertake for the love of their children.

I wish them all Godspeed on their perilous journeys and pray that, like us, they reach freedom and safety.